MARY BERRY
& LUCY YOUNG
COOK UP A
FEAST

MARY BERRY
& LUCY YOUNG
COOK UP A
FEAST

LONDON, NEW YORK, MELBOURNE,
MUNICH, AND DELHI

Project Editor
Michael Fullalove

Designers
Carolyn Hewitson, John Round

Photography
William Reavell

DK LONDON

Project Editor
Andrew Roff

Project Art Editor
Kathryn Wilding

Senior Jacket Creative
Nicola Powling

Senior Presentations Creative
Caroline de Souza

Managing Editors
Dawn Henderson, Angela Wilkes

Managing Art Editors
Christine Keilty, Marianne Markham

Production Editor
Ben Marcus

Production Controller
Alice Sykes

Creative Technical Support
Sonia Charbonnier

DK INDIA

Head of Publishing
Aparna Sharma

Managing Art Editor
Romi Chakraborty

Senior Editor
Saloni Talwar

DTP Designer
Tarun Sharma

First published in Great Britain in 2010
by Dorling Kindersley Limited
80 Strand, London WC2R 0RL

A Penguin Company
Text copyright © 2010 Mary Berry
Copyright © 2010 Dorling Kindersley

2 4 6 8 10 9 7 5 3 1

A CIP catalogue record for this book
is available from the British Library.

ISBN 978-1-4053-4445-6

Colour reproduction by MDP, Bath
Printed and bound in Singapore by Star Standard

Discover more at
www.dk.com

Contents

In the 20 years we've worked together we've written cookery books on a vast range of subjects. One of the many joys of publishing them is the feedback we get from you, our readers. We take your comments extremely seriously. And if there's one request that's kept on coming, it's for a book to serve numbers – a party book, with recipes for anything from a family get-together in the kitchen to a full-on feast. It's an area we feel well qualified to write on – in our personal lives as well as in our professional lives, there's nothing we like so much as cooking for family, friends, and neighbours – no matter the number.

At the same time, we're well aware of the worries that many of you have about cooking for more than six – you tell us about them at our cookery demonstrations and in your letters and emails. "What can I make for so many people?" "How can I keep the food hot and will there be enough?" These are the sorts of question we're asked and these are the sorts of question we bore in mind as we wrote this book.

In *Cook up a Feast*, we give you all the advice you need to make cooking for a crowd easy and stress free. There are recipes for summer and winter, for formal occasions and informal occasions, inside the home and out. We give timings for Agas as well as conventional ovens, together with prepare-ahead and freezing information. And at the back of the book there's a choice of menus for lots of different kinds of event.

We kick off with **the basics** – how to plan your feast and how to guarantee there's enough for everyone to eat. We tell you ways to get the most from your kitchen (the centre of the action at any special occasion) and let you in on a few cheats and shortcuts to make life easier. We also give you ideas on setting the scene and on how to keep your cool on the day itself. Then it's on to the recipes.

To get your feast off to a flying start, we begin with a chapter on **Party bites** – the mouthwatering mouthfuls you serve with drinks. Following hot on its heels there's a selection of **Starters**, then a chapter on **Special main courses**. We've long been fans of the kind of casual gathering where various people bring along a dish. It's a style of entertaining that's now so popular it's got its own name – the **Pot luck party** – and in that chapter we give you a collection of all-in-one dishes that are ideal for preparing ahead and transporting to your chosen venue. **Buffets** are another classic way of entertaining and we've teamed our buffet recipes with those for **Bowl parties**, a new kind of get-together, where guests can tuck into hearty food served in individual bowls. **Italian food** is such a perennial crowd-pleaser, it seemed only fitting to devote an entire chapter to it, while in **Summer in the Garden** you'll find our favourite dishes for picnics, barbecues, and other al fresco meals. The finale to any feast is the pudding, so towards the back of the book there's a selection of **Desserts** with that all-important wow factor. Which leaves just one meal uncatered for – tea. There are so many occasions when a cup of tea and a choice of sweet and savoury treats hit exactly the right note. The recipes in **Tea for a Crowd** are just the job.

To take the effort out of estimating quantities, for the vast majority of recipes we give a list of ingredients to serve six and a list of ingredients to serve 12, with notes on any special equipment you'll need. And because celebrations are often larger than that, throughout the book we flag up dishes that are particularly suitable for cooking for a dozen people upwards.

So here it is – the much-requested long-awaited book to answer all your party needs and put your mind at rest when cooking for a crowd. We hope each and every one of you enjoys it and finds the inspiration and confidence you're looking for as you plan your special day.

Remember – no feast is worth stressing over. Whatever happens, fun will be had by everyone – including you!

The mere thought of cooking up a feast is enough to send many people into a spin. So what better place to start than with answers to seven of the questions most commonly put to us.

Preparing a feast Q&A

Q *"I'm only used to cooking for four or six and am a bit daunted by the idea of feeding lots of people. What's the best way of going about it?"*

A "The recipes in this book are all designed with entertaining in mind, so that's already a great starting point. Begin with some forward planning and get yourself organized – decide what kind of occasion you'd like it to be, where you'll have it, and when. Then it's time to draw up some lists – write down the names of your guests and what you'll give them to eat. Plan your shop and work out the cooking times, so that you know when the dishes need to go into the oven or on to the hob. There's more information on planning on pages 10–11."

Q *"I'm worried there won't be enough for everyone to eat. How can I be sure I'll get it right?"*

A "If you follow our recipes to the T, everything will be fine – we have worked out all the quantities for you. Serve plenty of bread or potatoes with your main course, and offer a second pudding. If you know your guests have really huge appetites, make extra quantities of the main-course recipe, but make sure you choose a dish that can be frozen after the party in case there's some left. To double-check you're on the right lines, turn to pages 12–13."

Q *"My kitchen's tiny. Will I have enough space to prepare food for lots of people?"*

A "Don't let the size of your kitchen put you off – you can turn out delicious food even from the galley kitchen of a boat. As long as you have a standard-sized cooker, a fridge, freezer, and a surface to work on, you'll be fine. Keep the menu simple and prepare ahead. Store food you've made in advance in your fridge or freezer. If you're short on space, ask a neighbour if you can make use of their fridge for a few hours. For more advice from us on getting the most from your kitchen, turn to pages 14–15."

Q *"I don't have the right equipment to cook large quantities of food. Will I have to go out and buy lots of new stuff?"*

A "In a word, 'no'. You can entertain on a large scale – and without spending lots of money – with just the minimum of equipment. Inexpensive throwaway dishes are one option (not very green, we know, but then you probably don't have parties all that often). Alternatively, you could borrow from friends or you could improvise – we do that the whole time. On pages 16–17 you'll find our guide to the equipment you need for a party."

Q *"I'd like to give my party a theme, but I'm a bit stuck for ideas. Do you have any suggestions?"*

A "Themed parties are such fun and they can be as formal or as informal as you like. Forget about the theme to begin with and plan your party as you would any other. What's the reason for it, who's coming, and where's the venue? Think of a few of your favourite things to do and eat and see if they are an inspiration. What's happening in the world at large? Is there a TV show you love? Pick a country, then choose recipes that come from there. You'll find some of our ideas on page 19. Once you've chosen your theme, make sure you spell it out when you're sending out the invitations. Then get down to the planning, so that you carry your theme through to the decorations, music, and food."

"To stop last-minute panics, prepare well ahead. That way, you'll be able to relax, knowing that everything is organized."

Q *"I love having people round for a meal, but it always seems like so much hard work. How can I make life easier for myself?"*

A "Keeping your menu simple is the best way of cutting down on the amount of work. Serve one course – an all-in-one dish, say – plus a pudding. Another way is to organize a pot luck meal, where the cooking is shared among the guests – you ask people to bring a salad or pudding, for example, which means you only need to provide a main course. Pot luck parties share the cost, too. The other option is to do a spot of cheating. You'll find some of our crafty shortcuts on pages 20–21."

Q *"I just know I'll lose my nerve the minute our guests arrive and end up ruining the food. How can I avoid a last-minute panic?"*

A "Simple. Prepare the food well ahead, so that all you need to do is take it out of the fridge or reheat it. Plenty of the recipes in this book fit that bill. With your menu taken care of, you'll be free to spend the day of your party making all the final preparations. For a guide to the things you need to think about then, turn to pages 22–23."

Whatever the occasion, when we're having a party the first thing we always do is sit and plan it. Careful planning and meticulous organization are key to success. These are our seven golden rules.

Planning the occasion

Cook with the seasons

A visit to the shops can be just the inspiration you need when you're planning your menu. The bright pink shoots of young rhubarb, for instance, are irresistible in spring, and perfect for the creamy, lemony pudding on page 254. Soft fruits such as strawberries and raspberries follow close behind in midsummer. Leeks, chicory, and parsnips are at their best in winter, while tomatoes are wishy washy and anaemic. Steer well clear is our advice.

For an early summer menu, you can't beat asparagus.

1 Choose what kind of feast

Decide between formal and informal. Will it be supper in the kitchen or the conservatory, a bowl party or a buffet? Is your feast in honour of a special event such as a birthday or anniversary? If it isn't, invent one – we often do! Do you have enough space to entertain the number of people you would like to invite? Do you have the room for all your guests to sit down or would you rather they mingled and munched? Do you have a contingency plan if you're hoping to eat in the garden and the weather turns bad?

2 Be realistic

There's always the temptation to pull out all the stops to give your guests the best time you can. But, from experience, we'd say you are probably making more work for yourself than you need to.

Instead of pushing yourself to the very limit (and exhausting yourself in the process), it's far better to stay inside your comfort zone. Be realistic rather than ambitious. Remember, simple well-cooked dishes will always outshine more complicated recipes that might not go according to plan. And your guests would much rather find you relaxed and ready to chat than stressed out – and flat out – in the kitchen.

3 Look at your guest list

Keep firmly in mind who your guests are and devise a menu to suit them. Are there children coming? Or vegetarians? Theirs might not be the only dietary considerations – certain ingredients, such as raw eggs, are best avoided by pregnant women, the elderly, and the young alike. Nuts are a problem for some allergy-sufferers, as is shellfish. This is such a perennial favourite, however, that

rather than taking it completely off the menu, we tend to provide an alternative dish for those guests with the allergy.

The number of guests you've invited is also likely to determine what you cook. If you're inviting lots of people, for instance, a buffet, bowl party, or drinks party would fit the bill. If people will be standing up as they eat, it makes sense to prepare something that's easy for them to eat with a fork.

To give you a helping hand, at the back of the book, you'll find menus we've put together for all sorts of occasions. Take a look through them – at least one is bound to suit yours!

4 Bear in mind the timing

Having guests for brunch or lunch is likely to be a much less elaborate affair than a smart dinner party. People will expect less to eat, too.

The time of year is another consideration – guests are generally starving on Christmas Eve, but rather more well fed by Boxing Day. In general terms, warming dishes will hit the spot in winter, while a selection of cold foods is good in summer.

5 Calculate the work load

With your proposed menu to hand, jot down what you can prepare ahead and what you can freeze in readiness for your big day. Will you be comfortable putting the finishing touches to dishes while your guests are there? Or would you rather it was just a simple matter of popping them in the oven?

Dishes you can reheat and serve are ideal if you want to spend as much time as you can with your guests or if you think you might get flustered. Even better are cold dishes that will be sitting there ready for you to bring out and serve.

For a fuss-free relaxed way of entertaining, have a bowl party. Your guests enjoy their main course in a bowl – standing up or sitting down.

"Your guests would much rather find you relaxed and ready to chat than stressed out – and flat out – in the kitchen."

6 Fine-tune your menu

When you've taken these factors into consideration, fine-tune your menu and plan the cooking times with military precision. Then write it down – not on the back of an old envelope, but on a proper piece of paper that you can keep somewhere safe for reference. And cross things off as you go along – it will inspire you with confidence.

Remember to make a note if a dish can't be served straight away – roasted meats, for instance, need 15–20 minutes to rest before you carve them, and some tarts are tricky to cut when hot. Check, too, that you'll have enough room in your oven or on your hob and that you won't be trying to finish off too many dishes at once.

7 Head for the shops

If you have lots of shopping to do, tackle it in two hits. Make a list of those things you can buy well in advance – storecupboard ingredients, for instance – and compile a second list of all the produce such as fruit and vegetables that you need to get at the last minute so they are as fresh as possible. Run through the big day in your head, trying to think of items such as ice cubes, matches, and napkins that you might otherwise forget until it's too late.

Consider having a pot luck party

If reading all of this is making you realize you don't really have enough time to organize a feast on your own, think about throwing a pot luck party, where you ask friends, family, neighbours, or colleagues to share the load by bringing along a dish. These pot luck parties are all the rage right now – and for good reason. They are an excellent way of cutting down on the amount of work and expense involved for everyone. For more information, turn to page 132.

All-in-one dishes like our shepherd's pie (page 141) are ideal for transporting to a pot luck party.

From experience, we know it's better to serve too much food than not enough. That said, you don't want so much left over that you do not know what to do with it. Here's how to get the quantities right.

Serving the right amount

Almost every recipe in this book is designed to serve six or 12. These quantities depend to some extent, of course, on who your guests are – if you have invited a group of your girlfriends over for lunch, for instance, they are unlikely to eat as much as a gang of growing teenagers or the lads from the local rugby club.

In general, though, we tend to err on the generous side. And to make doubly sure that there will be enough food, we always provide a plentiful supply of bread or potatoes, so that guests with a healthy appetite can tuck in and help themselves.

Time of day
How much food we serve depends on the time of day. Lunch, for instance, is generally a lighter meal than supper. Here's what we serve when.

Brunch One course with salad or bread.

Informal lunch A light main course plus a fruit salad or simple pudding.

Sit-down lunch A main course and a pudding, with a first course for very special occasions.

Kitchen supper A main course and a pudding, with a first course for very special occasions.

Formal dinner Party bites, first course, main course, and pudding. In other words, the works!

Main courses
Unless you're serving a buffet, you are only making extra work for yourself by offering a choice of main courses. The one exception is curries – a selection of two or three always goes down a storm. When serving 12 people, never be tempted to make two different dishes for six – the servings can look rather mean. Prepare two dishes for 12 – you can bank on most people wanting to sample both.

Puddings
Even if it's only one sumptuous dessert plus a fruit salad, we always serve a choice of puddings at any gathering of eight people or more. That way, anyone with a corner to fill can do just that. Most people have a sweet tooth, in any case. And if you're still worried about guests leaving with an empty tummy, place a cheese board on the table.

Cooking for more than a dozen people
If you're planning on entertaining more than a dozen guests, look out for our "Great for a crowd" stamp throughout the book. These are our favourite recipes for larger gatherings. To make life easier for ourselves, they are often dishes we can prepare in advance and freeze. For some of them, you'll need to invest in a big 11 litre (20 pint) pan.

Buy a long-handled spatula, too, and remember that food in a large pan needs stirring more frequently, as it is much more likely to catch on the bottom. The large plastic storage boxes you find in DIY shops are perfect for storing cooked food in – but check that they will fit into your fridge or freezer before you transfer the food into them.

SERVING QUANTITIES FOR LARGE NUMBERS

To help you serve side dishes, garnishes, and accompaniments in the right amounts to large numbers of people, here are our suggested serving quantities.

FIRST COURSES

Soup
300ml (10fl oz) per serving, although the exact amount depends on the vessels you are serving it in. Soup bowls usually hold 300ml; mugs a little less. For 12, you will need 3.5 litres (6 pints) soup; for 20–25, 6 litres (10½ pints) soup

Rocket (as a garnish)
200g (7oz) for 12; 400g (14oz) for 20–25

MAIN-COURSE SIDE DISHES

Baby new potatoes
1.5kg (3lb 3oz) for 12; 2.5kg (5½lb) for 20–25

Jacket potatoes
1 medium potato per person

Mashed potatoes
225g (8oz) (unpeeled weight of potatoes) per serving. So 2.7kg (6lb) for 12; 4.5kg (10lb) for 20–25

Roast potatoes
Three small potatoes per serving

Green salad/mixed leaf salad
300g (11oz) for 12; 500g (1lb 2oz) for 20–25

Tomato salad
1 small or ½ large tomato per serving

Rice/bulghur wheat/couscous
600g (1lb 5oz) for 12; 1.25kg (2¾lb) for 20–25

Noodles
1 nest per person

Bread
1 large baguette cuts into 10–12 slices

Green vegetables
About 75g (2½oz) per serving. So 900g (2lb) for 12; 1.5kg (3lb 3oz) for 20–25

Gravy
1.2 litres (2 pints) for 12; 1.4–1.7 litres (2½–3 pints) for 20. If your guests are helping themselves from the gravy boat, make a little more, as they may serve themselves rather generously

FOR A BUFFET

Poached salmon
2.7–3kg (6–6½lb) salmon (head on, gutted) for 12; 6kg (13lb) salmon for 20–25

Ham
2 slices per serving (if accompanied by another meat or fish); 3 slices per serving (if served on its own)

Roast fillet of beef
140–175g (5–6oz) per serving when hot; 100g (3½oz) per serving when cold (cold beef is easier to carve thinly)

FOR PUDDINGS

Pouring cream
600ml (1 pint) for 12; 1.2 litres (2 pints) for 20–25

Crème fraîche/yogurt
400ml tub for 12; 2 x 400ml tubs for 20–25

Custard
1.2 litres (2 pints) for 12; 2.4 litres (4 pints) for 20–25

Ice cream
1 scoop per person as an accompaniment; 2 scoops per person served on its own

FOR A CHEESE BOARD

Serve 3–5 cheeses, about 750g (1lb 10oz) in total for 12; 1kg (2¼lb) for 20–25. The most popular is Cheddar. Accompany with your favourite savoury biscuits, a good chutney, and some fresh figs or grapes

Never is the kitchen more the heart of the home than when you're entertaining. Everything needs to run like clockwork, especially if it is also the setting for your feast. So time for some kitchen knowhow.

Kitchen knowhow

When you're cooking for a crowd, you need every spare inch of your kitchen. Big pots and pans and large serving platters all require space, so start by clearing away as much clutter as you can. The more surfaces you have to work on, the better. And you may well need them later to serve or arrange the food out on.

Unless all the dishes you're serving are cold, you'll need to think about how you'll use your cooker. With lots of party food to prepare, it's likely to be working flat out. What will you be cooking in your oven and what will you be cooking on the hob? And when? Maximizing the space in your fridge and freezer calls for careful planning, too.

"When you're planning your menu, aim to spread the work load between your oven and your hob."

If your fridge is chock-a-block, put bottles in buckets of ice and water. Don't submerge the labels or they might come off, making it tricky to know what's inside.

Get the most from your cooker

When you're planning your menu, aim to spread the work load between your oven and your hob. Pick one dish you can cook on the hob and a couple in the oven, or vice versa.

The tasks you're likely to need to perform at the last minute include cooking, reheating, and keeping dishes hot. Make sure you have all the room you need, and adapt your menu if you foresee a problem. Not every dish is suitable for reheating, remember – lasagnes and fish pies, for instance, need to be served freshly cooked, although they can often be prepared up to a certain point in advance and then cooked to serve. This is the sort of information you'll find in the Prepare ahead box on each recipe, so check there.

A second oven or a hot plate makes life easier (even if you only use it for warming the plates) and a microwave is great for reheating dishes you have made in advance. Remember that it may be impossible to get large containers into it, and the reheating time can be quite long for big dishes.

Keeping food hot

It is essential to keep hot food hot. Use the top of your hob to keep pans on a gentle simmer or pop things into a low oven, but only after they have come to the boil on the hob. Turn to page 23 for our guide to reheating food.

Get the most from your fridge

Platters and serving dishes make poor use of the space in a fridge. They might even be too big to fit in. We keep food we've prepared in advance in polythene food bags or plastic containers. It helps to put sweet things and savoury things on separate shelves to make them easier to find.

If you do put plates or dishes of food in the fridge, cover them carefully with cling film or foil and then sit them flat on a shelf.

Insulated containers – the kind you use for picnics – are ideal for keeping food cool. Make sure you have plenty of ice blocks ready in the freezer.

If you're running out of space in your fridge, there are some items you can take out until everything is back to normal. There are also items that must definitely stay in.

• You can take any beer, wine, and soft drinks out. You can still serve these chilled by putting them into buckets of icy water. Be careful not to cover the labels – particularly if the bottles are on sale or return – as they will soak off in time. If you have lots of people coming, you could fill the bath with cold water and ice. Spread an old towel out in the bottom beforehand to prevent scratching and to stop the bottles falling over. Ground coffee, bottled sauces, and jars of pickles and chutney will also be fine out of the fridge for a few hours. The same is true of fresh fruit and vegetables.

• Cooked meats, salamis, and pâtés should be kept in the fridge until you come to serve them. Salads with pasta, rice, or vegetables in them also need to be kept chilled, as do ready-to-eat seafood and dips.

If you've cleared out everything you can and still don't have enough space in the fridge, make sure the dishes you're going to serve last stay in there. The rest should be okay at room temperature for up to 4 hours – unless it's a blisteringly hot day.

Get the most from your freezer

Transfer food to plastic containers or polythene bags. Small portions freeze quickest. They take less time to defrost, too. And make sure you label them so that you know what they are when you come to defrost them. You don't want to reheat what you think is a chicken and leek pie only to find when you come to serve it that there's rhubarb inside.

Make use of your freezer as a back-up for extra bread, rolls, butter, petits pois, and ice cream, just in case the number of guests increases. And clear space for freezing any leftovers.

Fridge safety

The average domestic fridge isn't that big and when it's full to capacity, it has to work overtime to cope. As a result, the temperature inside can rise, even if the weather outside isn't that warm. A fridge that's full to capacity doesn't allow the cold air to circulate freely either, which can sometimes mean foods are inadequately chilled.

Check frequently that yours is working at the correct temperature – 4–5°C (39–41°F) – and adjust the controls to lower the temperature, if necessary. If your fridge doesn't have a temperature display, invest in a fridge thermometer – it's an inexpensive piece of equipment that could potentially save you and your guests from food poisoning.

Defrosting food

If you've frozen food ahead of time, it's important to defrost (thaw) it completely before cooking. We always advise defrosting in the fridge because it's the safest method of doing it. Overnight should be fine for small dishes, but a large deep dish can take up to two days. If time is against you, however, you can defrost non-meat and non-fish dishes at room temperature for a maximum of six hours. Once thawed, transfer to the fridge until needed. Never defrost in a warm oven or warm cupboard – the risk of attracting bacteria is high.

Clearing up

The kitchen is also the place where you'll pile all the dirty china and cutlery. Ask someone to help you clear and wash the dishes or to put them in the dishwasher while you get on with the next course. And ask someone else to put leftover food in the fridge or freezer. This is where family comes in!

Transfer food into polythene bags or plastic containers to keep it in the fridge or freezer – they make better use of the limited space available.

Once you've fine-tuned your menu, check you have all the pots, pans, and dishes you'll need. If you don't have absolutely everything, don't worry – there are often ways round it.

The right equipment

If you haven't cooked for a crowd before, there's a chance your kitchen might not be geared up for it. When money's no object, of course, you can simply go out and buy all the new kit you need. But that may not be an option. It might not be necessary in any case. Help is at hand – in various guises.

The majority of recipes for 12 in this book can be cooked in two standard dishes for six rather than in a single huge one. There's even an advantage to doing this – smaller dishes are a lot less heavy

"Our preserving pan has saved the day on so many occasions – we've used it as a mixing bowl, cooked potatoes or a ham in it, even used it to stir a cake in."

Perfect timing

With so much going on in the kitchen when you're cooking for a crowd, it's worth putting your mind at rest by investing in a good digital kitchen timer. They are relatively inexpensive, extremely simple to use, and the best models can time up to four dishes at once.

to handle. If you don't have a second dish, borrow one from a friend or buy a foil dish. The cooking times for two dishes should be the same as for one large dish, but keep an eye on the food towards the end of cooking – the important thing is that it's cooked right through to the middle.

Foil dishes
You can buy a whole range of inexpensive foil dishes at your local supermarket or department store. They are available online, too. They're not as sturdy as porcelain cookware, so always sit them on a baking sheet, particularly when you're taking them in and out of the oven, and take care not to puncture them.

Because they are made of metal, cooking times are slightly less. Again, check towards the end of cooking to see if the food is done.

Improvising
Take a look around your kitchen to see if there are any pieces of equipment you can improvise with. A roasting tin, for example, can stand in as an ovenproof dish, and we find no end of uses for our preserving pan. To check the capacity of a dish, fill it with water from a measuring jug. Slightly too big is better than too small – for obvious reasons.

For serving
Presentation is so important. If you don't own any serving platters, you could use trays covered in foil, bamboo mats, or leaves – vine or banana leaves for savoury dishes, currant or fig leaves for sweet dishes. A wooden chopping board or marble pastry board would do the job, too. Even a jug can come in handy as a container for breadsticks.

If you're worried about breakages, consider using non-breakable options. It's not only bread that looks appetizing in a basket – our party bites look spectacular presented in a shallow wicker tray, as do cupcakes, muffins, and scones. Pretty plastic or melamine serving dishes are another option. You'll find lots to choose from in the shops. There are even some trendy designer versions.

Glasses
Don't have enough glasses to go round? Then pop to your local supermarket or off licence – they'll be happy to loan you all the glasses you need, so long as you're buying your wine or beer from them. Throwaway glasses are another option and are a particularly sensible idea if you're eating outside.

Some basic cookware and tableware

Walk into a department store or kitchen shop and you'll see a bewildering array of equipment. There's a pot or pan, it seems, for every method of cooking and a utensil for each technique. In this book we've aimed to keep fancy equipment to a minimum and to use standard-sized pieces whenever possible – ovenproof dishes, for example, should have a capacity of 2 litres (3½ pints) for six and 4 litres (7 pints) for 12. Here is some of the other equipment you'll need to cook up and serve up a feast.

Bowls
There are so many things you can put in pretty bowls at a party – dips and salads, to name but two.

Ramekins
Size 1 (150ml/5fl oz) ramekins are ideal for serving individual soufflés and crème brûlées.

Salad bowl
For tossing and serving salads, use a large glass, wooden, or china bowl – deep or shallow.

Loaf tin
You can do more than bake bread in a 450g (1lb) loaf tin. It's great for loaf cakes, terrines, and pâtés.

Muffin tin
You need a deep-holed muffin tin for muffins, a mini muffin tin for cupcakes and tartlet cases.

Tart tin
A 28cm loose-bottomed tart tin is essential for quiches and tarts. It should be 4cm (1½in) deep.

Foil dishes
Platters, casserole dishes, and tart tins made of foil are a godsend, not least because they cut down on the amount of washing up.

Casserole
A 5 litre (8½pint) casserole that's heavy and deep is a versatile piece of kit that can be used over direct heat as well as in the oven.

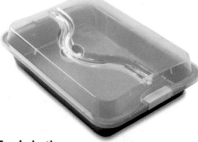

Traybake tin
A 30 x 23cm (12 x 9in) tin will yield enough cake – or sticky toffee pudding – for a dozen people. Some makes come with a storage lid.

Preserving pan
Not essential, but if you have a preserving pan you could stir a cake or boil a ham in it.

Fish kettle
Many large supermarkets and fishmongers will lend you a fish kettle to poach salmon in.

Platters
Serving dishes come in all shapes and sizes. We particularly like thin banana-shaped dishes.

Whatever the occasion you're cooking for, you'll want to create the right atmosphere by setting the scene. Flowers, candles, and music all have their part to play. You could give the event a theme, too.

Setting the scene

Start off by deciding which area of your home you are going to entertain your guests in and, whether it's your kitchen, sitting room, conservatory, or dining room, set it up as much as you can the day before. That way, you'll have plenty of time to make any last-minute adjustments.

If you're having a stand-up party, remove any unneeded furniture and arrange what's left so that guests can move easily around the room. If there isn't enough seating to go round, clear as many surfaces as you can for people to perch on. One large rectangular or oval table placed close to a wall is best for the food. Smaller tables dotted around the walls of the room work well if you have more space, as they encourage people to move and mingle. Provide a separate table for drinks and glasses, and make space here and there for dishes for guests to dispose of their cocktail sticks and olive stones in and for them to put their glasses down.

Lighting

The right lighting will instantly establish the mood for your party. Avoid overhead lights at all costs – they're very unflattering, especially for an evening

Tealights twinkling in glasses add a touch of romance to any table and cost next to nothing.

"We kick off with some easy listening, then – as the party revs up – Mary reaches for the Rod Stewart and Lucy puts her iPod on Party shuffle."

Make the table look pretty with napkins and china in a coordinating accent colour.

do when it's all about glamour. Stick to strategically placed table lamps and standard lamps. Candlelight is particularly lovely, lending sparkle and romance to any occasion. Place candles in clusters around the room. Ideal spots for them are at the back of a table (so they can't be knocked over easily), around the hearth of a fireplace, and on a mantlepiece.

Flowers

A simple arrangement of flowers makes a stunning centrepiece for the table. Even a small vase of blooms will add the finishing touch if you're short on space. We generally choose posies of one kind of flower, and often decorate the table with a pot plant, such as an orchid, geranium, or cyclamen, depending on the time of year.

Music

Music is great for creating an ambience, but never play it so loud that people have to shout, and be careful about what you choose – straight-ahead jazz or heavy metal would be too intrusive and not to everyone's taste. We like to kick off with some easy listening then – as the party gets in full swing – Mary reaches for the Rod Stewart and Lucy puts her iPod on Party shuffle.

Themed parties

We love coming up with different themes for parties. But rather than full-on fancy dress, we'll often ask people to colour-code their clothes to black and white or to come in a wig – something simple for people to do, but with a large element of fun. Of course, many occasions already have a theme – you could be entertaining guests after the christening of the newest member of the family, for instance, or celebrating the landmark birthday of a friend. Match the decorations – and the food – to the event. Curries would be perfect at a Bollywood bash, chilli for a Mexican theme, and pasta for an Italian party.

Flower arrangements don't need to be big. This posy of anemones, hellebores, and roses would look magical at Christmas.

It's all in the details

One of the lovely things about entertaining is sitting down after your guests have gone and looking back at the day, thinking of all the little things that went well. It could be how succulent the lamb was, how pretty the flowers looked on the table, and how happy people looked as they stood around and chatted. That's why we think that setting the scene is so important – joyful memories for you and joyful memories for them.

If you're on the last minute, you might appreciate a helping hand. Luckily, cutting the odd corner won't affect the final quality of the dish – so long as you choose the right corners to cut.

Cheats and shortcuts

There are many ways you can cheat and make cooking for a party easier. A quick visit to your local supermarket or delicatessen will provide you with all the ready-prepared ingredients you need to rustle up a speedy dish like the Express Mediterranean platter on page 83, for instance. Hummus, vine leaves, olives, and a selection of cold meats – what could be more delicious and trouble free to serve as your first course.

Bags of prepared salads are an excellent timesaver, too. Buy the different varieties of leaves in separate packets, then you don't end up getting enormous amounts of shredded iceberg lettuce (not our favourite), and mix them together when you are about to serve them. A bottle of good-quality vinaigrette won't go amiss, too.

You can also get ready-prepared vegetables in bags – broccoli and cauliflower trimmed and broken up into florets, carrots peeled and chopped, peas and beans podded. Serving a vegetable side dish has never been so easy. You could also team frozen vegetables with fresh vegetables – frozen peas go well with softened leeks or courgettes, for instance, and frozen baby broad beans can be mixed with any variety of fresh bean.

On the facing page, you'll find a list of the cheat ingredients we always have to hand in our fridge, freezer, and storecupboard. From ready-baked tartlet cases to cans of chickpeas and sweetcorn, they're all designed to take some of the pressure off the busy cook.

Think simple and in season – if you have no time to make an elaborate pudding in the summer, serve fresh strawberries or raspberries with cream or make our Magenta fruit compote with white chocolate sauce on page 264. Simplicty itself.

Equipment
Certain pieces of equipment can save you time and effort as well. Cake-tin liners take the fiddle out of lining cake tins. They are also guaranteed to be a perfect fit. Throwaway foil containers, such as tart tins, casserole dishes, roasting tins, and platters are not only convenient, they don't need washing up either. You might appreciate that more than you think at the end of the day.

Other than a bit of chopping and some stirring, little preparation is required to turn out a dish as spectacular as our 21st-century coronation chicken on page 187.

CHEAT INGREDIENTS

These shop-bought items are perfectly acceptable to use when you're cooking up a feast and want to reduce the amount of work you have to do.

IN CANS

apricots (in natural juices)

black-eyed beans (in water)

butter beans (in water)

chickpeas (in water)

flageolet beans (in water)

pears (in natural juices)

red kidney beans (in water)

sweetcorn

white peaches (in natural juices)

IN PACKETS/BAGS

crispy bacon rashers

French bread (part-baked)

meringues

ready-to-eat dried apricots

soft bread dough

stock cubes

trifle sponges

IN JARS/BOTTLES

chargrilled artichokes

chargrilled peppers

mayonnaise

onion marmalade

passata

pepperdew peppers

pesto

salad dressing

tapenade

FROM THE CHILLER CABINET

bacon lardons

celeriac remoulade

crayfish tails

custard

dough balls

filo pastry

puff pastry

quail's eggs (cooked and ready peeled)

salad leaves

shortcrust pastry

soft bread dough

tartlet cases

FROM THE FREEZER

baby broad beans

chestnuts (ready peeled)

onions (ready chopped)

petits pois

soft fruits such as raspberries

And to drink…

For a delicious soft drink that's almost as good as home-made lemonade, we mix together bottles of shop-bought fizzy apple juice with grapefruit or cranberry juice (two-thirds fizzy apple juice to one-third fruit juice is about right). Then we float a few lemon or orange slices on top. Hey presto! Some sliced strawberries and tiny sprigs of mint look pretty in summer.

"All it takes to rustle up a dish like the Express Mediterranean platter on page 83 is a quick trip to the supermarket."

Preparing ahead

Okay, so preparing food in advance isn't exactly cheating, but it is a simple way of making life easier for yourself on the day. Throughout this book we give you advice on preparing ahead, but there are other little shortcuts, too. When you're making the gravy for the Mini pork en croûtes on page 120, for instance, you can mix all the ingredients together, ready to add the juices from the meat at the last minute. We do this all the time.

We also keep fresh white breadcrumbs, grated Cheddar, grated Parmesan, and nuts in separate plastic containers in the freezer. They thaw in minutes, ready to cook with, and taste as fresh as the moment you put them in there.

Our top 10 speedy dishes

Smoked salmon on rye (page 46)	10–15 mins prep
Express Mediterranean platter (page 83)	10 mins prep
Chicken with pesto and Taleggio (page 104)	10 mins prep
Teriyaki steak (page 113)	5 mins prep
Seafood linguine (page 164)	5–10 mins prep
Mushroom stroganoff (page 198)	10 mins prep
Rhubarb and lemon pots (page 254)	10–15 mins prep
Heavenly lemon cheesecake (page 259)	10–15 mins prep
Mango Eton mess (page 273)	10–15 mins prep
Lemon and lime possets (page 274)	10 mins prep

It's the day of your feast and the countdown's on. If you've prepared ahead and kept yourself well organized, the pressure shouldn't be too intense. It's now time to make the final preparations.

On the day

Take a look at your menu. What's sitting in the fridge waiting to be transferred to a dish or platter? What needs to be reheated or have the finishing touches put to it? And what has to be put together from scratch? Even if it's only the potatoes you're serving with your main course or a salad you have to dress, make sure they're on your list.

Organize the equipment

Clear a space next to your cooker and lay out all the equipment you'll need – knives, utensils, oven gloves, a kitchen timer. Try to think of everything.

Well ahead of time, get out all the plates, bowls, serving platters, and cutlery you will need.

Clear a space on a counter and pile the serving platters on it. Don't forget dishes for sauces and a basket for bread.

Sort out all the plates, bowls, cutlery, napkins, and serving utensils you'll require and place them on your dining table or buffet table. If you're serving food hot, have the plates or bowls ready to pop in the oven to heat through.

Lay the table

If you're having a buffet, arrange a stack of plates or bowls at one end of the table, with the cutlery and napkins at the other end. The flow of traffic can go from right to left or from left to right, depending on the layout of your room. To show you how this works, we've laid the table for a buffet on pages 212–213 and for a bowl party on pages 178–179.

For a large sit-down meal, it's a good idea to have a seating plan. For special occasions, you might want to have name cards. If it's a family affair and you have young children, get them to decorate the cards for you. If you're having flowers in the centre of the table, arrange them in tall vases or low vases so that people can still see each other and chat.

Ask for help if you need it

If you think you'll need help at some point during the party, make sure you line up volunteers in plenty of time. You might need someone to take people's coats and bags, for instance (we usually put them on a bed), or someone to go round with a plate of canapés or a bottle of wine. If you have any last-minute cooking to do, you might well appreciate a helping hand in the kitchen, too, even if it's only asking someone to toss the salad. But beware of enlisting too much help – people could end up getting in your way.

Warm the plates and platters

Plates must be piping hot for food you're serving hot. Platters may need heating, too. The easiest way to do this is in a low oven or in the warming oven of the Aga. If your oven's already in use, you could either run them through a quick wash in the dishwasher (there's no need for any detergent) or stack them over a pan of simmering water. Swap them around every so often so they all get hot. Hot plates and hostess trolleys may not be high fashion any more, but they will certainly come in handy if you have one.

Taste the food

In the same way that you taste food as you're making it, it's important to taste it again before you serve it. Adjust the seasoning, if need be – that way, you can present it with confidence.

Serving cold food

If you've prepared food ahead and kept it in the fridge ready to serve cold, transfer it to platters just before serving. If you want to cover the platters with cling film, make sure it's only lightly secured under the rim – when too tightly wrapped, it can be time-consuming to remove and there's always the risk of damaging the arrangement as you do so.

"Don't provide outsized serving utensils – they are practical, but the food will go in no time."

Portion control

Whether you're serving individual plates of food or letting guests help themselves, it's important to keep an eye on the size of the portions.

If you're serving guests, make sure the portions are a sensible size – you don't want to overwhelm people (particularly women) by putting too much on their plate to begin with. They can always have more.

If you're serving food on platters for guests to help themselves, don't provide outsized utensils – they may seem practical, but guests will make full use of them and the food will be gone in no time. When serving pies and lasagnes, we often lightly mark portion sizes on the surface with a knife so guests know where to cut. This works well with whole fish, too. Again, don't make the portions too large.

The drink and glasses

At a buffet, set the drink and glasses out on a separate table. Site it well away from the door – the first thing guests generally do at a party is pour themselves a drink and you don't want them blocking the entrance to the room. Provide the right glasses for the drinks on offer – wine glasses (both red and white), beer glasses, and glasses for water or soft drinks – and make sure there are plenty of them. Some non-breakable glasses or plastic beakers are a good idea if there are going to be children present. You might want to supply an ice bucket and some straws, too. A corkscrew and a bottle opener are essential items, as is a container for corks and caps.

Red wine can be swirled easily in a large-bowled glass to release aromas.

White wine will keep cooler in a narrow glass with a stem to hold it by.

Beer tastes better from a chalice glass, which also maintains the head.

Soft drinks or water are best served in tall highball glasses.

Reheating food

If you're going to reheat food, it needs to be done thoroughly. There can be serious health risks if you don't. We've indicated in the recipes when you can prepare a dish ahead and reheat it. If it doesn't say you can do this, don't do it – you'll spoil a dish like our beef stir-fry, for example.

If you've kept food you've prepared ahead in the fridge, allow time for it to come to room temperature before you reheat it. This can take much longer than you think – up to a few hours for a big dish. It depends to some extent on the temperature in your kitchen.

Whenever possible, reheat food in a wide shallow pan or dish – it will heat up more quickly than in a small deep one.

On the hob, use a large-based pan that covers the whole of the hot plate. If you are reheating a casserole, bring it up to the boil, then cover with a lid and leave it to simmer gently, stirring occasionally to prevent it burning.

Before you preheat the oven, arrange the shelves so that you know the dishes will all fit in. Preheat it well ahead of time and, halfway through cooking, switch the dishes around in case your oven has hotter parts to it.

Remember that the more dishes you're reheating in the oven at the same time, the longer they'll take. Check towards the end of cooking to see if they're done – they must be piping hot in the middle.

From left Golden dough balls with cheese and chutney (page 35), Crostini with slow-roasted tomatoes and herbs (page 51), Pork meatballs with oriental dipping sauce (page 38).

Party bites

Party bites is our name for the tiny dishes that delight the eye and excite the palate at the start of a special occasion. To get your feast off with a flourish, choose the right ones and present them with flair.

Party bites

Antipasti, tapas, mezze, canapés – there are so many names for party bites. Little surprise then that the recipes for this chapter come from all around the world. At their most sophisticated, party bites are exquisite tartlets topped with half a quail's egg. Somewhat humbler – but no less satisfying – are slices of baguette baked in the oven till golden and crisp, then topped with a mouthwatering mixture of slow-roasted tomatoes and herbs. Which you choose depends to some extent on the occasion – formal or informal – as well as who your guests are. But here are some general guidelines.

What to serve

● Offer a selection of meat, fish, and vegetarian canapés. That way, you can guarantee you're catering for all tastes.

● Unless you're having a drinks party, offer just a small selection of bites. People are much more likely to remember them if you don't give too much choice.

● Offer a selection of hot and cold eats. The advantage of doing this is that you'll be able to prepare the cold canapés completely ahead of time, which will help you spread your work load and leave you free to put the finishing touches to the hot canapés. In summer, though, it's perfectly acceptable to serve just cold canapés.

● Think about the dishes that follow. If you're serving fish as your starter or main course, you might want to ring the changes and have party bites that are vegetarian or have meat in them. If you're serving curry, it might be fun to extend the theme with some oriental-style canapés, such as chicken satay or meatballs with a hot dipping sauce.

What to serve them on

● Use light platters or plates to serve the canapés on. In our experience, heavy platters can soon become a bore to hold, particularly when guests want to stand and chat.

● China, wood, melamine, thin slate, or flat wicker trays are ideal.

● Throwaway foil serving dishes are another option. You'll find them in supermarkets and department stores, as well as online. We often cover them with redcurrant or blackcurrant leaves so you can't see the foil. Vine leaves also work well – ask for them at the greengrocer's or at oriental shops.

● Think about the colour. Food always looks appetizing against white, but it can look equally stunning on black or silver. Avoid colours that will overpower the food or make it look anaemic.

● Small mugs are ideal for serving soup when guests are standing up, but don't fill them to the brim or you'll take too much of the edge off their appetites.

● If you have the time, decorate the serving platters – fresh herbs tied in bundles with raffia look pretty. Sprigs of holly add a festive touch at Christmas and a posy of sweet peas or roses is good in summer. Even some wedges of lemon or lime would do.

Other things you might need

● If the party bite comes with a dipping sauce, serve it in a ramekin or small bowl.

● Some party bites call for cocktail sticks or skewers. Use a selection of cocktail sticks – wooden, bamboo, glass, or plastic (but not for hot food). Even though they have to be soaked in water for a few hours before use, we prefer wooden skewers to metal ones because they're nice to handle and don't get hot.

● Place piles of small napkins – fabric or paper – in obvious places around the room for people to help themselves.

> **CHEAT** *If you've run out of serving dishes, take a look around your kitchen to see what you can use instead. A chopping board, tray, or pastry board will do the job. If it's seen better days, give it a quick makeover with some foil, sushi mats, or vine leaves.*

How many party bites to serve

Whatever party bites you choose to prepare from the recipes in this chapter, these are the numbers to serve per guest.

● **8–10 per person** at an occasion such as a drinks party where you're serving no other food. Serve up to five different types – cold and/or hot – depending on the number of people you've invited.

● **3 per person** at a meal with no first course. Serve two different types of canapé – cold and/or hot.

● **1–2 per person** at a meal with a first course. Serve just one kind of party bite, either cold or hot.

How to serve party bites

● If you've kept the canapés in the fridge, take them out about an hour before you want to serve them so they have a chance to come up to room temperature. The flavours will improve as a result.

● When serving hot canapés, work out timings carefully in advance – you don't want to keep people waiting. Nor do you want everything in the oven at once. And allow a little time for them to cool down before you take them out to serve.

● Assemble the canapés completely and then transfer them to the plate or platter. If you try to assemble them directly on the platter, it can get rather messy – and you won't have time for mishaps.

● Arrange the canapés in neat lines. For some reason, odd numbers – three, five, seven, and so on – look better than even numbers.

FOR KIDS *If you have a troop of ravenous children or teenagers on the prowl, your party bites will be wolfed down in a flash. We always steer them towards a batch of sandwiches or bigger canapés that we've prepared especially for them.*

"Start with your most stunning party bite – just like the curtain going up at the theatre, this is your signal that the action is about to commence."

● Canapés always look more appetizing if they're served without a cocktail stick stuck in them – even if you need one to eat them. We always pop the sticks in a separate container on the serving platter. A shot glass is ideal. Remember to dot little bowls here and there for people to dispose of them.

● Serve dipping sauces in a separate bowl or ramekin and let guests help themselves.

When to bring out the party bites

● Don't bring out your canapés until most of your guests have arrived. You don't want them to have been gobbled up by the time everyone gets there.

● If you need a hand to take them round, ask a good friend – anyone who's single, there without their partner, or who doesn't know many people will probably jump at the chance.

● Start with your most stunning party bite – just like the curtain going up at the theatre, this is your signal that the action is about to commence.

● To begin with, serve one kind of canapé per plate or platter, so you can keep a track of which guests have had what.

● Once the party bites have started to disappear, serve mixed plates or platters rather than half-empty ones – these can look rather sad and uninviting.

● Allow 45 minutes to an hour for guests to enjoy their canapés before you serve your first course or main course. Don't rush things – you want to keep the atmosphere relaxed.

● At a drinks party you expect to last for 2–3 hours, serve the party bites for a couple of hours and then wind down.

● As a sign that it's knocking-off time and the curtain's about to come back down, we serve something sweet – brownies or cupcakes presented in paper truffle cases.

These are smart enough to impress royalty! They're quick to assemble, too. Buy the goat's cheese in a tub (not a roll) and use vacuum-packed Parma ham, as you need evenly cut slices. Serve the rolls hot or warm.

Asparagus, goat's cheese, and Parma ham filo rolls

Makes 48–60

18 asparagus spears, trimmed
12 slices Parma ham
6 tbsp soft spreadable goat's cheese
6 sheets filo pastry
   (each about 18 x 25cm/7 x 10in in size)
100g (3½oz) butter, melted

1 Cook the asparagus in boiling salted water for 2–3 minutes or until just tender. Drain and refresh in cold water, then dry on kitchen paper.

2 Lay two slices of ham next to each other lengthways on a board. One edge should overlap slightly. Spread 1 tablespoon of the goat's cheese over the top so the ham is completely covered.

3 Arrange three asparagus spears end to end along one of the long edges of the ham. Trim them slightly if they are too long, then roll the ham up tightly.

4 Brush one sheet of filo with melted butter, sit the ham along one end, and roll tightly into a long sausage. Make five more sausages in the same way, then transfer to the fridge to firm up.

5 To serve, preheat the oven to 200°C (180°C fan/400°F/Gas 6). Slice each sausage diagonally into 8–10 slices, then arrange on a baking sheet and bake for 8–10 minutes or until golden and crisp.

PREPARE AHEAD
The rolls can be made up to the end of step 4 up to 12 hours ahead. Not suitable for freezing.

IN THE AGA
Bake on the grid shelf on the floor of the roasting oven for 8 minutes, keeping a careful eye on them.

These are divine. They are also very tiny, but you could make them larger if you prefer. Just remember to bake them for a few minutes longer – and keep your eye on them.

Sausage and apple filo rolls

Makes 80

450g (1lb) pork sausagemeat
1 small Bramley apple, peeled, cored, and coarsely grated
1 tbsp grainy mustard
1 tbsp freshly chopped sage
salt and freshly ground black pepper
10 sheets filo pastry
(each about 18 x 25cm/7 x 10in in size)
100g (3½oz) butter, melted

1 Put the sausagemeat, apple, mustard, and sage into a mixing bowl, season with salt and freshly ground black pepper, and mix well.

2 Divide the mixture into 10, then roll each one into a sausage about the diameter of a chipolata and as wide as a sheet of filo.

3 Brush one sheet of filo with melted butter. Arrange a sausage down one side and roll it up. Repeat with the remaining filo and sausages, then chill in the fridge for 30 minutes.

4 To serve, preheat the oven to 200°C (180°C fan/400°F/Gas 6). Slice each roll into eight diagonally and arrange on two baking sheets lined with non-stick baking parchment.

5 Bake for 8–10 minutes or until golden and crisp. Serve hot or warm.

PREPARE AHEAD AND FREEZE
The rolls can be made up to the end of step 4 up to 12 hours ahead. Alternatively, you can bake them and reheat to serve. Freeze the uncooked rolls for up to 2 months.

IN THE AGA
Bake on the grid shelf on the floor of the roasting oven for 8 minutes.

Dough balls are available in most supermarkets. They often come in a box with garlic butter, but you can also buy them in bags without the butter. They make an excellent base for hot canapés.

Golden dough balls with cheese and chutney

Makes 32

16 ready-to-cook dough balls
25g (scant 1oz) butter
100g (3½oz) mature Cheddar cheese, grated
1 tbsp milk
salt and freshly ground black pepper
1 egg yolk
2 tbsp freshly snipped chives
3 tbsp mango chutney

VARIATION

As a variation on this scrummy recipe, cut small slices of chargrilled red peppers from a jar and arrange them in a cross on the top of each dough ball when they come out of the oven.

1 Slice each dough ball in half horizontally, then cut a small piece off the rounded base so they'll sit flat on the baking sheet without toppling over.

2 Melt the butter in a saucepan, add the cheese, and stir to melt. Add the milk and stir until smooth. Leave to cool slightly, then season with salt and freshly ground black pepper and stir in the egg yolk and chives. Transfer to the fridge to firm up – when the mixture looks like soft butter, it will be easier to spread.

3 Preheat the oven to 200°C (180°C fan/400°F/Gas 6). Line a baking sheet with non-stick baking parchment or foil. Spread the cheese mixture over the flat side of each ball, spreading right to the edges. Spoon a small blob of the chutney on top.

4 Bake for 10–12 minutes or until golden brown and hot. Arrange on a platter and serve straightaway.

PREPARE AHEAD AND FREEZE

The dough balls can be made up to the end of step 3 up to 12 hours ahead. Freeze without the chutney for up to 1 month.

IN THE AGA

Bake the dough balls on the top set of runners in the roasting oven for 10 minutes.

These warm canapés always go down a storm and they're a cinch to make. If you'd like to serve them as a starter, you'll need three to four per person. Serve them with a little ramekin of satay sauce.

Mini chicken satays

Makes 24

Special equipment *24 skewers (see below)*

4 large skinless boneless chicken breasts
4 tsp white wine vinegar or rice vinegar
4 tsp caster sugar
2 tbsp sunflower oil or sesame oil
a little olive oil, to fry
a sprig of coriander, to garnish

For the satay sauce

1½ tbsp olive oil
1 large onion, finely chopped
1 large red chilli, deseeded
   and finely chopped
3 garlic cloves, crushed
1 tbsp medium curry powder
6 heaped tbsp crunchy peanut butter
360ml (12fl oz) water
1 heaped tsp caster sugar
juice of ½ large lime
salt and freshly ground black pepper

SKEWERS

We prefer wooden skewers to metal ones. Soak them in water for about 8 hours before use so that they don't burn during cooking.

1 Slice each chicken breast into six thin strips, then place them in a mixing bowl. Add the vinegar, sugar, and oil and toss together well. Leave to marinate in the fridge for about an hour.

2 To make the sauce, heat the oil in a frying pan over a high heat, add the onion, chilli, and garlic and fry for 1 minute. Cover with a lid, lower the heat, and cook for 5 minutes or until the onion is starting to soften.

3 Stir in the curry powder and fry for 1 minute. Add the peanut butter, water, sugar, and lime juice and stir over a high heat until the sauce is quite thick and shiny, then season with salt and freshly ground black pepper. Spoon into a serving bowl and leave to cool completely.

4 Thread each strip of chicken on to a skewer – it should be fairly flat so that it will fry evenly, with room at one end so it can be held comfortably.

5 Heat a little olive oil in a large frying pan and fry the chicken skewers for 1–2 minutes on each side or until golden all over and cooked through. You may need to do this in batches. Garnish the sauce with the coriander sprig and serve with the warm chicken skewers.

PREPARE AHEAD

The sauce can be made up to 3 days ahead. The skewers can be threaded up to 2 days ahead. Not suitable for freezing.

IN THE AGA

At step 2, start on the boiling plate, then cover with a lid and transfer to the simmering oven for 10 minutes.

Oriental food always goes down well at a party. The consistency of the sauce is thin – as is traditional – but you can thicken it at the end with half a teaspoon of cornflour mixed with two teaspoons of water.

Pork meatballs with oriental dipping sauce

Makes about 50

450g (1lb) lean minced pork
1 red chilli, halved, deseeded, and finely diced (see below right)
1 tsp freshly grated root ginger
½ onion, coarsely grated
50g (1¾oz) cream crackers, finely crushed
1 tsp five-spice powder

1 egg yolk
small bunch of coriander, roughly chopped
zest and juice of ½ lime
salt and freshly ground black pepper
a little sunflower, to fry

For the dipping sauce

juice of ½ lime
2 tbsp light muscovado sugar
100ml (3½fl oz) plum sauce
1 tbsp soy sauce
4 tbsp cold water

1 Put the first nine ingredients into a bowl and mix together with your hands. Season well with salt and freshly ground black pepper, then shape into about 50 small meatballs.

2 Heat a little oil in a large frying pan, add the meatballs, and fry slowly for 10 minutes or until lightly golden and cooked through. You might need to do this in batches. Keep warm while you make the dipping sauce.

3 Put all the ingredients for the sauce into a small saucepan and heat until the sugar dissolves. Transfer to six tiny ramekins or two larger bowls and serve them next to the meatballs on the plate.

DESEEDING CHILLIES

Cut the chilli in half lengthways, then scrape out the seeds with a spoon. You might want to wear plastic gloves if you have sensitive skin.

PREPARE AHEAD AND FREEZE
The meatballs can be made and fried up to 2 days ahead. The sauce can be made up to 3 days ahead. Freeze the uncooked meatballs for up to 2 months.

We've been serving a version of this canapé for years and they are still one of our most popular. Our assistant, Lucinda, also has a catering company and she says these are always the first to go.

Sausages and mustard mash

Makes 20

20 cocktail sausages
100g (3½oz) mashed potatoes
a little milk (optional)
a little butter (optional)
salt and freshly ground
　black pepper

grainy mustard
a little freshly grated
　Parmesan cheese
paprika, to dust

1 Grill the sausages, turning them halfway through, until cooked and evenly brown. Set aside to cool completely.

2 Heat the mashed potatoes in a pan (if they are a bit stiff, stir in a little milk and butter – the mixture should be smooth and fairly loose). Season with salt and freshly ground black pepper and add grainy mustard to taste. Transfer to a piping bag fitted with a plain narrow nozzle (don't worry if you don't have one – you can use a teaspoon).

3 Slice each sausage open lengthways. Squeezing the ends of each one together gently, pipe or spoon the mashed potato into the opening.

4 Arrange on a baking tray, sprinkle with the Parmesan, and lightly dust with paprika.

5 To serve, preheat the oven to 200°C (180°C fan/400°F/Gas 6). Reheat the sausages for 10 minutes or until hot right the way through. Transfer to a platter and serve. Do warn your guests they may be hot!

PREPARE AHEAD AND FREEZE
The bangers and mash can be prepared up to the end of step 3 up to 1 day ahead. Freeze at the end of step 3 for up to 1 month.

IN THE AGA
Reheat on the second set of runners in the roasting oven for 8 minutes.

These are our take on the crispy duck pancakes you get in Chinese restaurants. And very good they are, too. We use filo pastry because it is much easier to roll than shop-bought pancakes.

Duck and hoisin spring rolls

Makes 18

1 boneless duck breast, skin removed
a little olive oil
salt and freshly ground black pepper
6 sheets filo pastry
50g (1¾oz) butter, melted
3 tbsp hoisin sauce, plus a little extra
  for dipping
¼ cucumber, sliced in half lengthways,
  seeds removed, then cut into
  6cm (2½in) long matchsticks
3 spring onions, cut into 6cm (2½in)
  long matchsticks

1 Preheat the oven to 200°C (180°C fan/400°F/Gas 6). Meanwhile, rub both sides of the duck breasts with a little olive oil, season with salt and freshly ground black pepper, then fry over a high heat for 2 minutes on each side or until golden brown on the outside and still pink on the inside. Allow to cool slightly, then cut into very thin slices.

2 Lay a sheet of filo on the work surface and cut it into three 10 x 12cm (4 x 5in) strips (the dimensions of the filo will depend on the make, but cut strips that are roughly this size). Brush the edges of each strip with melted butter.

3 Spoon a little hoisin sauce near the bottom of each strip (leaving a gap around the edges), then sit a couple of slices of duck on top, followed by a few of the cucumber and spring onion matchsticks.

4 Fold the sides of each strip in, then, starting at the bottom, roll them up into neatly shaped spring rolls. Make 15 more in the same way.

5 Brush the spring rolls with a little more melted butter, arrange on a baking sheet, and bake, turning them halfway through cooking, for 10 minutes or until golden. Serve warm with extra hoisin sauce to dip into.

PREPARE AHEAD
The spring rolls can be made up to the end of step 4 up to 8 hours ahead. Not suitable for freezing.

IN THE AGA
Bake on the second set of runners in the roasting oven for 7–10 minutes.

Every can of water chestnuts we open seems to contain 21, but you may end up with one more or one less. It doesn't matter in the slightest for these, our version of the traditional devils on horseback.

Bacon and water chestnut bites with mango chutney

Makes about 21

7 rashers thin unsmoked streaky bacon
4 tbsp mango chutney
220g can water chestnuts, drained
   and dried

1 Preheat the oven to 220°C (200°C fan/425°F/Gas 7). Lay a rasher of bacon on a chopping board. Hold on to one end of it with one hand and place the back of a knife on it near your hand. Pressing the knife down firmly, pull the bacon towards you so that the entire length of it runs underneath the knife, stretching as it does so. Cut across into three equal pieces. Repeat with the other rashers.

2 Lay all the rashers on the board. Spoon ½ teaspoon of the chutney on one end, sit a water chestnut on top, then roll the rashers up and arrange them on a baking sheet.

3 Spoon a little more chutney on top of each bite, then bake, turning them halfway through, for 20 minutes or until crisp and golden. Serve hot with a cocktail stick.

PREPARE AHEAD
The bites can be made up to the end of step 2 up to 24 hours ahead. Not suitable for freezing.

IN THE AGA
Roast on the floor of the roasting oven for 15 minutes, turning them halfway through.

These are utterly delicious – crispy bacon and egg mayonnaise tartlets, each topped with half a quail's egg. To make the eggs easier to peel, do it when they are just cool enough to handle.

Crispy bacon and quail's egg tartlets

Makes 24

12 large hen's eggs
12 quail's eggs
2 tbsp mayonnaise
dash of Tabasco
2 tbsp freshly snipped chives
salt and freshly ground black pepper
4 rashers streaky bacon
24 shop-bought pastry canapé cases
celery salt, for sprinkling

1 Put the hen's eggs in a saucepan. Cover with cold water, bring to the boil, and boil for 5 minutes. Add the quail's eggs and boil for a further 3 minutes. Drain and cover with cold water. Peel as soon as they are cool enough to handle.

2 Put the mayonnaise, Tabasco, and half the chives into a bowl with some salt and freshly ground black pepper and mix together. Quarter the large eggs, add to the mayonnaise, and mash well with a fork. Cut the quail's eggs in half and set aside.

3 Fry the bacon in a non-stick frying pan until crisp, then drain on kitchen paper and set aside.

4 Spoon the egg mayonnaise mixture into the pastry cases and sit half a quail's egg cut side up on top of each one. Snip the bacon into pieces and arrange a piece next to the quail's eggs.

5 Sprinkle with a pinch of celery salt, garnish with the remaining chives, and serve at once.

PREPARE AHEAD
The tartlets can be prepared up to 3 hours ahead.
Not suitable for freezing.

Made a little larger, these fritters are also great for brunch. You'll find the crispy bacon in a packet at the deli counter of the supermarket. Fry some streaky bacon rashers yourself, if you prefer.

Sweetcorn and feta fritters

Makes 30

100g (3½oz) self-raising flour

2 eggs

100ml (3½fl oz) milk

salt and freshly ground black pepper

4 tbsp freshly snipped chives

150g can sweetcorn, drained

50g (1¾oz) feta cheese, finely crumbled

a little sunflower oil, to fry

200g (7oz) half-fat cream cheese

100g (3½oz) crispy bacon rashers, broken into pieces

1 Put the flour into a mixing bowl, make a well in the centre, and add the eggs. Whisk by hand, gradually adding the milk, until you have a smooth batter. Season with salt and freshly ground black pepper, then stir in half the chives along with the sweetcorn and feta.

2 Heat the oil in a non-stick frying pan, add the batter to the pan half a teaspoon at a time, then fry for 2–3 minutes on each side or until golden and cooked through. You may need to do this in batches. Set aside to cool.

3 Put the cream cheese into a bowl, add the remaining chives, and season with salt and freshly ground black pepper.

4 Using a teaspoon, spoon the cream cheese mixture on top of the fritters, then top with a piece of crispy bacon. Arrange on a platter and serve.

PREPARE AHEAD

The fritters can be made up to 1 day ahead and assembled up to 6 hours ahead. Not suitable for freezing.

ON THE AGA

Fry the fritters on the simmering plate (grease it or cover it with non-stick baking parchment first) or in a non-stick frying pan.

Matchsticks of celeriac coated in mustardy mayonnaise, remoulade is a classic starter. Here, the mixture is teamed with rocket and wrapped in wafer-thin slices of rare fillet steak.

Beef remoulade rolls

Makes 24

2 large fat fillet steaks (weighing about 175g/6oz each)
1 tbsp olive oil
salt and freshly ground black pepper
1 small celeriac
4 tbsp good-quality mayonnaise
1 tbsp Dijon mustard
large handful of rocket

1 Rub the steaks with the oil and season with salt and freshly ground black pepper. Heat any remaining oil in a non-stick frying pan, add the steaks, and fry for 3 minutes on each side or until still rare (this will depend on the thickness). Set aside to cool completely.

2 Peel the celeriac with a sharp knife, chop into pieces, then cut into very thin matchsticks with the matchstick attachment of a food processor. Immerse in boiling salted water for 3 minutes or until soft. Drain and dry on kitchen paper.

3 Put the mayonnaise and mustard into a bowl, season with salt and freshly ground black pepper, and mix well. Stir in the celeriac.

4 Slice each cold steak into 12 thin slices (you may get more depending on the size of the steak). Spoon a little remoulade on one end of each slice, put a few rocket leaves on top, then roll them up and arrange on a platter. Serve with cocktail sticks, if you wish.

CHEAT

If you are short of time, buy 225g (8oz) ready-made remoulade from the deli counter of the supermarket.

PREPARE AHEAD

The remoulade can be made up to 3 days ahead. The rolls can be made up to 8 hours ahead. Not suitable for freezing.

These are always a hit. As a twist on the traditional recipe, we use rye bread, pumpernickel, or pumpkin-seed bread. You'll find the cucumbers in jars near the gherkins and olives at the supermarket.

Smoked salmon on rye with cucumber pickle

Makes 60

4 tbsp light mayonnaise
2 tsp grainy mustard
1 tsp lemon juice
1 tbsp freshly chopped dill, plus extra
  to garnish
4 rectangular slices of rye bread,
  pumpernickel, or pumpkin seed bread
200g (7oz) smoked salmon slices
4 cucumber dill pickles, drained
  and very finely chopped

1 Mix the mayonnaise, mustard, lemon juice, and dill in a small bowl.

2 Lay the bread on a chopping board and spread evenly with the mixture.

3 Cover the mayonnaise with smoked salmon, then cut each piece of bread into 15 squares. Top each one with chopped pickle, arrange on a serving plate, then garnish with dill and serve.

PREPARE AHEAD
The bites can be made up to 6 hours ahead.
Not suitable for freezing.

Dips are so easy to serve at a party. Here are two of our favourites. The scorching chilli one will certainly sort the men from the boys!

Dip platter

Garlicky herb dip

Serves 6–12 (depending on what you serve it with)

1 green chilli, halved, deseeded, and cut into three

3 small spring onions, finely chopped

3 garlic cloves, halved

small handful of flat-leaf parsley

small bunch of chives

200ml tub full-fat crème fraîche

1 tsp Dijon mustard

1 tbsp lemon juice

salt and freshly ground black pepper

1 Put the chilli, spring onions, garlic, and parsley into a processor and whiz until very finely chopped. Add the remaining ingredients, season with salt and freshly ground black pepper, and whiz again until smooth.

2 Spoon the dip into a bowl or ramekin and chill. To serve, place in the centre of a large plate, with your choice of dippers (see right) around the edge. The dip also goes well with potato wedges or dolloped on a jacket potato.

Scorching chilli dip

Serves 6–12 (depending on what you serve it with)

10 pepperdew peppers, drained, rinsed, and cut in half

1 red chilli, cut in half

2 tsp freshly grated root ginger

6 tbsp mayonnaise

2 tbsp mango chutney

100g (3½oz) full-fat cream cheese

a few drops of Tabasco

salt and freshly ground black pepper

1 Put all the ingredients into a processor and whiz until smooth. Season with salt and freshly ground black pepper.

2 Spoon the dip into a bowl or ramekin and place in the centre of a large plate. Arrange your choice of dippers (see above right) around the edge.

PREPARE AHEAD
The dip can be made up to 4 days ahead. The flavours will get stronger the longer it keeps. Not suitable for freezing.

DIPPERS
Vegetables are the classic dippers and always popular. Our favourites are peppers, carrots, cucumber, fennel, and celery – all cut into matchsticks or thin slices. Halved baby corn and small Little Gem lettuce leaves are also ideal.

If you're serving crisps, tortillas, or bread, choose plain varieties so they don't overpower the flavour of the dip. Toasted naan and pitta bread are perfect for dipping.

Breadsticks are inexpensive and come plain or flavoured. They are great for dipping as they hold their shape.

We like our blinis quite thin, but the thickness is entirely up to you. If you make them too thick by mistake, simply slice them in half horizontally and you'll have twice the number.

Home-made blinis with salmon and crème fraîche

Makes 30

100g (3½oz) self-raising flour
½ tsp baking powder
2 eggs
4 tbsp milk
2 tbsp freshly snipped chives
1 tbsp sunflower oil

For the topping

100g (3½oz) full-fat cream cheese
3 tbsp crème fraîche
2 tbsp freshly chopped dill, plus a few sprigs to garnish
1 tsp lemon juice
200g (7oz) smoked salmon

1 Put the flour, baking powder, eggs, milk, and chives into a bowl and mix to make a smooth batter. Heat the oil in a frying pan, add the batter half a teaspoon at a time, and fry for 1–2 minutes or until little bubbles form and the blinis start to curl at the edges. Turn over and lightly brown the other side, then transfer to a wire rack to cool. You may need to do this in batches.

2 For the topping, mix the cream cheese, crème fraîche, chopped dill, and lemon juice in a small bowl, then spoon a little on to each blini.

3 Top the blinis with a small swirl of smoked salmon and a tiny sprig of dill. Arrange on a platter and serve.

PREPARE AHEAD AND FREEZE
The blinis can be made up to the end of step 1 up to 2 days ahead. They can be assembled up to 6 hours ahead. Freeze at the end of step 1 for up to 3 months.

ON THE AGA
Fry the blinis directly on the simmering plate (grease it well beforehand) or in a frying pan on the simmering plate.

The time spent roasting the tomatoes is worth every moment – the depth of flavour they acquire is wonderful. Teamed with a herby cream cheese, they make a wonderful cold canapé.

Crostini with slow-roasted tomatoes and herbs

Makes 30

1 stick of soft bread dough or a very
  thin baguette
a little olive oil
15 small cherry tomatoes
salt and freshly ground black pepper
dash of caster sugar
2 tbsp full-fat cream cheese
2 heaped tsp freshly chopped mint
2 heaped tsp freshly chopped basil

1 Preheat the oven to 140°C (120°C fan/275°F/Gas 1). Meanwhile, cut the bread into 30 thin slices and brush both sides with a little of the oil.

2 Slice the tomatoes in half and arrange cut side up on a baking sheet. Sprinkle with a little salt, some freshly ground black pepper, and a dash of sugar. Cook in the oven for 30 minutes or until just softened and beginning to shrivel.

3 Heat a little olive oil in a frying pan and fry the slices of bread over a high heat until golden brown on both sides. Set aside to cool.

4 Mix the cream cheese and herbs together in a bowl and season with salt and freshly ground black pepper. Spoon on to the cold crostini and top each one with a cold tomato half.

PREPARE AHEAD AND FREEZE
The crostini can be assembled up to the end of step 4 up to 6 hours ahead. Freeze without the topping for up to 4 months.

IN THE AGA
Slide the tomatoes into the simmering oven and cook for 1 hour.

These are so popular whenever we serve them. Boursin cheese comes in packets and is flavoured either with pepper or garlic – we use the pepper version (Boursin Poivre) for this recipe.

Crostini with Parma ham and peppered cream cheese

Makes 30

For the onion marmalade
1 tbsp olive oil
1 red onion, thinly sliced
½ tsp balsamic vinegar
1 tsp brown sugar
salt and freshly ground black pepper

1 soft bread dough (see below) or thin white baguette
a little olive oil
½ x 150g packet Boursin Poivre
6 slices Parma ham

1 Preheat the oven to 160°C (140°C fan/325°F/Gas 3). Meanwhile, make the onion marmalade. Heat the oil in a saucepan, add the onion, and fry over a high heat, stirring, for 5 minutes or until lightly coloured. Cover with a lid and cook slowly for 20 minutes or until soft. Add the vinegar and sugar and stir over a high heat for a few minutes until combined and glossy. Season with salt and freshly ground black pepper, then set aside to cool.

2 Cut the bread into 30 slices. Brush each side with a little olive oil, then arrange on a baking sheet. Bake for 30–45 minutes or until crisp. Leave to cool.

3 To serve, spread a little Boursin on top of each of the crostini. Snip each slice of Parma ham into 5 pieces and arrange on top of the Boursin. Top with a little marmalade, arrange on a platter, and serve.

CHEAT
If you are short on time, use onion marmalade from a jar. Soft bread dough is available from supermarkets. It is half cooked and very thin – perfect for making crostini. Use a thin white baguette if you can't find it.

PREPARE AHEAD AND FREEZE
The marmalade and crostini can be made up to 1 week ahead. The topping can be added to the crostini up to 6 hours ahead. Freeze the crostini without the topping for up to 4 months.

IN THE AGA
Start the onions on the boiling plate, then cover with a lid and transfer to the simmering oven for 30 minutes. If there is any excess liquid left in the pan, return to the boiling plate for a couple of minutes. Bake the slices of bread on the floor of the roasting oven for 8 minutes on each side.

The addition of Parmesan cheese and pesto makes the pastry for these tarlet cases out of this world! For more filling ideas for tartlets, see pages 54–55.

Hummus and feta tartlets

Makes 48

Special equipment 12-hole mini muffin tin; 5cm (2in) round pastry cutter

For the tartlet cases
175g (6oz) plain flour, plus
   a little extra to dust
75g (2½oz) freshly grated
   Parmesan cheese
75g (2½oz) cold butter, cubed
2 tbsp pesto
2 tbsp cold water

For the filling
200g tub hummus
4 small carrots, grated
juice of ½ lemon
salt and freshly ground black pepper
200g (7oz) feta cheese, crumbled
200g (7oz) mixed pitted olives,
   sliced in half

1 Preheat the oven to 180°C (160°C fan/350°F/Gas 4). Meanwhile, put the flour, cheese, and butter into a food processor and whiz until the mixture resembles fine breadcrumbs. Add the pesto and water and whiz until the dough just comes together. Turn out on to a floured work surface and knead lightly into a ball. Roll out very thinly and then stamp out 48 rounds with a 5cm (2in) round cutter (don't worry if you don't get exactly 48). Use 12 of these to line the muffin tin.

2 Bake for 12–15 minutes or until golden brown. Turn out on to a wire rack to cool and bake the remaining tartlet cases in the same way.

3 When the tartlet cases are completely cold, spoon a little hummus into the base of each one. Mix the carrots and lemon juice together in a bowl and season with salt and freshly ground black pepper. Pile a little carrot on top of the hummus, then arrange some feta and half an olive on top. Serve cold.

PREPARE AHEAD AND FREEZE
The tartlet cases can be made up to 10 days ahead and kept in the fridge. The tartlets can be filled up to 4 hours ahead. Freeze the empty tartlet cases for up to 2 months.

IN THE AGA
Bake the tartlets on the grid shelf on the floor of the roasting oven for 10 minutes.

Four delicious toppings for blinis or crostini. Each is enough to top 30. Prepare the blinis according to the method on page 50 and the crostini according to the method on page 52.

Toppings for blinis and crostini

Mozzarella, pesto, and cherry tomato

6 heaped tbsp pesto
150g (5½oz) mozzarella, broken
  into pieces
8 cherry tomatoes, quartered

Spoon a little pesto on to each blini or crostini, top with a piece of mozzarella and then a quartered tomato. You should have two quarters left over.

Quail's egg, hollandaise, and asparagus

15 quail's eggs
30 asparagus tips
salt and freshly ground black pepper
170ml jar hollandaise sauce

Put the quail's eggs into a pan, cover with cold water, and bring to the boil. Boil for 3 minutes, then plunge into cold water. When cool, peel and cut in half. Cook the asparagus tips in boiling salted water for 2–3 minutes or until tender. Drain and refresh in cold water. Spoon a blob of hollandaise on to each blini or crostini, sit half a quail's egg and an asparagus tip on top, then sprinkle with freshly ground black pepper. Serve cold or reheat in an oven preheated to 160°C (140°C fan/325°F/Gas 3) for 10 minutes or until warmed through.

Crab, cream cheese, and chilli dipping sauce

170g can white crabmeat, drained
3 heaped tbsp cream cheese
3 tsp chilli dipping sauce
salt and freshly ground black pepper

Mix the ingredients together in a bowl, season with salt and freshly ground black pepper, then spoon on to the blinis or crostini.

Parma ham, pepperdew pepper, and cream cheese

8 tbsp cream cheese
10 slices Parma ham, each cut into three
6 red baby bell pepperdew peppers,
  drained and cut into five slices

Spread the cream cheese on to the blinis or crostini, then arrange a swirl of ham and a slice of pepper on top.

Four excellent fillings for tartlets. Each recipe makes enough to fill 48 cases. Prepare the tartlets according to the recipe on page 53, but leave out the pesto.

Fillings for tartlets

Rare beef, beetroot, and horseradish

½ tbsp olive oil
225g (8oz) fillet steak
1 large cooked beetroot, coarsely grated
6 heaped tbsp creamed
  horseradish sauce

Heat the oil in a frying pan, add the steak, and fry for 3 minutes on each side or until cooked on the outside and rare on the inside. Leave to cool, then cut into 48 thin slices and arrange in the tartlet cases. Sprinkle with grated beetroot and a blob of horseradish sauce.

Goat's cheese and Mediterranean vegetables

2 medium courgettes, cut in half
  lengthways and thinly sliced
2 red peppers, halved, deseeded,
  and cut into tiny dice
olive oil, to roast
salt and freshly ground black pepper
100g (3½oz) firm goat's cheese,
  cut into cubes

Preheat the oven to 200°C (180°C fan/400°F/Gas 6). Toss the courgettes and peppers with a little olive oil and season with salt and freshly ground black pepper. Roast in the oven for 15 minutes or until golden and tender. Spoon into the tartlet cases and top with the goat's cheese. Serve cold or reheat in an oven preheated to 160°C (140°C fan/325°F/Gas 3) for 10 minutes or until warmed through.

Prawn cocktail with mango

350g (12oz) cooked prawns
8 tbsp mayonnaise
1 tbsp tomato ketchup
2 tsp creamed horseradish sauce
1 tbsp lemon juice
salt and freshly ground black pepper
1 small mango, halved, stoned, and the
  flesh cut into 48 cubes (see page 273)

Mix the prawns with the mayonnaise, ketchup, horseradish sauce, and lemon juice. Season with salt and freshly ground black pepper and spoon into the tartlet cases. Top each with a cube of mango.

Dolcelatte, watercress, and pear

70g packet watercress
450g (1lb) dolcelatte cheese, cut into
  48 small cubes
1 ripe pear, peeled, cored, and cut into
  48 small cubes

To serve cold, divide the watercress among the tartlets, then top with a cube of cheese and a cube of pear. To serve warm, top with the cheese and pear, then reheat in an oven preheated to 160°C (140°C fan/325°F/Gas 3) for 10 minutes or until the cheese has melted. Add the watercress before serving.

A selection of blinis, crostini, and tartlets (see overleaf) •••▶

Our best starters

If you haven't served nibbles with drinks, the first course is your opportunity to get off to a good start with a dish your guests can't wait to tuck into. The recipes in this chapter fit that bill perfectly.

Our best starters

When you're choosing a first course, look at your menu as a whole.

● If you're serving fish as a main course, offer a meat or vegetarian dish as your starter, and vice versa.

● A simple first course is good before a more elaborate main course – you don't want to spoil people's appetites or fill them up before the meal has barely begun. But a rich or elaborate starter is fine before a simple main course.

Hot or cold?

A cold first course makes life easy when you're serving large numbers of people and is ideal in summer. Hot soup is perfect in winter, but bear in mind that if you're working singlehandedly it can be trickier than you think to serve soup to a crowd – it has to be piping hot, as have the bowls you pour it into.

Again, look at your menu as a whole. You might feel more relaxed if you know one course is made, ready to take out of the fridge and serve.

*"If your guests are sitting down to eat,
put the starter on the table before they
come in so the scene is set."*

Serving cold starters

● Remember to put out any accompaniments, such as bread and butter, toast, or rolls.

● Dress salad garnishes at the last minute so the leaves don't go limp.

● If guests are sitting down to eat, put the starter on the table before they come into the room so the scene is set.

● At a more informal occasion, where guests are not sitting down at a table to eat, go round with the first course on a platter – this is a very sociable way to entertain.

Serving hot starters

● Before you serve the food, have everything you need to hand – oven gloves, utensils, kitchen timer, and so on.

● If you're serving your first course on individual plates, place them on a work surface and arrange any garnish on them, then all you need to do is add the hot food.

● It's quicker, easier, and less messy to pour soup from a large jug rather than trying to serve it with a ladle.

● Make sure soup bowls are piping hot – soup gets cold extremely quickly.

● Assemble your guests before you do any last-minute reheating or cooking.

FOR LUNCH *Some of our starters, such as the tartlets on page 67 and the mousseline creams on page 71, are substantial enough to serve as a light lunch. For hungry friends, you might want to serve a couple, but one is fine for us.*

Vibrant in colour and quick to make, this soup is ideal for any winter party. Serve with croûtons or crispy bread.

Sweet potato soup with cumin and ginger

Serves 6

1 tbsp olive oil

900g (2lb) sweet potatoes, peeled and cut into 1cm (½in) cubes

450g (1lb) carrots, cut into 1cm (½in) cubes

2cm (¾in) piece fresh root ginger, peeled and finely grated

1 tsp ground cumin

1.4 litres (2½ pints) vegetable stock

salt and freshly ground black pepper

double cream, to garnish

chopped chives, to garnish

Serves 12

2 tbsp olive oil

1.8kg (4lb) sweet potatoes, peeled and cut into 1cm (½in) cubes

900g (2lb) carrots, cut into 1cm (½in) cubes

5cm (2in) piece fresh root ginger, peeled and finely grated

2 tsp ground cumin

3 litres (5¼ pints) vegetable stock

salt and freshly ground black pepper

150ml (5fl oz) double cream, to garnish

chopped chives, to garnish

1 Heat the oil in a deep saucepan, add the sweet potatoes, carrots, ginger, and cumin and fry over a high heat, stirring, for 10 minutes or until starting to brown.

2 Add the stock, bring to the boil, then season with salt and freshly ground black pepper. Cover with a lid and simmer over a low heat for 20–30 minutes (35–40 minutes for 12) or until the sweet potatoes and carrots are tender.

3 Carefully scoop out half the vegetables into a bowl using a slotted spoon. Whiz the remainder in a processor or blender until smooth, then return to the pan.

4 Add the reserved vegetables, bring to the boil again, and check the seasoning.

5 To serve, garnish with a swirl of double cream and some chopped chives.

PREPARE AHEAD AND FREEZE

The soup can be made up to 3 days ahead. Freeze for up to 3 months.

IN THE AGA

At step 2, cover with a lid and transfer to the simmering oven for 30 minutes (40 minutes for 12) or until tender.

The onions are caramelized in sugar in this traditional recipe. We toast the croûtons to make a perfect winter starter or lunch dish.

French onion soup with mustard Gruyère croûtons

Serves 6

25g (scant 1oz) butter

4 large onions (about 675g/1½lb), thinly sliced

2 tsp soft light brown sugar

1.7 litres (3 pints) chicken stock

1 tbsp cornflour

salt and freshly ground black pepper

1½ tbsp balsamic vinegar

For the croûtons

1 small thin soft bread stick

25g (scant 1oz) butter, at room temperature

2 tbsp Dijon mustard

50g (1¾oz) Gruyère, finely grated

Serves 12

50g (1¾oz) butter

8 large onions (about 1.35kg/3lb), thinly sliced

2 tbsp soft light brown sugar

3.6 litres (6¼ pints) chicken stock

2 tbsp cornflour

salt and freshly ground black pepper

4 tbsp balsamic vinegar

For the croûtons

1 large thin soft bread stick

50g (1¾oz) butter, at room temperature

4 tbsp Dijon mustard

100g (3½oz) Gruyère, finely grated

1 Melt the butter in a deep saucepan, add the onions, and fry for 5 minutes, stirring. Lower the heat, cover with a lid, and cook for 20 minutes or until completely soft.

2 Remove the lid, stir in the sugar, and continue to fry the onions over a high heat for 10 minutes or until lightly browned. Add the stock, bring to the boil, cover with a lid again, and simmer for 5–10 minutes.

3 Mix the cornflour in a cup with a little cold water to make a thin paste, then stir into the soup. Season with salt and freshly ground black pepper, add the vinegar, and stir well. Bring to the boil, stirring continuously, until slightly thickened.

4 To make the croûtons, preheat the grill. Slice the bread into 18 thin slices (36 for 12), butter both sides, then toast on one side until golden. Turn the croûtons over, spread a little mustard on the untoasted side and top with the cheese. Slide back under the grill for 3–5 minutes or until the cheese is golden and melted.

5 Serve the soup in hot bowls with three croûtons per person.

PREPARE AHEAD AND FREEZE

The soup can be made up to 3 days ahead. The croûtons can be assembled up to 6 hours ahead and popped under the grill to serve. Freeze the soup without the croûtons for up to 3 months.

IN THE AGA

At step 1, cover with a lid and soften the onion in the simmering oven for 15 minutes or until tender. Continue on the boiling plate.

This is a hearty, healthy soup full of flavour and goodness. Serve it piping hot with some crusty bread.

Puy lentil and pearl barley soup

Serves 6

1 tbsp olive oil
1 large onion, finely chopped
2 carrots, finely diced
2 garlic cloves, crushed
100g (3½oz) dried Puy lentils
100g (3½oz) pearl barley
680g jar passata

1.5 litres (2¾ pints) chicken stock
  or vegetable stock
salt and freshly ground
  black pepper
2 tsp sugar
1 tbsp balsamic vinegar

Serves 12

2 tbsp olive oil
2 onions, finely chopped
2 large carrots, finely diced
4 garlic cloves, crushed
225g (8oz) dried Puy lentils
225g (8oz) pearl barley
2 x 680g jars passata

3 litres (5¼ pints) chicken stock
  or vegetable stock
salt and freshly ground
  black pepper
1 tbsp sugar
2 tbsp balsamic vinegar

1 Heat the oil in a deep frying pan, add the onion and carrots, and fry over a high heat, stirring, for 10 minutes or until lightly brown.

2 Add the garlic, lentils, and barley and fry for 1 minute. Blend in the passata and stock and season with salt and freshly ground black pepper.

3 Bring to the boil, cover with a lid, and simmer for 40–45 minutes (50–55 minutes for 12) or until the lentils and barley are tender.

4 Add the sugar and vinegar, check the seasoning, and serve.

PREPARE AHEAD
The soup can be made up to 3 days ahead.
Not suitable for freezing.

IN THE AGA
At step 3, cover with a lid and transfer to the simmering oven for 45–55 minutes.

Our lovely friend Jane gave us the idea for this recipe. It's creamy and luxurious – ideal before a light meal. Serve with croûtons.

GREAT FOR A CROWD

Honey-glazed parsnip soup

Serves 6

1 tbsp olive oil

900g (2lb) parsnips, roughly chopped

2 large onions, roughly chopped

4 celery sticks, sliced

1 leek, roughly chopped

1½ tbsp runny honey

1.4 litres (2½ pints) vegetable stock

salt and freshly ground black pepper

150ml (5fl oz) double cream

Serves 12

2 tbsp olive oil

1.5kg (3lb 3oz) parsnips, roughly chopped

4 large onions, roughly chopped

8 celery sticks, sliced

2 leeks, roughly chopped

3 tbsp runny honey

2.8 litres (5 pints) vegetable stock

salt and freshly ground black pepper

300ml (10fl oz) double cream

1 Heat the oil in a deep saucepan, add the vegetables, and fry over a high heat for a few minutes. Stir in the honey and fry for 4–5 minutes or until the vegetables are becoming golden brown and caramelized.

2 Add the stock and season with salt and freshly ground black pepper. Cover with a lid, lower the heat, and simmer for 20–30 minutes (35–40 minutes for 12) or until the parsnips are completely tender.

3 Transfer to a processor or blender and whiz until completely smooth.

4 Return to the pan to reheat, stir in the cream, and check the seasoning. Serve piping hot.

Great for a crowd... At the end of step 2, pour the contents of the pan through a sieve into a large bowl. Transfer the vegetables to a processor and whiz till smooth. Add a little of the cooking liquid and whiz again, then put the purée and the rest of the cooking liquid into a pan, stir well, and continue to step 4. The soup freezes well.

SERVING SUGGESTION

If you really want to impress your guests, serve a few mouthfuls of this soup in little coffee cups between your first and main courses, as they do in posh restaurants.

PREPARE AHEAD AND FREEZE

The soup can be made up to the end of step 3 up to 2 days ahead. Freeze at the end of step 3 for up to 1 month.

IN THE AGA

At step 2, cover with a lid and transfer to the simmering oven for 30 minutes (45 minutes for 12) or until the parsnips are tender.

These are perfect as a first course, but you could equally serve them as a light lunch. Serve warm with dressed salad leaves.

Fennel and smoked salmon tartlets

Makes 8

Special equipment 2 x 4-hole Yorkshire pudding trays or 8 x 10cm (4in) tart tins

For the pastry

175g (6oz) plain flour, plus a little extra to dust
85g (3oz) butter
1 egg
1 tbsp water

a knob of butter
1 large fennel bulb, roughly chopped
1 small red chilli, deseeded and chopped
150g (5½oz) smoked salmon, chopped
large handful of freshly chopped parsley
200ml (7fl oz) pouring double cream
2 eggs
salt and freshly ground black pepper
50g (1¾oz) mature Cheddar cheese, grated

Makes 12

Special equipment 3 x 4-hole Yorkshire pudding trays or 12 x 10cm (4in) tart tins

For the pastry

350g (12oz) plain flour, plus a little extra to dust
175g (6oz) butter
1 egg
1–2 tbsp water

a knob of butter
2 medium fennel bulbs, roughly chopped
1 large red chilli, deseeded and chopped
200g (7oz) smoked salmon, chopped
large handful of freshly chopped parsley
300ml (10fl oz) pouring double cream
3 eggs
salt and freshly ground black pepper
75g (2½oz) mature Cheddar cheese, grated

1 To make the pastry, put the flour and butter into a processor and whiz until the mixture resembles breadcrumbs. Add the egg and water and whiz until it forms a ball. Roll the pastry out thinly on a lightly floured work surface, then cut circles with a 12cm (5in) cutter or the bottom of a saucer. Place in the trays or tins and chill for 20 minutes.

2 Heat the knob of butter in a frying pan, add the fennel and chilli, and fry for 1 minute. Cover with a lid and cook over a low heat for 15 minutes or until soft. Set aside to cool.

3 Preheat the oven to 200°C (180°C fan/400°F/Gas 6) and put a baking sheet in to get hot (two sheets for 12). Meanwhile, divide the cooled fennel mixture among the pastry cases, then sprinkle over the smoked salmon and parsley. Whisk the cream and eggs together in a measuring jug, season with salt and freshly ground black pepper, and stir in half the cheese. Pour into the cases, then sprinkle over the remaining cheese.

4 Bake for 20 minutes (25 minutes for 12) or until golden brown and the pastry is crisp.

CHEAT
If you don't have time to make the pastry yourself, you can use shop bought – use 225g (8oz) shortcrust pastry for eight tartlets and 350g (12oz) for 12 tartlets.

PREPARE AHEAD AND FREEZE
You can make the tartlets up to 2 days ahead. Freeze for up to 2 months.

IN THE AGA
Bake on the floor of the roasting oven for 15–20 minutes. If you're making 12 tartlets, bake a batch of eight and then a batch of four.

Mary was given this recipe by a friend in Portugal who makes full use of fruits in season. We use vacuum-packed dry-cured ham, as it comes in convenient even-sized slices.

GREAT FOR A CROWD

Roasted figs with Parma ham and goat's cheese

Serves 6

2 x 100g rolls firm goat's cheese, such as Capricorn
6 fresh figs
12 slices Parma ham

rocket or salad leaves, to serve
balsamic vinegar, to serve
olive oil, to serve

Serves 12

4 x 100g rolls firm goat's cheese, such as Capricorn
12 fresh figs
24 slices Parma ham

rocket or salad leaves, to serve
balsamic vinegar, to serve
olive oil, to serve

1 Pop the goat's cheese in the freezer for about an hour or until firm.

2 Preheat the oven to 220°C (200°C fan/425°F/Gas 7). Cut off the pointed stem at the top of each fig, then stand the figs upright on a board. Cut a cross in the top of each one, but don't cut right down to the base.

3 Trim the ends off the cheese and discard, then cut each roll into three slices. Cut each slice in half to give semi-circles. Cut half the semi-circles in half again to give quarters.

4 Lie each slice of ham out flat and trim off any excess fat.

5 Put a semi-circle of cheese into each fig where you've made the cross. Use the quarters to fit in either side, so the complete cross is filled with goat's cheese.

6 Wrap each fig in a piece of ham, then wrap it in another piece, working in the other direction. Squeeze the ham together at the top.

7 Roast for 8 minutes (10 minutes for 12) or until the cheese has melted and the ham is crisp.

8 Arrange the figs on serving plates with some rocket or salad leaves, drizzle with a little balsamic vinegar and olive oil, and serve at once.

Great for a crowd... Replace the goat's cheese with a blue cheese such as Stilton. You can simply grate this and use it to fill the cross in the figs.

PREPARE AHEAD
You can prepare the figs up to the end of step 6 up to 12 hours ahead. Not suitable for freezing.

IN THE AGA
Bake on the second set of runners in the roasting oven for 6–8 minutes.

VARIATION
When figs are not in season, we use skinned, medium-sized, slightly under-ripe tomatoes prepared in the same way. Spoon a teaspoon of pesto over the cheese and tomato before wrapping it in the Parma ham.

This is such an easy first course for when asparagus is plentiful and at its best in the months of May and June.

Asparagus with Parmesan and mustard sauce

Serves 6

750g (1lb 10oz) asparagus spears, woody ends removed

salt and freshly ground black pepper

50g (1¾oz) Parmesan cheese, freshly grated

For the mustard sauce

2 tsp Dijon mustard

2 tsp white wine vinegar

4 tbsp sunflower oil

2 tbsp mayonnaise

juice of ½ lemon

1 tsp caster sugar

Serves 12

1.5kg (3lb 3oz) asparagus spears, woody ends removed

salt and freshly ground black pepper

100g (3½oz) Parmesan cheese, freshly grated

For the mustard sauce

1 heaped tbsp Dijon mustard

1½ tbsp white wine vinegar

8 tbsp sunflower oil

4 tbsp mayonnaise

juice of 1 lemon

2 tsp caster sugar

1 Preheat the oven to 220°C (200°C fan/425°F/Gas 7). Meanwhile, put the asparagus spears into a shallow pan of boiling salted water and bring back up to the boil. Boil for 3 minutes, then drain, refresh in cold water, and dry on kitchen paper.

2 Arrange six bundles of asparagus on a large baking sheet lined with parchment paper (12 bundles on two baking sheets for 12), season with salt and freshly ground black pepper, and sprinkle with the cheese.

3 Bake for 8 minutes (12 minutes for 12) or until the cheese has melted and browned and the asparagus is piping hot.

4 Meanwhile, make the sauce: put all the ingredients into a bowl and whisk with a hand whisk until well combined, then season with salt and freshly ground black pepper.

5 Carefully transfer the bundles on to hot plates and serve with the mustard sauce.

VARIATION

We like to cook the asparagus on a baking sheet and serve them in individual portions, but you can bake them in a large ovenproof dish and take it to the table if you prefer.

PREPARE AHEAD

The asparagus can be prepared up to the end of step 2 up to 1 day ahead. The sauce can be made up to 4 days ahead. Not suitable for freezing.

IN THE AGA

Bake on the top set of runners in the roasting oven for 7–8 minutes (8–10 minutes for 12).

These make a delicious creamy starter. Serve them in ramekins with crusty bread to mop up all the sauce.

Roquefort and parsley mousseline creams

Serves 6

Special equipment 6 x size 1 (150ml/5fl oz) ramekins, greased

45g (1½oz) butter
45g (1½oz) plain flour
300ml (10fl oz) hot milk
3 large eggs, separated

100g (3½oz) Roquefort, coarsely grated
1 tbsp freshly chopped parsley
salt and freshly ground black pepper
dash of Tabasco

Serves 12

Special equipment 12 x size 1 (150ml/5fl oz) ramekins, greased

75g (2½oz) butter
75g (2½oz) plain flour
600ml (1 pint) hot milk
6 large eggs, separated

225g (8oz) Roquefort, coarsely grated
2 tbsp freshly chopped parsley
salt and freshly ground black pepper
dash of Tabasco

1 Preheat the oven to 190°C (170°C fan/375°F/Gas 5). Meanwhile, melt the butter in a large saucepan, add the flour and then the milk, and whisk until the mixture thickens to a smooth white sauce. Remove from the heat and allow to cool slightly.

2 Meanwhile, whisk the egg whites in a bowl with an electric hand whisk until stiff.

3 Stir the cheese and parsley into the warm sauce and season with salt and freshly ground black pepper (not too much salt, as the cheese is salty). Add the egg yolks and Tabasco and stir to combine.

4 Mix a spoonful of the egg whites into the sauce until smooth, then fold in the rest so the mixture is light and combined. Spoon evenly into the ramekins and sit on a baking sheet.

5 Bake for 15–20 minutes (20–25 minutes for 12) or until risen and golden.

PREPARE AHEAD
The creams can be made up to the end of step 4 up to 6 hours ahead. Not suitable for freezing.

IN THE AGA
Bake on the second set of runners in the roasting oven for 15 minutes (15–20 minutes for 12).

A warming first course that's full of flavour. The bruschette are also perfect for a light lunch. Serve with dressed rocket leaves.

Bruschette with Reblochon and roasted vegetables

Serves 6

2 yellow peppers, halved, deseeded, and chopped into 2.5cm (1in) pieces

1 red onion, sliced into wedges

3 small courgettes, cut into 1cm (½in) slices

4 tbsp olive oil

salt and freshly ground black pepper

2 tsp balsamic vinegar

small bunch of basil, roughly chopped

½ ciabatta or white baguette

2 garlic cloves, crushed

200g (7oz) Reblochon de Savoie

paprika, to dust

Serves 12

4 yellow peppers, halved, deseeded, and chopped into 2.5cm (1in) pieces

2 red onions, sliced into wedges

6 small courgettes, cut into 1cm (½in) slices

8 tbsp olive oil

salt and freshly ground black pepper

4 tsp balsamic vinegar

large bunch of basil, roughly chopped

1 ciabatta or white baguette

4 garlic cloves, crushed

400g (14oz) Reblochon de Savoie

paprika, to dust

1 Preheat the oven to 220°C (200°C fan/425°F/Gas 7). Mix the vegetables in a roasting tin (two tins for 12), add half the oil, and season with salt and freshly ground black pepper. Toss together well, then roast for 30 minutes (45 minutes for 12) or until soft and tinged golden brown. Remove from the oven and stir in the vinegar and basil.

2 Meanwhile, cut the ciabatta or baguette into six slices (12 slices for 12). Mix the remaining oil with the garlic in a small bowl, then brush both sides of the bread with it. Place on a baking sheet and bake on a shelf under the vegetables, turning them halfway through, for 10–12 minutes or until lightly golden and crisp.

3 Remove the crispy bruschette from the oven and top with the vegetables. Keeping the rind on, slice the cheese into six wedges (12 wedges for 12), put one on top of each pile of vegetables, then dust lightly with paprika.

4 Return to the oven for 10–12 minutes (12–15 minutes for 12) or until the cheese has melted. If some runs off the sides of the bread, quickly scoop it back on top. Serve hot.

VARIATION

Reblochon de Savoie is a French cheese from the Alps. It is aged in cellars or caves in the mountains and is similar to Brie, but with a nuttier flavour. You can use Brie or goat's cheese instead, if you prefer.

PREPARE AHEAD

The ciabatta can be baked up to 3 days ahead. The vegetables can be roasted up to 8 hours ahead. Assemble up to the end of step 3 up to 3 hours ahead. Not suitable for freezing.

IN THE AGA

Roast the vegetables on the floor of the roasting oven for 25 minutes. Cook the bruschette at the top of the roasting oven for 8–10 minutes, turning them halfway through. At step 4, slide on to the second set of runners in the roasting oven for 8–10 minutes.

You can prepare this attractive starter ahead and have it ready and waiting in the fridge. Serve with lightly buttered brown bread.

Prawn and crayfish cocktail

Serves 6

8 tbsp mayonnaise

juice of ½ lemon

2 tbsp tomato ketchup

2 tsp creamed horseradish sauce

3 tbsp capers, drained, rinsed, dried, and roughly chopped

salt and freshly ground black pepper

300g (11oz) small cooked shelled North Atlantic prawns

175g (6oz) tub cooked crayfish tails, drained

4 Baby Gem lettuces

2 tbsp freshly chopped parsley

Serves 12

240ml (8fl oz) mayonnaise

juice of 1 lemon

4 tbsp tomato ketchup

1 heaped tbsp creamed horseradish sauce

6 tbsp capers, drained, rinsed, dried, and roughly chopped

salt and freshly ground black pepper

600g (1lb 5oz) small cooked shelled North Atlantic prawns

2 x 175g (6oz) tubs cooked crayfish tails, drained

8 Baby Gem lettuces

4 tbsp freshly chopped parsley

1 Mix the first five ingredients together in a bowl and season with salt and freshly ground black pepper.

2 Dry the prawns and crayfish tails on kitchen paper and stir into the sauce.

3 Peel the lettuce leaves from the heart and arrange 18 leaves (36 for 12) on a platter or on individual plates, allowing three leaves per person. Spoon the prawn mixture into the leaves and sprinkle with a little of the parsley.

PREPARE AHEAD

The sauce can be made up to 4 days ahead.

The dish can be assembled up to 6 hours ahead.

Not suitable for freezing.

A first course with wow factor, yet it is surprisingly easy to make. Serve cold with warm brown rolls or some good brown bread.

GREAT FOR A CROWD

Smoked salmon and prawns in dill mayonnaise

Serves 6

200g (7oz) shelled cooked North Atlantic prawns
200g (7oz) sliced smoked salmon
small bunch of fresh dill
170ml tub soured cream
finely grated zest of 1 lemon
juice of ½ lemon

dash of Tabasco
freshly ground black pepper
lamb's lettuce, a little vinaigrette, and 6 lemon wedges, to serve

Serves 12

400g (14oz) shelled cooked North Atlantic prawns
400g (14oz) sliced smoked salmon
large bunch of fresh dill
2 x 170ml tubs soured cream
finely grated zest of 2 lemons
juice of 1 lemon

generous dash of Tabasco
freshly ground black pepper
lamb's lettuce, a little vinaigrette, and 12 lemon wedges, to serve

1 Lay the prawns on kitchen paper and squeeze out any excess liquid.

2 Cut one long strip, about 1 x 5cm (½ x 2in), per serving from the salmon slices and put to one side. Cut the remaining smoked salmon into small pieces about 1cm (½in) in size.

3 Set aside a sprig of dill per serving, then chop the rest of the bunch finely and tip into a mixing bowl. Add the soured cream, lemon zest, lemon juice, Tabasco, and some freshly ground black pepper and stir to combine.

4 Add the prawns and chopped salmon pieces.

5 Arrange the lamb's lettuce on individual plates, drizzle with vinaigrette, then pile the prawn mixture in the centre.

6 Twist the reserved pieces of salmon into half-bow shapes and arrange on the top. Garnish with a sprig of dill and a wedge of lemon.

Great for a crowd... These are perfect for a crowd because they are individual servings, so you'll always know you have the right number.

PREPARE AHEAD
The prawn and salmon mixture can be made up to the end of step 4 up to 8 hours ahead – the flavours will actually improve. The plates can be arranged up to 3 hours ahead. Not suitable for freezing.

VARIATION
For very special occasions, arrange a fresh king prawn in the shell on the top of each portion. This recipe was given to us by Rosie, a private caterer, and we have adapted it to make it our own.

A delicious and impressive starter, which looks stunning at a dinner party, wedding, or other celebration. Serve with dressed salad leaves, lemon wedges, and buttered brown bread.

Crab, avocado, and smoked salmon tians

Serves 6

Special equipment *6 x 7cm (2¾in) metal cooking rings arranged on a baking sheet lined with cling film*

300g (11oz) fresh crab meat
100g (3½oz) full-fat cream cheese
bunch of dill, finely chopped
juice of 1 lemon
dash of Tabasco

½ tsp Dijon mustard
salt and freshly ground
   black pepper
3 small ripe avocados, halved,
   stoned, and peeled
6 handfuls of salad leaves such
   as watercress, rocket, or lamb's
   lettuce, to garnish
6 slices smoked salmon

Serves 12

Special equipment *12 x 7cm (2¾in) metal cooking rings arranged on a baking sheet lined with cling film*

600g (1lb 5oz) fresh crab meat
200g (7oz) full-fat cream cheese
large bunch of dill, finely chopped
juice of 2 lemons
generous dash of Tabasco

1 tsp Dijon mustard
salt and freshly ground
   black pepper
6 small ripe avocados, halved,
   stoned, and peeled
12 handfuls of salad leaves such
   as watercress, rocket, or lamb's
   lettuce, to garnish
12 slices smoked salmon

1 Mix the crab meat, cream cheese, dill, half the lemon juice, the Tabasco, and mustard in a bowl and season with salt and freshly ground black pepper.

2 Mash one avocado with a fork until smooth (two avocados for 12) and cut the remaining avocados into small pieces. Mix the mashed and chopped avocado together, stir in the remaining lemon juice, and season with salt and freshly ground black pepper.

3 Spoon the avocado mixture into the base of each cooking ring and press down with the back of a spoon.

4 Divide the crab mixture among the rings and spread to the edges to cover the avocado entirely. Cover with cling film and chill in the fridge for a few hours.

5 When ready to serve, arrange a handful of salad leaves on each plate, place a ring on top, then carefully remove the cling film and ring. Top each tian with a swirl of smoked salmon.

IMPROVISING

If you don't have metal cooking rings to shape the tians, don't worry – you can use ramekins lined with cling film. Lift the tians out carefully before serving and remove the cling film.

PREPARE AHEAD
The tians can be made up to 6 hours ahead.
Not suitable for freezing.

This is ideal for any occasion – buffet, picnic, even a smart dinner party. Serve it with toast or on individual plates with dressed rocket leaves.

Double salmon and egg terrine

Serves 6

Special equipment *450g (1lb) loaf tin lined with cling film*

100g (3½oz) fresh salmon fillet, skinned

a knob of butter, plus 25g (scant 1oz), at room temperature

salt and freshly ground black pepper

100g (3½oz) smoked salmon trimmings

100g (3½oz) full-fat cream cheese

3 tbsp light mayonnaise

1 tbsp freshly chopped chives

2 tbsp lemon juice

4 large hard-boiled eggs, chopped fairly finely

cress, to garnish

Serves 12

Special equipment *900g (2lb) loaf tin lined with cling film*

225g (8oz) fresh salmon fillet, skinned

a large knob of butter, plus 50g (1¾oz), at room temperature

salt and freshly ground black pepper

170g packet smoked salmon trimmings

200g (7oz) full-fat cream cheese

6 tbsp light mayonnaise

2 tbsp freshly chopped chives

juice of ½ lemon

8 large hard-boiled eggs, chopped fairly finely

cress, to garnish

1 Preheat the oven to 180°C (160°C fan/350°F/Gas 4). Place the salmon on some foil, spoon the knob of butter on top, and season with salt and freshly ground black pepper. Scrunch the sides of the foil together at the top to make a parcel, place on a baking sheet, and bake for 12–15 minutes (15–20 minutes for 12) or until just cooked. Set aside to cool in the foil.

2 Pick out the nicest pieces of smoked salmon (around half) and put the rest into a food processor with the cream cheese, the remaining butter, mayonnaise, chives, and lemon juice. Break up the cold salmon in the foil and add to the processor with the juices. Season with salt and freshly ground black pepper, then whiz until smooth. Spoon into a mixing bowl.

3 Add the eggs and stir until combined. Scatter the remaining smoked salmon trimmings (chopped, if necessary) on top of the cling film in the base of the loaf tin.

4 Spoon the mousse mixture on top and level the surface. Cover with cling film and chill in the fridge for at least 6 hours to firm up.

5 To serve, pop the terrine in the freezer for about 30 minutes to make slicing easier, then turn it out of the tin and cut into slices. Scatter with cress and serve.

PREPARE AHEAD
The terrine can be made up to the end of step 4 up to 2 days ahead. Not suitable for freezing.

IN THE AGA
Cook the salmon parcel in the simmering oven for 15 minutes or until just cooked.

A quick-to-prepare starter served with smoked trout. You'll find it in the chiller cabinets at the supermarket. Serve with warm rolls.

Smoked mackerel and watercress pâté

Serves 6

Special equipment *19cm (7½in) square cake tin, lined with cling film*

100g (3½oz) butter, at room temperature

175g (6oz) full-fat cream cheese

1 tbsp creamed horseradish

juice of ½ lemon

300g (11oz) smoked mackerel, skin removed

a few drops of Tabasco

25g (scant 1oz) fresh watercress, plus a little extra to garnish

freshly ground black pepper

6 small slices smoked trout

6 lemon wedges, to garnish

Serves 12

Special equipment *23 x 30cm (9 x 12in) traybake tin or roasting tin, lined with cling film*

225g (8oz) butter, at room temperature

350g (12oz) full-fat cream cheese

2 tbsp creamed horseradish

juice of 1 lemon

600g (1lb 5oz) smoked mackerel, skin removed

a few drops of Tabasco

50g (1¾oz) fresh watercress, plus a little extra to garnish

freshly ground black pepper

12 small slices smoked trout

12 lemon wedges, to garnish

1 Put the butter, cream cheese, horseradish, and lemon juice into a processor and whiz until completely smooth.

2 Remove any tiny bones from the mackerel, then break the flesh into pieces and add to the processor. Add the Tabasco and watercress, season with freshly ground black pepper, and whiz again until just blended.

3 Spoon into the tin and level the top. Cover with cling film and chill overnight.

4 To serve, pop the pâté in the freezer for about 30 minutes to make slicing easier, then turn it out and cut into squares, triangles, slices, or rounds. Arrange a piece on each plate, top with a slice of smoked trout in a swirl, then garnish with watercress and a lemon wedge.

PREPARE AHEAD
The pâté can be made up to the end of step 3 up to 2 days ahead. Not suitable for freezing.

Mary made this as part of a New Year's Eve pot luck supper party. The tray was quick to prepare and easy to bundle into the car with a plate of brown bread and butter.

Celebratory fish platter

Serves 6

For the gravadlax

500g (1lb 2oz) piece salmon fillet, from the thick end, skin on

2 tbsp dried dill

2 tbsp coarse sea salt

2 tbsp caster sugar

salt and freshly ground black pepper

6 tbsp mayonnaise

1 tsp Dijon mustard

2 tsp freshly chopped dill

For the prawn cocktail

300g (11oz) small cooked shelled North Atlantic prawns

6 tbsp light mayonnaise

juice of ½ lemon

2 tbsp tomato ketchup

2 tbsp creamed horseradish sauce

To serve

75g (2½oz) lamb's lettuce or rocket

6 large Little Gem lettuce leaves

6 large cooked king prawns, shell and head on

225g (8oz) smoked eel, cut into 2cm (¾in) pieces

lemon wedges

Serves 12

For the gravadlax

1kg (2¼lb) piece salmon fillet, from the thick end, skin on

4 tbsp dried dill

4 tbsp coarse sea salt

4 tbsp caster sugar

salt and freshly ground black pepper

12 tbsp mayonnaise

1 tbsp Dijon mustard

1 tbsp freshly chopped dill

For the prawn cocktail

600g (1lb 5oz) small cooked shelled North Atlantic prawns

12 tbsp light mayonnaise

juice of 1 small lemon

4 tbsp tomato ketchup

4 tbsp creamed horseradish sauce

To serve

175g (6oz) lamb's lettuce or rocket

12 large Little Gem lettuce leaves

12 large cooked king prawns, shell and head on

400g (14oz) smoked eel, cut into 2cm (¾in) pieces

lemon wedges

1 To make the gravadlax, place the salmon skin side down on a large piece of foil, then pull out any bones with tweezers or a small knife. Sprinkle over the dill, salt, sugar, and some freshly ground black pepper, making sure all the salmon is covered. Wrap in the foil and place on a tray or baking sheet. Place another baking sheet on top and put some heavy weights or tinned food on it to weigh the fish down. Transfer to the fridge for 12 hours or overnight.

2 Take the salmon from the fridge and pour away any juices. Place in the freezer for 30 minutes to make slicing easier. Then, using a sharp knife, cut into thin slices (see right).

3 To make the prawn cocktail, dry the prawns thoroughly with kitchen paper. Mix the mayonnaise, lemon juice, ketchup, and horseradish in a bowl, add the prawns, and season with salt and freshly ground black pepper.

4 To serve, scatter the lamb's lettuce or rocket over the base of a platter. Spoon the prawn cocktail into the lettuce leaves, garnish with a king prawn, then arrange around the edge. Put the smoked eel in a pile at the opposite end, arrange the gravadlax in the centre, then place the lemon wedges alongside. Mix the mayonnaise for the gravadlax with the mustard and dill, season with salt and freshly ground black pepper, and serve in a bowl.

SLICING THE SALMON

Cut the salmon into thin slices. Keep the knife angled at about 45° so the slices are wide. Discard the skin.

PREPARE AHEAD AND FREEZE

The gravadlax can be made up to 2 days ahead. Freeze for up to 1 month. The cocktail sauce can be made up to 12 hours ahead. Not suitable for freezing. The platter can be assembled up to 4 hours ahead.

This is so easy to make in a food processor. What's more, it requires no oven-baking – instead, it's cooked on the hob. Serve with toast.

Rustic mushroom liver pâté

Serves 6

Special equipment *450g (1lb) loaf tin, lined with cling film*

15g (½oz) dried porcini mushrooms

2 tbsp olive oil

1 onion, roughly chopped

50g (1¾oz) smoked streaky bacon, snipped into small pieces and rind removed

1 garlic clove, crushed

50g (1¾oz) chestnut mushrooms, thinly sliced

1 tsp each freshly chopped parsley and thyme leaves

200g (7oz) fresh chicken livers

25g (scant 1oz) fresh white breadcrumbs

50g (1¾oz) butter, at room temperature

100g (3½oz) full-fat cream cheese

2 tsp Worcestershire sauce

salt and freshly ground black pepper

a little freshly chopped parsley, to garnish

Serves 12

Special equipment *900g (2lb) loaf tin, lined with cling film*

25g (scant 1oz) dried porcini mushrooms

4 tbsp olive oil

1 large onion, roughly chopped

100g (3½oz) smoked streaky bacon, snipped into small pieces and rind removed

2 garlic cloves, crushed

100g (3½oz) chestnut mushrooms, thinly sliced

2 tsp each freshly chopped parsley and thyme leaves

400g (14oz) fresh chicken livers

50g (1¾oz) fresh white breadcrumbs

50g (1¾oz) butter, at room temperature

200g (7oz) full-fat cream cheese

1 tbsp Worcestershire sauce

salt and freshly ground black pepper

a little freshly chopped parsley, to garnish

1 Put the porcini into a bowl and pour over just enough boiling water to cover. Set aside to soften for about 30 minutes, then drain and dry well with kitchen paper.

2 Heat half the oil in a frying pan, add the onion, bacon, and porcini, and fry for 1 minute. Cover with a lid and cook over a low heat for 10 minutes or until the bacon is cooked. Add the garlic, mushrooms, parsley, and thyme and fry for 5 minutes or until the mushrooms are just cooked. Transfer to a mixing bowl.

3 Heat the remaining oil in the unwashed pan and fry the chicken livers for 1–2 minutes on each side or until brown on the outside and still pink in the centre. Add to the bowl with the porcini mixture and leave to cool.

4 Spoon half the cold chicken liver mixture into a processor, add the breadcrumbs, butter, cream cheese, and Worcestershire sauce, and whiz until smooth. Season with salt and freshly ground black pepper and whiz again until smooth and combined. Tip into a bowl.

5 Chop the remaining cold chicken liver mixture coarsely, then add to the bowl with the smooth pâté and stir to combine. Spoon into the prepared tin and level the top. Cover with cling film and chill for a minimum of 6 hours or overnight.

6 To serve, turn the tin upside down on to a serving plate and remove the cling film. Press some chopped parsley on top, cut the pâté in fairly thick slices, and serve.

PREPARE AHEAD
The pâté can be made up to 3 days ahead. Not suitable for freezing.

IN THE AGA
At step 2, cover with a lid and transfer to the simmering oven for 20 minutes to soften.

A very sociable first course that's also a bit of a cheat. If you are serving 12, arrange the food on two platters or tart plates.

Express Mediterranean platter

Serves 6

8 pepperdew peppers, drained and sliced

1 tbsp freshly chopped parsley

200g tub hummus

salt and freshly ground black pepper

6 stuffed vine leaves

200g (7oz) feta cheese, cut into bite-sized cubes

200g (7oz) marinated chargrilled artichokes in oil, drained and oil reserved

200g (7oz) Kalamata olives in oil, drained and oil reserved

6 pitta breads

Serves 12

16 pepperdew peppers, drained and sliced

2 tbsp freshly chopped parsley

2 x 200g tubs hummus

salt and freshly ground black pepper

12 stuffed vine leaves

400g (14oz) feta cheese, cut into bite-sized cubes

400g (14oz) marinated chargrilled artichokes in oil, drained and oil reserved

400g (14oz) Kalamata olives in oil, drained and oil reserved

12 pitta breads

1 Take a large flat platter or round tart plate and put a small bowl in the centre. Mix the pepperdew pepper slices and parsley with the hummus, season with salt and freshly ground black pepper, and spoon into the bowl.

2 Arrange the vine leaves, feta, artichokes, and olives in piles around the platter.

3 Toast the pitta and slice into fingers, then arrange in a pile next to the artichokes.

4 Drizzle the feta with some of the oil from the olives or artichokes and serve chilled or at room temperature.

KALAMATA OLIVES

We love the sweetness and rich flavour of Kalamata olives, but you can use your favourite olives instead.

PREPARE AHEAD

The hummus can be mixed with the parsley and peppers up to 4 days ahead. The platter can be assembled up to 8 hours ahead.

When you're serving numbers at a smart dinner party, it's always a good feeling to know the first course is made and waiting in the fridge. This recipe is perfect for that. Serve with brown bread rolls.

Fillet of beef with beetroot and horseradish dressing

Serves 6

300g (11oz) middle-cut fillet steak, trimmed

1 tbsp olive oil, plus a little extra to serve

salt and freshly ground black pepper

4 medium-sized cooked beetroot, thinly sliced

50g (1¾oz) rocket

50g (1¾oz) piece Parmesan cheese

For the horseradish dressing

2 tbsp creamed horseradish sauce

3 tbsp light mayonnaise

2 tbsp lemon juice

Serves 12

2 x 300g (11oz) middle-cut fillet steaks, trimmed

2 tbsp olive oil, plus a little extra to serve

salt and freshly ground black pepper

8 medium-sized cooked beetroot, thinly sliced

100g (3½oz) rocket

100g (3½oz) piece Parmesan cheese

For the horseradish dressing

4 tbsp creamed horseradish sauce

6 tbsp light mayonnaise

4 tbsp lemon juice

1 Rub the steak with the oil and season with salt and freshly ground black pepper.

2 Heat a frying pan until very hot, then fry the fillet for 2½ minutes on each side (fry each fillet separately for 12). This will give you a rare steak. If you prefer medium, cook for another minute on each side. Remove from the pan and leave to cool.

3 To make the dressing, put the ingredients into a small bowl and whisk with a hand whisk until smooth and combined. Season with salt and freshly ground black pepper.

4 When the steak is cold, carve into very thin slices – you're aiming to get 30 slices per fillet. Arrange five thin slices in a star shape on each plate. Arrange five slices of beetroot in the middle of the plate in a spiral shape, then drizzle with the horseradish dressing.

5 Gather together a little bundle of rocket leaves for each plate and place on top of the beetroot. Using a potato peeler, shave little shavings of Parmesan over the top.

6 Drizzle with a little olive oil and serve straightaway.

MIDDLE-CUT FILLET

When you carve the fillet, you want the slices to be long and thin rather than round. Which is why we use two middle-cut fillets to serve 12 instead of one whole fillet, which would be thinner at one end. The middle-cut fillets give you the correct shape.

PREPARE AHEAD

The plates can be prepared up to the end of step 5 up to 6 hours ahead. Drizzle with oil just before serving. Not suitable for freezing.

You can use any variety of sliced meats you like for this appetizing selection of roasted vegetables with an aubergine and mint dip. Serve with chunky bread, flat bread, or toasted pitta bread.

Moroccan platter

Serves 6

For the aubergine and mint dip

2 large aubergines

2 tbsp olive oil

3 fat garlic cloves (unpeeled)

100ml (3½fl oz) Greek yogurt

juice of ½ lemon

3 tbsp freshly chopped mint, plus a sprig to garnish

salt and freshly ground black pepper

For the roasted vegetables

4 courgettes, thickly sliced

1 yellow pepper, halved, deseeded, and sliced into large chunks

1 red pepper, halved, deseeded, and sliced into large chunks

2 tbsp olive oil

2 tbsp balsamic vinegar

Sliced meats

6 slices Parma ham

6 slices salami

6 slices chorizo

Serves 12

For the aubergine and mint dip

4 large aubergines

4 tbsp olive oil

6 fat garlic cloves (unpeeled)

200ml (7fl oz) Greek yogurt

juice of 1 lemon

6 tbsp freshly chopped mint, plus 2 sprigs to garnish

salt and freshly ground black pepper

For the roasted vegetables

8 courgettes, thickly sliced

2 yellow peppers, halved, deseeded, and sliced into large chunks

2 red peppers, halved, deseeded, and sliced into large chunks

4 tbsp olive oil

4 tbsp balsamic vinegar

Sliced meats

12 slices Parma ham

12 slices salami

12 slices chorizo

1 Preheat the oven to 220°C (200°C fan/425°F/Gas 7).

2 To make the aubergine and mint dip, slice the aubergines in half lengthways, arrange cut side up in a roasting tin, and drizzle with the oil. Add the garlic to the tin and roast for 30–35 minutes or until the aubergine flesh is soft.

3 Scoop the flesh out of the aubergines and place in a processor. Discard the skins. Squeeze the garlic from their skins and add to the aubergines, then whiz together until smooth. Add the yogurt, lemon juice, and mint, season with salt and freshly ground black pepper, and whiz again until combined. Spoon into a serving bowl (two bowls for 12) and set aside to cool.

4 Meanwhile, make the roasted vegetables. Arrange the courgettes, yellow pepper, and red pepper in a roasting tin, drizzle over the oil, and roast in the preheated oven for 30–35 minutes or until just cooked. Drizzle over the vinegar, season with salt and freshly ground black pepper, and set aside to cool.

5 To assemble the dish, arrange the cold meats in piles on a platter (two platters for 12), garnish the dip with mint and place in the centre, then arrange the roasted vegetables and the bread of your choice at the ends.

PREPARE AHEAD

The dip can be made up to 3 days ahead. The vegetables can be roasted up to 1 day ahead. The platter can be assembled up to 8 hours ahead. Not suitable for freezing.

IN THE AGA

Roast the aubergines, courgettes, and peppers on the floor of the roasting oven for 25–30 minutes or until tender.

SERVING PITTA BREAD

Pitta bread goes really well with this platter. Toast until lightly golden and handle with care – it gets very hot.

"A platter of tasty ingredients passed around the table makes a sociable starter. If you're serving 12, prepare two identical platters. If your guests are going to be standing up to eat, dot several platters around the room so they can help themselves."

Moroccan platter (see overleaf) ●●●▶

Special
main courses

There are often times when we want our guests to sit together at a table and eat. To give such events a real sense of occasion, we like to serve a main course that's that little bit special.

Special main courses

Main courses don't have to be tricky to be special – it's presentation that's key. Guests couldn't fail to be impressed by a whole side of salmon served on a platter with a glistening tarragon butter sauce, yet it's relatively straightforward to make. The same is true of duck breasts roasted till golden on the outside and pink in the middle, then sliced and arranged in a fan with a piquant lime and ginger sauce.

The other recipes in this chapter all follow suit. They are low on effort, but high on impact – just what you want when you're cooking for a crowd.

Special side dishes

Special main courses call for special side dishes, so on pages 123–129 we've included a selection of potato dishes and vegetable dishes for supper parties, dinner parties, or lunch. These are so delicious, they could almost be served as a course by themselves.

● If you want to keep the main course lighter, however, stick with some simply cooked vegetables or a green salad. Buy what's in season and pick out the freshest you can.

● In general, serve one or two side dishes. If you're cooking for large numbers, you might want to restrict it to just one – too much choice can quickly translate into too much preparation and too many dishes to serve hot.

"Our special main course recipes are low on effort, but high on impact – just what you want when you're cooking for a crowd."

Serving the main course

We like to serve our guests with the main course at a sit-down meal and always bear in mind the size of their appetites – you can generally count on a farmer or tree surgeon being famished, for instance, but our girlfriends usually aren't. The side dishes we bring to the table so people can help themselves.

Gently does it

Although you don't want to keep your guests hanging around, you don't want to hurry proceedings either.

● If you're not serving a starter, seat people before you bring out your main course.

● If you are serving a starter and your main course needs reheating, do it while you're eating the first course. Remember to allow 15–20 minutes for roast meats to rest before you carve them.

● Reheat your pudding, if necessary, while you're eating the main course.

● Don't rush to clear people's plates as soon as they've finished. Keep the atmosphere leisurely and relaxed. You might even encourage guests to swap places around the table before you serve the next course.

TABLE TALK *Since you're pulling out the stops with the food, it makes sense to go to a little extra effort with the table decorations. Use your most impressive china, arrange fresh flowers in a vase, and light the candles before your guests come to the table to sit down.*

The tomato in the vegetable stock gives the sauce a wonderful colour. To allow the flavours to infuse, prepare it the day before. Serve with new potatoes and fresh green vegetables or salad.

Salmon fillet with tarragon butter sauce

Serves 6

1 onion, finely chopped
1 carrot, finely chopped
1 celery stick, finely chopped
1 large tomato, cut in half
360ml (12fl oz) water
1 heaped tbsp freshly chopped tarragon (stalks reserved)

a little olive oil, to grease
salt and freshly ground black pepper
750–900g (1lb 10oz–2lb) side of salmon fillet in one piece, skin on
150g (5½oz) cold butter (straight from the fridge), cut into cubes

Serves 12

2 onions, finely chopped
2 carrots, finely chopped
2 celery sticks, finely chopped
2 large tomatoes, cut in half
750ml (1¼ pints) water
2 heaped tbsp freshly chopped tarragon (stalks reserved)

a little olive oil, to grease
salt and freshly ground black pepper
1.8kg (4lb) side of salmon or 2 x 750–900g (1lb 10oz–2lb) sides of salmon
300g (11oz) cold butter (straight from the fridge), cut into cubes

1 Put the onion, carrot, celery, tomato, and water into a saucepan. Add the reserved tarragon stalks and bring to the boil. Cover with a lid and simmer over a low heat for 10 minutes. Set aside for a minimum of 1 hour (ideally overnight) for the flavours to infuse.

2 Preheat the oven to 180°C (160°C fan/350°F/Gas 4). Line a baking sheet with foil, oil it lightly, and sprinkle with salt and freshly ground black pepper.

3 Lay the salmon skin side down on a board. Using a sharp knife, divide it into equal serving portions, cutting through the flesh until the knife touches the skin, but not cutting through it. Lay skin side up on the foil and bake for 20 minutes (25–30 minutes for 12) or until matt pink and just done. The precise timing will depend on the thickness.

4 To make the sauce, strain the vegetable stock into a saucepan, then boil rapidly until it reduces by half. Put the butter into a heatproof bowl, pour over the boiling stock, and whiz with a hand blender or in a processor until smooth.

5 Peel the skin from the fish and discard (if it doesn't peel easily, it isn't quite cooked, so pop it back into the oven for a few minutes). Transfer the fish portions to a platter or plates. Add the tarragon to the hot sauce, pour over the fish, and serve.

VARIATION
You can cook individual salmon fillets if you like, but we prefer doing it this way, as the fish doesn't dry out.

PREPARE AHEAD
The sauce can be made up to 2 days ahead. Add the tarragon while reheating. The salmon can be cooked the day before and served cold. Not suitable for freezing.

IN THE AGA
At step 1, cover with a lid and transfer to the simmering oven for 15 minutes. Bake the salmon on the second set of runners in the roasting oven for 15 minutes (20 minutes for 12).

Salmon fillets, cooked simply and slowly, are complemented by a rich sauce of asparagus, cream, and pesto. Serve with baby new potatoes or, for a special occasion, Jersey Royals.

Salmon and asparagus with a basil sauce

Serves 6

6 x 150g (5½oz) centre-cut salmon fillets, skinned
salt and freshly ground black pepper
12 asparagus spears

300ml (10fl oz) double cream
juice of ½ lemon
4 tbsp pesto

Serves 12

12 x 150g (5½oz) centre-cut salmon fillets, skinned
salt and freshly ground black pepper
24 asparagus spears

600ml (1 pint) double cream
juice of 1 lemon
8 tbsp pesto

1 Preheat the oven to 140°C (120°C fan/275°F/Gas 1). Line a roasting tin with a large piece of foil and arrange the salmon fillets on top in a single layer. Season with salt and freshly ground black pepper, then scrunch the sides of the foil at the top so the fillets are enclosed.

2 Cook in the oven for 50 minutes (1 hour for 12) or until the salmon is matt pink and just done. Don't let it overcook or it will become dry.

3 Meanwhile, trim the woody ends from the asparagus spears and discard, then cut off 5cm (2in) from each tip and put to one side. Finely shred the stalks, cutting them diagonally into thin slices.

4 Bring a pan of salted water to the boil, add the asparagus tips and shredded stalks, then bring back to the boil and cook for 3 minutes. Drain, separate the tips from the stalks, and keep warm.

5 Heat the cream, lemon juice, and pesto in a pan until hot. Add the cooked shredded stalks and season with salt and freshly ground black pepper.

6 To serve, arrange the hot salmon fillets on a serving plate. Pour over the sauce and garnish each fillet with two asparagus tips. Serve any leftover sauce separately.

Great for a crowd... Don't be tempted to pile the fillets on top of each other to cook them – bake in a single layer in separate roasting tins.

PREPARE AHEAD

The asparagus can be cooked up to 8 hours ahead, then drained, refreshed in cold water, and drained again. Plunge the asparagus tips into boiling water for 30 seconds to warm through. The sauce can be made up 8 hours ahead. Not suitable for freezing.

IN THE AGA

Cook the salmon in the simmering oven for 45 minutes (55 minutes for 12).

Salmon and asparagus with a basil sauce (see overleaf) ●●●>

So many people love fishcakes, which is why we always invent a new recipe for them for each of our books.

Double salmon fishcakes with horseradish sauce

Serves 6

350g (12oz) cooked salmon, skin and bones removed
100g (3½oz) hot-smoked salmon
450g (1lb) mashed potato
3 tbsp mayonnaise
2 tbsp creamed horseradish
2 heaped tbsp freshly snipped chives
2 heaped tbsp freshly chopped parsley
salt and freshly ground black pepper
1 egg, beaten

50g (1¾oz) fresh breadcrumbs
1 tbsp olive oil
1 lemon, cut into 6 wedges, to garnish

For the horseradish sauce

150ml (5fl oz) soured cream or full-fat crème fraîche
3 tbsp creamed horseradish
2 tbsp mayonnaise
2 tbsp freshly snipped chives

Serves 12

700g (1lb 9oz) cooked salmon, skin and bones removed
200g (7oz) hot-smoked salmon
900g (2lb) mashed potato
6 tbsp mayonnaise
4 tbsp creamed horseradish
4 heaped tbsp freshly snipped chives
4 heaped tbsp freshly chopped parsley
salt and freshly ground black pepper
1 egg, beaten

100g (3½oz) fresh breadcrumbs
2 tbsp olive oil
2 lemons, each cut into 6 wedges, to garnish

For the horseradish sauce

300ml (10fl oz) soured cream or full-fat crème fraîche
6 tbsp creamed horseradish
4 tbsp mayonnaise
4 tbsp freshly snipped chives

1 Put both kinds of salmon, the mashed potato, mayonnaise, horseradish, and herbs into a mixing bowl, season with salt and freshly ground black pepper, and stir well to combine.

2 Divide the mixture into 12 (24 for 12) and shape into fishcakes. They shouldn't be too thick. Brush with beaten egg, coat with breadcrumbs, and chill for a minimum of an hour.

3 Meanwhile, make the sauce: put all the ingredients into a bowl, season with salt and freshly ground black pepper, and mix together well. Set aside.

4 Heat the oil in a non-stick frying pan and fry the fishcakes for 3–4 minutes on each side or until golden on the outside and hot in the middle. You may need to do this in batches and keep them warm in the oven.

5 Serve the fishcakes hot with a spoonful of the cold sauce and a lemon wedge.

PREPARE AHEAD AND FREEZE
The fishcakes can be made up to the end of step 2 up to 1 day ahead. Alternatively, fry them the day before and reheat. The sauce can be made up to 3 days ahead. Freeze the fishcakes at the end of step 2 for up to 2 months.

A wonderful all-in-one dish – new potatoes, onions, and courgettes with lightly cooked trout fillets and a fresh sauce.

Trout fillets with roasted vegetables and lemon sauce

Serves 6

750g (1lb 10oz) baby new
  potatoes, halved lengthways
3 medium onions, peeled and
  cut into 8 wedges
salt and freshly ground
  black pepper
3 tbsp olive oil
4 small courgettes, thinly sliced
6 trout fillets, skin on

For the sauce

6 tbsp freshly chopped parsley
finely grated zest and juice of
  1 large lemon
85g (3oz) butter, melted

Serves 12

1.5kg (3lb 3oz) baby new
  potatoes, halved lengthways
5 large onions, peeled and cut
  into 8 wedges
salt and freshly ground
  black pepper
6 tbsp olive oil
8 small courgettes, thinly sliced
12 trout fillets, skin on

For the sauce

large bunch of parsley, chopped
finely grated zest and juice of
  2 large lemons
175g (6oz) butter, melted

1 Preheat the oven to 200°C (180°C fan/400°F/Gas 6). Put the potatoes and onions in a pan, cover with cold salted water, bring to the boil, and cook for 10 minutes or until just tender.

2 Drain, toss in half the oil, season with black pepper, and arrange in a single layer in a large roasting tin or ovenproof dish (two tins or dishes for 12). Roast for 20 minutes (30 minutes for 12) or until the potatoes and onions are just tender.

3 Toss the courgettes in a bowl with the remaining oil and season with salt and freshly ground black pepper.

4 Season the flesh side of the trout with salt and freshly ground black pepper. Stir the contents of the roasting tin, then lay the trout skin side up in a single layer on top of them. Scatter the courgettes around the fish. Return to the oven and cook for 12–15 minutes (20–30 minutes for 12) or until the fish is tender.

5 Meanwhile, make the sauce: mix the parsley, lemon zest, and lemon juice together in a bowl. Stir in the butter and season with salt and freshly ground black pepper.

6 Peel the skin from the fish and discard. Transfer to a serving plate with the vegetables, then spoon some of the hot sauce over the top. Serve the rest of the sauce separately.

SKINNING THE TROUT

If the skin doesn't come off easily, the trout is not quite cooked, so pop it back into the oven for a few minutes.

PREPARE AHEAD

The vegetables can be cooked up to the end of step 2 up to 6 hours ahead. The sauce can be made up to 1 day ahead. Not suitable for freezing.

IN THE AGA

At step 2, roast on the floor of the roasting oven for 15 minutes (30 minutes for 12). At step 4, cook on the second set of runners in the roasting oven for 12 minutes (15 minutes for 12).

An impressive centrepiece for a dinner party or buffet table. Cooking the trout with the skin on gives it a fresher flavour and keeps it moist.

Hot baked trout with tomato and basil salsa

Serves 6

a little olive oil

salt and freshly ground
   black pepper

750g (1lb 10oz) trout fillet,
   skin on

3 tbsp freshly shredded basil

3 tbsp olive oil

1 tsp caster sugar

a good dash of Tabasco

1 tbsp lemon juice

For the salsa

500g (1lb 2oz) tomatoes

½ cucumber

3 spring onions, finely chopped

Serves 12

a little olive oil

salt and freshly ground
   black pepper

1.35kg (3lb) trout fillet or
   2 x 750g (1lb 10oz) trout
   fillets, skin on

6 spring onions, finely chopped

6 tbsp freshly shredded basil

6 tbsp olive oil

2 tsp caster sugar

a good dash of Tabasco

2 tbsp lemon juice

For the salsa

1kg (2¼lb) tomatoes

1 cucumber

1 Preheat the oven to 200°C (180°C fan/400°F/Gas 6). Line a baking sheet with foil, then brush it with a little olive oil and sprinkle with salt and freshly ground black pepper.

2 Lay the trout skin side down on a board. Using a sharp knife, cut it into equal serving portions, taking care not to cut through the skin. Lay it skin side up on the baking sheet and bake for 15–20 minutes (30 minutes for 12) or until just cooked.

3 Meanwhile, make the salsa: skin the tomatoes (see right), then slice in half, remove the seeds, and cut the flesh into small dice. Peel the cucumber with a vegetable peeler, then slice in half lengthways. Discard the seeds and cut the flesh into dice the size of the tomatoes.

4 Mix the tomatoes, cucumber, onions, and half the basil in a bowl. Whisk the oil, sugar, Tabasco, lemon juice, and some salt and freshly ground black pepper in a separate bowl, then pour over the tomatoes and stir to combine.

5 Peel the skin from the trout and discard (if it does not peel off easily, it is not quite cooked, so pop it back in the oven for a few minutes). Arrange on a serving platter.

6 Spoon the salsa down the centre of the fish and scatter with the remaining basil. If you have any salsa leftover, serve it in a separate bowl. Serve the trout hot or warm with the cold salsa.

SKINNING TOMATOES

STEP 1 Place the tomato in boiling water for 20 seconds or until the skin splits, then remove.

STEP 2 When cool enough to handle, carefully peel the skin from the tomato with a paring knife.

PREPARE AHEAD
The salsa can be made up to 8 hours ahead. Not suitable for freezing.

IN THE AGA
Bake on the second set of runners in the roasting oven for 12–15 minutes (20–25 minutes for 12).

These look impressive, yet are so easy. Buy pieces of haddock that are roughly the same shape. Serve with salad and new potatoes.

Haddock mousseline parcels

Serves 6

12 x 75g (2½oz) pieces of unsmoked haddock
salt and freshly ground black pepper
175g (6oz) undyed smoked haddock fillet, roughly chopped
50g (1¾oz) baby spinach
a little freshly grated nutmeg
2 tbsp freshly chopped parsley
finely grated zest of 1 lemon

500ml tub full-fat crème fraîche
1 egg
6 sheets filo pastry
melted butter, for brushing

For the spinach sauce

knob of butter
175g (6oz) baby spinach
juice of 1 lemon

Serves 12

24 x 75g (2½oz) pieces of unsmoked haddock
salt and freshly ground black pepper
350g (12oz) undyed smoked haddock fillet, roughly chopped
100g (3½oz) baby spinach
a little freshly grated nutmeg
4 tbsp freshly chopped parsley
finely grated zest of 2 lemons

2 x 500ml tubs full-fat crème fraîche
2 eggs
12 sheets filo pastry
melted butter, for brushing

For the spinach sauce

knob of butter
350g (12oz) baby spinach
juice of 2 lemons

1 Preheat the oven to 200°C (180°C fan/400°F/Gas 6). Pop a baking sheet in to get very hot (two sheets for 12). Arrange the unsmoked haddock pieces in pairs on a board and season well with salt and freshly ground black pepper.

2 Put the smoked haddock into a processor and whiz for 1 minute or until finely minced. Add the spinach, nutmeg, parsley, lemon zest, and 2 tablespoons of the crème fraîche (4 tablespoons for 12) and season well with freshly ground black pepper. Separate the egg(s), add the white(s) to the processor, and reserve the yolk(s) for the sauce. Whiz until fairly smooth.

3 Divide the mousseline mixture into six equal portions (12 portions for 12) and spoon on top of half the unsmoked haddock pieces. Sit another piece of haddock on top of each one.

4 Brush the sheets of filo with butter. Place half of them side by side on a board, then place the other half directly on top. Cut each into four lengthways to give 12 strips (24 strips for 12).

5 Sit each haddock sandwich in the middle of a strip of filo, then bring the sides up to meet at the top. Lay another strip of filo over the top in the opposite direction and tuck the sides underneath, so the haddock is wrapped in filo on all sides. Repeat with the others.

6 Brush the tops of the filo with melted butter and sit the parcels on the hot baking sheet(s). Bake for 15 minutes (25 minutes for 12) or until golden and crisp.

7 To make the sauce, melt the butter in a pan and cook the spinach for 2 minutes or until wilted. Add the rest of the crème fraîche, some salt and freshly ground black pepper, and bring to the boil. Transfer to a processor and whiz till smooth. Stir in the yolk(s) and lemon juice and reheat.

8 To serve, cut each haddock parcel in half diagonally to make two triangles. Spoon the hot sauce on to dinner plates and sit two triangles of haddock upright in the centre of each one.

PREPARE AHEAD
The parcels can be made up to the end of step 5 up to 5 hours ahead. The sauce can be made up to 8 hours ahead. Add the yolk(s) and lemon juice just before serving. Not suitable for freezing.

IN THE AGA
Bake on the floor of the roasting oven for 8–10 minutes, then transfer to the top of the roasting oven to brown for a further 8–10 minutes.

Fresh and healthy, this dish is great for garden parties. Marinate it overnight for maximum flavour. Serve with salad and new potatoes.

Marinated chicken with summer salsa

Serves 6

2 red chillies, halved, deseeded, and finely diced
4 garlic cloves, crushed
6 tbsp freshly chopped parsley
zest and juice of 1 large lemon
4 tbsp olive oil
2 tbsp runny honey
4 tsp paprika
6 skinless chicken breasts

6 spring onions, finely sliced
small bunch of coriander, roughly chopped
finely grated zest and juice of 1 lime
2 tsp balsamic vinegar
2 tbsp olive oil
1 tsp caster sugar
salt and freshly ground black pepper

For the salsa

2 large tomatoes, cut in half, deseeded, and diced
½ cucumber, peeled, halved, deseeded, and diced

Serves 12

4 red chillies, halved, deseeded, and finely diced
8 garlic cloves, crushed
bunch of parsley, chopped
zest and juice of 2 lemons
8 tbsp olive oil
4 tbsp runny honey
2 heaped tbsp paprika
12 skinless chicken breasts

12 spring onions, finely sliced
large bunch of coriander, roughly chopped
finely grated zest and juice of 2 limes
1 tbsp balsamic vinegar
4 tbsp olive oil
2 tsp caster sugar
salt and freshly ground black pepper

For the salsa

4 large tomatoes, cut in half, deseeded, and diced
1 cucumber, peeled, halved, deseeded, and diced

1 Mix the first seven ingredients together in a large bowl. Add the chicken breasts and turn to coat. Leave to marinate in the fridge for 1–2 hours or overnight.

2 Preheat the oven to 220°C (200°C fan/425°F/Gas 7). Heat a griddle pan until hot, add the chicken, and brown for 20–30 seconds on each side or until griddle marks are left. You may need to do this in batches. Arrange on a baking sheet lined with non-stick baking parchment.

3 Roast for 25 minutes (35 minutes for 12) or until golden and cooked through. Remove from the oven and allow to rest for 5 minutes.

4 Meanwhile, make the salsa: mix all the ingredients in a large bowl and season with salt and freshly ground black pepper.

5 Carve the chicken into thick slices and serve with the salsa.

PREPARE AHEAD
The chicken can be prepared up to the end of step 2 up to 1 day ahead. The salsa ingredients can be prepared up to 1 day ahead and mixed together 1 hour ahead. Not suitable for freezing.

IN THE AGA
Roast the chicken in the middle of the roasting oven for 25 minutes (35 minutes for 12).

This is truly scrumptious. It's also quick to make. Home-made pesto is best, but you can use good-quality pesto from a jar if you're short of time. Serve with potatoes and salad.

Chicken with pesto, Taleggio, and roasted tomatoes

Serves 6

6 skinless boneless
  chicken breasts
salt and freshly gound
  black pepper
175g (6oz) Taleggio cheese
  (straight from the fridge),
  cut into small cubes
3 tbsp pesto

2 tbsp freshly chopped basil
3 tbsp full-fat cream cheese
50g (1¾oz) fresh breadcrumbs
a pinch of paprika
400g (14oz) cherry tomatoes
  on the vine
2 tbsp olive oil
1 tbsp balsamic vinegar

Serves 12

12 skinless boneless
  chicken breasts
salt and freshly gound
  black pepper
300g (11oz) Taleggio cheese
  (straight from the fridge),
  cut into cubes
5 tbsp pesto

4 tbsp freshly chopped basil
5 tbsp full-fat cream cheese
75g (2½oz) fresh breadcrumbs
a pinch of paprika
900g (2lb) cherry tomatoes
  on the vine
3 tbsp olive oil
2 tbsp balsamic vinegar

1 Preheat the oven to 220°C (200°C fan/425°F/Gas 7). Arrange the chicken breasts in a single layer in an ovenproof dish or roasting tin and season with salt and freshly ground black pepper.

2 Mix the Taleggio, pesto, basil, and cream cheese in a bowl and season with salt and freshly ground black pepper. Spoon on to the chicken breasts, spreading the mixture out to cover them completely. Sprinkle with the breadcrumbs and dust with a little paprika.

3 Bake for 20 minutes, then arrange the tomatoes around the chicken, pour the oil and vinegar over them, and return to the oven for a further 10 minutes (30 minutes for 12) or until the chicken is just cooked through. Be careful not to overcook it.

4 To serve, arrange a chicken breast on each plate with a few tomatoes, then spoon over some of the juices from the dish.

PREPARE AHEAD AND FREEZE
The chicken can be prepared up to the end of step 2 up to 12 hours ahead. Freeze at the end of step 2 for up to 2 months.

IN THE AGA
Roast on the second set of runners in the roasting oven for 15 minutes, add the tomatoes, and cook for 10 minutes more (30 minutes for 12).

MAKING PESTO

STEP 1 Put a large bunch of basil, 2 crushed garlic cloves, 1 tbsp pine nuts, and 2 tbsp freshly grated Parmesan cheese in a blender.

STEP 2 With the motor running, slowly pour in 100ml (3½fl oz) extra virgin olive. Season to taste.

A quick recipe that you can either prepare ahead or at the last minute. Serve with new potatoes and green vegetables or salad.

Sun-blushed tomato and herb chicken

Serves 6

1 tbsp freshly chopped parsley
3 tbsp freshly snipped chives
1 tbsp freshly chopped basil
200g tub full-fat cream cheese
1 egg yolk
2 tsp lemon juice
50g (1¾oz) sun-blushed or
 sun-ripened tomatoes, snipped
 into small pieces

salt and freshly ground
 black pepper
6 boneless chicken breasts,
 skin on
a little runny honey

For the sauce

150ml (5fl oz) dry white wine
300ml (10fl oz) double cream
1 tbsp freshly chopped parsley

Serves 12

2 tbsp freshly chopped parsley
6 tbsp freshly snipped chives
2 tbsp freshly chopped basil
2 x 200g tubs full-fat
 cream cheese
2 egg yolks
1 tbsp lemon juice
100g (3½oz) sun-blushed or
 sun-ripened tomatoes, snipped
 into small pieces

salt and freshly ground
 black pepper
12 boneless chicken breasts,
 skin on
a little runny honey

For the sauce

300ml (10fl oz) dry white wine
600ml (1 pint) double cream
2 tbsp freshly chopped parsley

1 Preheat the oven to 200°C (180°C fan/400°F/Gas 6). Put the first seven ingredients into a bowl, season with salt and freshly ground black pepper, and stir until combined.

2 Loosen the skin from the chicken breasts, but keep it attached at one side. Spoon the filling underneath and replace the skin.

3 Arrange the chicken breasts in a roasting tin, season with salt and freshly ground black pepper, then drizzle with a little honey.

4 Roast for 25–30 minutes (35–40 minutes for 12) or until golden and cooked through.

5 Meanwhile, make the sauce: put the wine into a pan (use a wide-based pan for 12, to make the reduction quicker) and boil over a high heat until it has reduced to about 3 tablespoons (6 tablespoons for 12). Add the cream and boil for a couple of minutes to thicken. Season with salt and freshly ground black pepper.

6 Allow the chicken breasts to rest for a few minutes after roasting, then add any juices from the tin to the sauce. Carve each breast into three or serve whole. Add the parsley to the hot sauce and serve with the chicken.

SUN-BLUSHED TOMATOES

Partly dried (rather than completely dried) tomatoes are sold under different names in different shops, but sun-blushed and sun-ripened tomatoes are the same thing.

PREPARE AHEAD
The chicken can be prepared up to the end of step 2 up to 1 day ahead. The sauce can be made up to 2 days ahead. Not suitable for freezing.

IN THE AGA
Roast on the second set of runners in the roasting oven for 25 minutes (35 minutes for 12).

This is one of Lucy's fail-safe recipes that can be rustled up quickly while everyone is enjoying a glass of wine. Serve with plain rice.

Pan-fried chicken with mushrooms and tarragon

Serves 6

1 tbsp olive oil
5 small skinless boneless chicken breasts, cut into thin strips
salt and freshly ground black pepper
1 large onion, finely chopped

2 medium courgettes, cut into thick matchsticks
350g (12oz) button mushrooms, quartered
2 large garlic cloves
200ml (7fl oz) dry white wine

200ml (7fl oz) double cream
juice of ½ lemon
1 heaped tbsp freshly chopped tarragon

Serves 12

This dish is not suitable for more than six because the sauce would not reduce to a thick consistency and be wet from the large quantity of vegetables.

1 Heat the oil in a deep frying pan, add half the chicken strips, season with salt and freshly ground black pepper, and brown over a high heat until golden all over. Remove with a slotted spoon and set aside on a plate. Cook the rest of the chicken strips in the same way.

2 Add the onion and fry over a high heat for a few minutes or until golden. Cover with a lid, lower the heat, and cook for 15 minutes or until tender. Turn up the heat, add the courgettes, mushrooms, and garlic, and fry for 3 minutes or until the vegetables start to soften. Remove from the pan and set aside with the chicken.

3 Add the wine to the pan and boil over a high heat until it has reduced in volume to about 4 tablespoons. Stir in the cream and boil again for a few minutes until the sauce thickens. Stir in the lemon juice and season with salt and freshly ground black pepper. Return the chicken and vegetables to the pan for a couple of minutes to heat through.

4 Add the tarragon and serve immediately.

PREPARE AHEAD
This is best cooked to serve. Not suitable for freezing.

This is such a simple yet classy dish, easy to cook for a crowd on formal occasions. Serve with new potatoes and green vegetables.

Boursin-stuffed chicken with garlic and mint sauce

Serves 6

150g packet full-fat Poivre
   Boursin cheese
75g (2½oz) mature Cheddar
   cheese, grated
6 skinless boneless
   chicken breasts
salt and freshly ground
   black pepper
2 tbsp runny honey
a pinch of paprika
200ml (7fl oz) dry white wine

2 large garlic cloves, sliced in half
300ml (10fl oz) double cream
200g (7oz) French beans,
   trimmed and sliced into three
300g (11oz) frozen broad beans
300g (11oz) frozen petits pois
a knob of butter
2 tbsp freshly chopped mint

Serves 12

2 x 150g packets full-fat Poivre
   Boursin cheese
175g (6oz) mature Cheddar
   cheese, grated
12 skinless boneless
   chicken breasts
salt and freshly ground
   black pepper
4 tbsp runny honey
a pinch of paprika
400ml (14fl oz) dry white wine

4 large garlic cloves, sliced in half
600ml (1 pint) double cream
400g (14oz) French beans,
   trimmed and sliced into three
600g (1lb 5oz) frozen
   broad beans
600g (1lb 5oz) frozen petits pois
a large knob of butter
4 tbsp freshly chopped mint

1 Preheat the oven to 220°C (200°C fan/425°F/Gas 7). Mash the Boursin and Cheddar together with a fork in a small bowl. Make three diagonal slashes in the top of each chicken breast, cutting about half the way through. Season with salt and freshly ground black pepper, then spoon the cheese into the gaps. Arrange in a flat ovenproof dish.

2 Drizzle with the honey and sprinkle with paprika. Roast in the oven for 20–25 minutes or until cooked, then remove from the oven and leave to rest for 5 minutes.

3 Meanwhile, put the wine and garlic into a saucepan and boil until reduced by half. Add the cream and boil until reduced by one-third or until the sauce has thickened to a pouring consistency. Remove the garlic and season with salt and freshly ground black pepper.

4 Bring a pan of salted water to the boil. Add the French beans, broad beans, and petits pois and boil for 4 minutes or until just cooked. Drain and toss with the butter.

5 Reheat the sauce and add the mint. Spoon the vegetables on to plates and place a chicken breast on top of each one. Serve with a little of the sauce.

POIVRE BOURSIN

You'll find this in packets in the cheese section of the supermarket. Be sure to get the full-fat cheese and not the "light" version.

PREPARE AHEAD

The chicken breasts can be prepared up to the end of step 1 up to 1 day ahead. The sauce can be made up to 3 days ahead. Add the mint just before serving. Not suitable for freezing.

IN THE AGA

Roast the chicken on the second set of runners in the roasting oven for 18–20 minutes (25–30 minutes for 12).

A warming dish that's perfect for sharing with friends when game is in season. Serve with mash or red cabbage and green vegetables.

Pheasant breasts with mushrooms and Madeira

Serves 6

2 onions, sliced

3 thyme sprigs

3 young pheasants

600ml (1 pint) hot game stock or chicken stock

50g (1¾oz) butter

250g (9oz) small chestnut mushrooms, quartered

45g (1½oz) plain flour

4 tbsp cold water

150ml (5fl oz) Madeira

1 tbsp balsamic vinegar

1 tbsp freshly chopped thyme leaves

1 tbsp full-fat crème fraîche

salt and freshly ground black pepper

Serves 12

4 onions, sliced

6 thyme sprigs

6 young pheasants

1.2 litres (2 pints) hot game stock or chicken stock

100g (3½oz) butter

500g (1lb 2oz) small chestnut mushrooms, quartered

85g (3oz) plain flour

8 tbsp cold water

300ml (10fl oz) Madeira

2 tbsp balsamic vinegar

2 tbsp freshly chopped thyme leaves

2 tbsp full-fat crème fraîche

salt and freshly ground black pepper

1 Preheat the oven to 200°C (180°C fan/400°F/Gas 6). Line a large roasting tin with foil and scatter the onions over the base.

2 Put a sprig of thyme in the cavity of each bird. Arrange them breast side down on top of the onions in the tin.

3 Pour over the hot stock, cover with foil, and roast for 50 minutes (1 hour for 12) or until the breasts are tender. Remove from the tin and allow to rest. Reserve the stock.

4 Melt the butter in a saucepan, add the mushrooms, and fry over a high heat for a few minutes or until soft. Strain the stock from the roasting tin into a measuring jug until you have 450ml/15fl oz (900ml/1½ pints for 12).

5 Mix the flour to a runny paste with the cold water, then stir in with the mushrooms and fry for 1 minute. Gradually add the measured stock and Madeira, stirring until blended. Bring to the boil, add the vinegar, thyme, and crème fraîche, and season with salt and freshly ground black pepper.

6 Using a sharp knife, detach the pheasant breasts from the carcass and cut each into three diagonally. Arrange in an ovenproof dish and pour over the hot sauce. If the thighs are tender, they can also be served. If tough, use to make game stock with the carcass.

PREPARE AHEAD

The dish can be cooked up to the end of step 6 up to 1 day ahead. Not suitable for freezing.

IN THE AGA

Roast the pheasants in the centre of the roasting oven for 45 minutes (55 minutes–1 hour for 12).

This is an easy way to cook duck breasts, as you brown them well ahead. You then cook them at the last minute, without the worry about whether they will be golden or not. Serve with green beans.

Duck breasts with a piquant lime and ginger sauce

Serves 6

6 duck breasts, skinned

salt and freshly ground
   black pepper

1 tbsp olive oil

2 tsp freshly grated root ginger

300ml (10fl oz) full-fat
   crème fraîche

juice of 1 lime

small knob of butter, at
   room temperature

3 tbsp lime marmalade

chives, to garnish

Serves 12

12 duck breasts, skinned

salt and freshly ground
   black pepper

2 tbsp olive oil

4 tsp freshly grated root ginger

600ml (1 pint) full-fat
   crème fraîche

juice of 2 limes

large knob of butter, at
   room temperature

6 tbsp lime marmalade

chives, to garnish

1 Season the duck breasts with salt and freshly ground black pepper, then heat the oil in a frying pan and brown each one on its skinned side for a minute or so or until golden. Set aside. Add the ginger to the pan and heat over a low heat for 1 minute. Whisk in the crème fraîche and lime juice until smooth and combined. Set aside until needed.

2 Mix the butter and marmalade together in a bowl, then spread over the browned side of the cold duck breasts. Arrange in a roasting tin browned side up.

3 When ready to serve, preheat the oven to 220°C (200°C fan/425°F/Gas 7). Roast the duck for 12–15 minutes (15–20 minutes for 12) or until cooked but still pink. Set aside to rest.

4 Meanwhile, place the roasting tin on the hob, add the lime and ginger sauce, and heat until hot, scraping up any sticky bits from the bottom of the tin.

5 Carve each duck breast diagonally into three and serve on the hot sauce with a garnish of chives.

PREPARE AHEAD
You can prepare the duck up to the end of step 2 up to 1 day ahead. Not suitable for freezing.

IN THE AGA
Roast the duck on the top set of runners in the roasting oven for 12 minutes.

This is a joy because it can be prepared ahead and reheated just before serving. Lucy often cooks it at her Aga demonstrations, where it goes down a treat. Serve with new potatoes and a green vegetable.

Fillet steak with a creamy mushroom sauce

Serves 6

225g (8oz) chestnut mushrooms, thinly sliced

2 tbsp brandy

300ml (10fl oz) pouring double cream

salt and freshly ground black pepper

6 x 150g (5½oz) middle-cut fillet steaks

1 tbsp olive oil

225g (8oz) baby spinach

50g (1¾oz) fresh white breadcrumbs

a little paprika, to dust

Serves 12

450g (1lb) chestnut mushrooms, thinly sliced

4 tbsp brandy

600ml (1 pint) pouring double cream

salt and freshly ground black pepper

12 x 150g (5½oz) middle-cut fillet steaks

2 tbsp olive oil

450g (1lb) baby spinach

75g (2½oz) fresh white breadcrumbs

a little paprika, to dust

1 Put the mushrooms and brandy into a wide-based pan and toss over a high heat for 2–3 minutes or until the liquid has reduced slightly. Scoop out the mushrooms with a slotted spoon, add the cream, and boil for 5 minutes or until it has reduced by half and reached a coating consistency. Return the mushrooms to the pan, season with salt and freshly ground black pepper, then set aside to cool completely.

2 Heat a large non-stick frying pan over a high heat. Brush each steak with a little oil and season with salt and freshly ground black pepper. Pan-fry each steak for 1–2 minutes on each side or until golden and sealed. Transfer to a baking sheet. You will need to do this in batches.

3 Add the spinach to the pan and cook for a few minutes or until just wilted. Place a mound on top of each steak. Spoon the cold mushroom sauce on top of the spinach (just enough to cover – you should have some sauce left over to reheat and serve with the steaks).

4 Preheat the oven to 220°C (200°C fan/425°F/Gas 7). Sprinkle the steaks with the breadcrumbs and a dusting of paprika and bake for 8 minutes (11 minutes for 12) or until piping hot but just rare in the middle. Add 2 minutes for medium and 4 minutes for medium to well done. Rest for a couple of minutes before serving. Reheat the remaining mushroom sauce in a pan.

5 Serve the steaks piping hot with the sauce alongside.

PREPARE AHEAD
The steaks can be prepared up to the end of step 3 up to 12 hours ahead. Not suitable for freezing.

IN THE AGA
Cook on the top set of runners in the roasting oven for 8 minutes (11 minutes for 12). Add 2 minutes for medium, 4 for medium to well done.

Apart from the marinating – which is vital for the flavour of the sauce to come through – this is a very quick dish. Buy steaks of the same thickness, so they cook at the same rate. Serve with noodles.

Teriyaki steak

Serves 6

100ml (3½fl oz) mirin
3 tbsp soy sauce
2 tbsp light brown sugar
1 garlic clove, crushed
6 x 150g (5½oz) sirloin steaks
  or rump steaks

2 tbsp olive oil
225g (8oz) mixed wild
  mushrooms, such as oyster,
  shiitake, and chestnut, sliced

Serves 12

This dish is not suitable for more than six people because you would have to cook it in two batches, which would mean some steaks would end up being overcooked.

1 Put the mirin, soy sauce, sugar, and garlic into a wide shallow dish and stir together.

2 Add the steaks and turn to coat. Leave to marinate for a minimum of 30 minutes and up to 8 hours.

3 Heat half the oil in a non-stick frying pan. Remove the steaks from the marinade (reserving the marinade) and fry for 2½ minutes on each side – they should be medium rare. Transfer to a hot plate to rest. You may need to do this in batches.

4 Heat the remaining oil in the pan, add the mushrooms, and fry over a high heat for a few minutes or until just cooked. Pour in the reserved marinade and bring to the boil.

5 Serve the steaks whole or in slices with the mushrooms and sauce spooned on top.

MIRIN

You'll find mirin in a bottle in the oriental section of the supermarket. It is a traditional Japanese rice seasoning, similar to rice wine or sake, but with a low alcohol content.

PREPARE AHEAD
The marinade can be made up to 4 days ahead.
The steaks can be marinated for up to 8 hours.
Not suitable for freezing.

The advantage of using centre-cut beef fillet is that it's the same diameter all along, which means it roasts evenly and won't overcook at one end. This is delicious with our Thai green rice on page 116.

Thai beef with lime and chilli

Serves 6

900g (2lb) centre-cut beef fillet
1 tbsp olive oil
1 large red chilli, deseeded and roughly chopped
2.5cm (1in) fresh root ginger, peeled and roughly chopped
1 fat garlic clove, roughly chopped
small bunch of mint, stalks removed

finely grated zest and juice of 1 lime
100g (3½oz) coconut cream
200ml tub full-fat crème fraîche
1 tbsp sweet chilli dipping sauce
1 tbsp sugar
½ tbsp fish sauce
3 heaped tbsp light mayonnaise

Serves 12

1.8kg (4lb) centre-cut beef fillet
2 tbsp olive oil
2 large red chillies, deseeded and roughly chopped
5cm (2in) fresh root ginger, peeled and roughly chopped
2 fat garlic cloves, roughly chopped
large bunch of mint, stalks removed

finely grated zest and juice of 2 limes
200g carton coconut cream
2 x 200ml tubs full-fat crème fraîche
2 tbsp sweet chilli dipping sauce
2 tbsp sugar
1 tbsp fish sauce
6 heaped tbsp light mayonnaise

1 Preheat the oven to 220°C (200°C fan/425°F/Gas 7). Rub the beef with the oil and brown quickly on all sides in a large pan.

2 Transfer to a roasting tin and roast for 20 minutes (30 minutes for 12) – it should be medium rare – then cover loosely with foil and leave to rest for 15–20 minutes.

3 Meanwhile, put the chilli, ginger, garlic, mint, lime zest, and lime juice into a processor and whiz until finely chopped. Add the six remaining ingredients and whiz again.

4 Carve the beef, allowing 2–3 slices per person, and arrange on a platter with the Thai green rice, if serving. Place the sauce alongside in a bowl.

PREPARE AHEAD
The sauce can be made up to 3 days ahead. The beef can be browned up to 12 hours ahead. Not suitable for freezing.

IN THE AGA
Roast the beef in the centre of the roasting oven for the same timings as above.

This brightly coloured side dish is full of flavour. It is the perfect accompaniment to our Thai beef with lime and chilli on page 114.

Thai green rice

Serves 6

24 asparagus spears
100g (3½oz) baby corn
salt
225g (8oz) frozen petits pois
100g (3½oz) easy cook
    long-grain rice

4 spring onions, finely sliced
2 tbsp soy sauce
2 tbsp sweet chilli dipping sauce
a little olive oil, to fry

Serves 12

48 asparagus spears
200g (7oz) baby corn
salt
450g (1lb) frozen petits pois
200g (7oz) easy cook
    long-grain rice

8 spring onions, finely sliced
4 tbsp soy sauce
4 tbsp sweet chilli dipping sauce
a little olive oil, to fry

1 Trim the tough ends from the asparagus spears diagonally and discard, then cut the stalks into diagonal slices and set the tips to one side. Cut the corn into 3–4 diagonal slices, depending on their size.

2 Cook the asparagus stalks and corn in boiling salted water for 4 minutes or until just cooked, then drain and refresh in cold water.

3 Cook the asparagus tips and petits pois in boiling salted water for 2 minutes, then drain and refresh in cold water. Cook the rice in boiling salted water according to the packet instructions, then drain.

4 Mix the rice with the cooked vegetables and spring onions, then toss with the soy sauce and chilli dipping sauce.

5 Heat the olive oil in a wok or non-stick frying pan and stir-fry the rice for 5 minutes or until hot. Serve at once – if kept hot, the vegetables will lose their vibrant green colour.

PREPARE AHEAD
The rice can be prepared up to the end of step 4 up to 12 hours ahead. Not suitable for freezing.

IN THE AGA
Cook the rice on the lowest set of runners in the roasting oven for 15 minutes (25 minutes for 12).

Light and fresh, this stir-fry is the perfect dish to rustle up as a speedy supper for up to six people. Serve with noodles or rice.

Sirloin steak and vegetable stir-fry

Serves 6

350g (12oz) thin sirloin steak or fillet steak, sliced into very thin strips

1 tbsp runny honey

salt and freshly ground black pepper

2 tbsp olive oil

2 carrots, sliced into matchsticks

6 spring onions, sliced

150g (5½oz) baby corn, cut into thick slices

150g (5½oz) sugarsnap peas, sliced in half lengthways

250g (9oz) pak choi, white and green separated and cut into thick slices

For the sauce

3 tbsp mirin

2 tbsp soy sauce

2 tbsp hoisin sauce

2 tbsp water

2 tsp cornflour

Serves 12

This dish is not suitable for more than six people because the vegetables would release too much water and make the stir-fry soggy.

1 Toss the steak in the honey and season well with salt and freshly ground black pepper.

2 Heat the oil in a large frying pan or wok over a high heat, add the steak, and stir-fry for 1–2 minutes or until brown and just cooked. Transfer to a plate with a slotted spoon.

3 Add the carrots, spring onions, and corn and stir-fry over a high heat for 3 minutes. Add the sugarsnap peas and the white part of the pak choi and stir-fry for 3 minutes.

4 Put the mirin, soy sauce, and hoisin sauce in a small bowl. Mix the water and cornflour to a smooth paste in another bowl, then add to the sauce. Pour the sauce into the frying pan with the steak and the green leaves of the pak choi and fry for 1–2 minutes or until the green leaves have just wilted.

5 Season with salt and freshly ground black pepper and serve at once.

PREPARE AHEAD

You can prepare all the ingredients up to 4 hours ahead. The sauce can be made up to 1 day ahead. Not suitable for freezing.

Lamb loin fillet is lean, tender, and very quick to cook. It's also quite expensive, so this recipe is for extra special occasions. Serve with creamy mashed potatoes and a green vegetable.

Marinated marmalade and whisky lamb fillet

Serves 6

3 large lamb loin fillets, trimmed
3 heaped tbsp thin-cut Seville orange marmalade
finely grated zest of ½ lemon
1 garlic clove, crushed
2 tbsp whisky
2 tbsp olive oil
salt and freshly ground black pepper

For the sauce

300ml (10fl oz) chicken stock
1½ tbsp soy sauce
2 tsp balsamic vinegar
2 level tsp cornflour
1 tbsp cold water

Serves 12

6 large lamb loin fillets, trimmed
6 heaped tbsp thin-cut Seville orange marmalade
finely grated zest of 1 lemon
2 garlic cloves, crushed
4 tbsp whisky
4 tbsp olive oil
salt and freshly ground black pepper

For the sauce

600ml (1 pint) chicken stock
3 tbsp soy sauce
4 tsp balsamic vinegar
4 level tsp cornflour
2 tbsp cold water

1 Arrange the lamb fillets in a flat dish. Put the marmalade, lemon zest, garlic, and whisky into a small bowl and mix together. Pour over the lamb, cover, and leave to marinate in the fridge for about an hour or up to 6 hours.

2 Preheat the oven to 220°C (200°C fan/425°F/Gas 7). Heat the oil in large frying pan. Scrape the marinade off the fillets and reserve for the sauce. Season the lamb with salt and freshly ground black pepper, then fry quickly until brown on all sides. You may need to do this in batches. Arrange on a baking sheet.

3 Roast for 8 minutes (12 minutes for 12) or until cooked but still pink in the middle. Set aside to rest.

4 Meanwhile, rinse the frying pan, add the reserved marinade along with the stock, soy sauce, and balsamic vinegar, and bring to the boil. Put the cornflour into a cup, add the cold water, and mix until smooth. Add a little of the hot sauce and mix again, then stir into the frying pan and bring to the boil to thicken it slightly.

5 Carve the lamb into slices, strain the sauce, and serve alongside.

PREPARE AHEAD AND FREEZE
The lamb can be marinated for up to 6 hours.
The sauce can be made up to 3 days ahead.
Freeze the sauce for up to 3 months.

IN THE AGA
Roast the lamb fillets on the second set of runners in the roasting oven for 8 minutes (10 minutes for 12).

Slow-roasted lamb is ideal for a crowd – it looks after itself in the oven, it's tender, and easy to carve. No wonder it's Mary's family lunch most Sundays. Serve with mint sauce and redcurrant jelly.

Slow-roast leg of lamb

Serves 6

1.5kg (3lb 3oz) half-boned
   leg of lamb
8 garlic cloves, thinly sliced
bunch of fresh thyme
2 red onions, roughly chopped
1 tbsp olive oil
salt and freshly ground
   black pepper

750ml (1¼ pints) water mixed
   with 1 beef stock cube
1 heaped tbsp plain flour
3 tbsp water
1 heaped tbsp redcurrant jelly
a little gravy browning (optional)

Serves 12

2 x 1.5kg (3lb 3oz) half-boned
   legs of lamb
16 garlic cloves, thinly sliced
large bunch of fresh thyme
4 red onions, roughly chopped
2 tbsp olive oil
salt and freshly ground
   black pepper

1.5 litres (2¾ pints) water mixed
   with 2 beef stock cubes
2 heaped tbsp plain flour
6 tbsp water
2 heaped tbsp redcurrant jelly
a little gravy browning (optional)

1 Preheat the oven to 220°C (200°C fan/425°F/Gas 7). Lay the lamb on a board and use a small sharp knife to make holes in the flesh. Push the garlic and thyme into the holes.

2 Arrange the onions in the base of a large roasting tin. Sit a grill rack over the onions and place the lamb on top. Drizzle over the oil and season with salt and freshly ground black pepper.

3 Roast for 30–40 minutes (40–50 minutes for 12) or until brown. Remove the tin from the oven and reduce the oven temperature to 140°C (120°C fan/275°F/Gas 1).

4 Pour the stock around the lamb, cover the tin with foil, and return to the oven for 4 hours (4½ hours for 12) or until the meat is tender and just falling off the bone.

5 Transfer the lamb to a board, cover with foil, and leave to rest while you make the gravy.

6 Put the flour into a cup and mix to a smooth runny paste with the water. Heat the roasting tin on the hob, whisk in the flour mixture and the redcurrant jelly, and bring to the boil, stirring all the time until smooth. Check the seasoning and add a little gravy browning if you'd like the gravy to be a rich brown colour.

7 Carve the lamb and serve with the hot gravy.

VARIATIONS

If you're cooking on a budget, use shoulder of lamb, which is much more reasonably priced, although it can be a little fatty. Make sure you skim off any fat at the end of cooking. If you prefer thin gravy, leave out the flour – just use the juices in the tin.

PREPARE AHEAD
The lamb can be prepared up to the end of step 2 up to 1 day ahead. Not suitable for freezing.

IN THE AGA
At step 3, roast on the second set of runners in the roasting oven for 30 minutes (40 minutes for 12). At step 4, transfer to the simmering oven for 5–6 hours.

As a team, we like to go to the pub occasionally, to chat and have a moment off from cooking. One evening we had a recipe similar to this – delicious and beautifully presented. Serve with spinach.

Mini pork en croûtes

Serves 6

75g (2½oz) mature Cheddar
  cheese, grated
50g (1¾oz) fresh white
  breadcrumbs
2 tbsp freshly chopped parsley
1 tsp freshly chopped thyme
1 egg
salt and freshly ground
  black pepper

dash of Tabasco
2 x 350g (12oz) pork fillets,
  trimmed
8 slices Parma ham
a little plain flour, to dust
375g packet ready-rolled
  puff pastry
1 egg, beaten with
  a little milk

Serves 12

150g (5oz) mature Cheddar
  cheese, grated
100g (3½oz) fresh white
  breadcrumbs
4 tbsp freshly chopped parsley
2 tsp freshly chopped thyme
2 eggs
salt and freshly ground
  black pepper

generous dash of Tabasco
4 x 350g (12oz) pork fillets,
  trimmed
16 slices Parma ham
a little plain flour, to dust
2 x 375g packets ready-rolled
  puff pastry
1 egg, beaten with
  a little milk

1 Put the cheese, breadcrumbs, herbs, and egg into a small bowl. Season with salt and freshly ground black pepper, add the Tabasco, and mix well.

2 Slice each pork fillet in half horizontally, then cover with cling film and bash with a rolling pin until they are slightly thinner. Spread the cheese mixture on top of the halved fillets, then put the fillet halves together again, with the cheese mixture in the middle.

3 Arrange four slices of the ham side by side on a board. With the edges overlapping slightly, they should be about as wide as one of the pork fillets. Sit a fillet across the ham at one end and roll it up so the pork is encased in the ham. Do the same with the other fillet(s).

4 On a lightly floured work surface, roll the pastry out into a 33 x 40cm (13 x 16in) rectangle (two rectangles for 12). Slice in half widthways and brush with egg. Wrap each fillet in pastry and place join side down on a baking sheet. Brush with egg and chill for an hour.

5 Preheat the oven to 220°C (200°C fan/425°F/Gas 7). Bake the parcels for 25–30 minutes (45 minutes for 12) or until golden and crisp. Allow to rest for 5–10 minutes before carving. Meanwhile, make the apple gravy (see right).

6 Slice each en croûte in three, then slice each piece in half diagonally and stand them on a dinner plate. Serve hot with the apple gravy. Serve any extra gravy separately.

FOR THE APPLE GRAVY

For six, heat a knob of butter in a saucepan, add 1 finely chopped large onion, and fry for 2 minutes. Cover with a lid and cook over a low heat for 15 minutes or until the onion is soft. Sprinkle in 50g (1¾oz) plain flour, blend in 400ml (14fl oz) chicken stock and the same quantity of unsweetened apple juice, and bring to the boil, stirring. Season with salt and freshly ground black pepper, add 2 tbsp Worcestershire sauce and a little gravy browning as well if you'd like the gravy to be a rich brown colour. Push through a sieve and discard the onion. For 12, double the quantities, so you need a large knob of butter, 2 large onions, 100g (3½oz) flour, 750ml (1¼ pints) each of chicken stock and apple juice, and 4 tbsp Worcestershire sauce.

PREPARE AHEAD AND FREEZE

The pork can be prepared up to the end of step 3 up to 12 hours ahead. Not suitable for freezing. The gravy can be made up to 2 days ahead. Freeze for up to 1 month.

IN THE AGA

Bake on the second set of runners in the roasting oven for 30 minutes. Slide the baking sheet on to the floor of the roasting oven 8 minutes before the end of cooking.

A variation on one of Mary's best-loved pork recipes. Lucy's family adores it and always puts in a request for it on special occasions. Serve with mashed potatoes and green vegetables.

Paprika pork fillet

Serves 6

2 tbsp olive oil

900g (2lb) pork fillet, trimmed and cut into 1cm (½in) slices

25g (scant 1oz) butter

1 large onion, roughly chopped

1 level tbsp paprika

2 level tbsp plain flour

300ml (10fl oz) chicken stock

5 tbsp sherry

1 tsp tomato purée

175g (6oz) button mushrooms, halved

salt and freshly ground black pepper

200g tub full-fat crème fraîche

Serves 12

4 tbsp olive oil

1.8kg (4lb) pork fillet, trimmed and sliced into 1cm (½in) slices

50g (1¾oz) butter

2 large onions, roughly chopped

2 level tbsp paprika

4 level tbsp plain flour

600ml (1 pint) chicken stock

150ml (5fl oz) sherry

2 tsp tomato purée

350g (12oz) button mushrooms, halved

salt and freshly ground black pepper

2 x 200g tubs full-fat crème fraîche

1 Heat the oil in a large non-stick frying pan or casserole. Add the pork and brown quickly on all sides. Remove with a slotted spoon and set aside. You may need to do this in batches.

2 Add the butter and onion to the pan, cover with a lid, and leave to soften over a low heat for 15 minutes or until tender.

3 Stir in the paprika and flour and fry over a high heat for 1 minute. Add the stock and sherry and bring to the boil, stirring all the time, to thicken slightly. Add the tomato purée and mushrooms.

4 Return the pork to the pan, season with salt and freshly ground black pepper, cover with a lid, and simmer over a low heat for 15 minutes (25–30 minutes for 12) or until the pork is tender.

5 Stir in the crème fraîche and serve piping hot.

Great for a crowd... When cooking larger quantities, use just enough oil to coat the bottom of the pan and take care not to overcook the pork or it will be dry. Freezes well.

PREPARE AHEAD AND FREEZE
The dish can be prepared up to the end of step 4 up to 1 day ahead. Freeze at the end of step 4 for up to 1 month.

IN THE AGA
Soften the onion in the simmering oven for 20 minutes. At step 4, cover with a lid and transfer to the simmering oven for 15 minutes (25 minutes for 12).

This is one Mary's favourite ways of serving potatoes. She's been cooking them for over 25 years and they're as popular now as they were then. Serve with chops, grilled meat, or fish.

Heavenly potato gratin

Serves 6

Special equipment 1 litre (1¾ pint) shallow ovenproof dish, buttered

900g (2lb) even-sized waxy potatoes, such as Desiree
1 tsp salt

freshly ground black pepper
45g (1½oz) butter, melted, plus a little extra to grease
150ml (5fl oz) single cream

Serves 12

Special equipment 2 litre (3½ pint) shallow ovenproof dish, buttered

1.8kg (4lb) even-sized waxy potatoes, such as Desiree
1 tsp salt

freshly ground black pepper
75g (2½oz) butter, melted, plus a little extra to grease
300ml (10fl oz) single cream

1 Preheat the oven to 220°C (200°C fan/400°F/Gas 7). Rub off any excess dirt from the potatoes and put them unpeeled into a pan. Cover with cold water and add the salt. Cover with a lid, bring to the boil, and cook until just tender. The timing will depend on their size, but they should be soft around the edges and slightly firm in the centre. Set aside for them to cool completely.

2 Peel the skins from the potatoes and discard. Using a coarse grater, grate the potatoes into the buttered dish, seasoning between the layers with salt and freshly ground black pepper. Do not press down – they should be light and fluffy.

3 Pour over the melted butter and cream, then bake for 20–25 minutes (40 minutes for 12) or until crisp and golden brown.

THE RIGHT DISH
Make sure you use an ovenproof dish that's wide and shallow, so you get more of the delicious crispy golden crust.

PREPARE AHEAD
The potatoes can be made up to the end of step 2 up to 1 day ahead. Not suitable for freezing.

IN THE AGA
Bake on the second set of runners in the roasting oven for 20–25 minutes (35 minutes for 12).

These are best prepared a day ahead. Make more than you need and freeze them for another occasion – they're great when there are just two or four of you. Serve with chops, grilled meat, or fish.

Cheese-topped dauphinois potatoes

Serves 6

Special equipment *18cm (7in) square shallow metal tin lined with non-stick paper and greased*

750g (1lb 10oz) large King Edward potatoes or other floury potatoes

150ml (5fl oz) chicken stock or vegetable stock

100ml (3½fl oz) double cream

salt and freshly ground black pepper

knob of butter

25g (scant 1oz) mature Cheddar cheese, grated

Serves 12

Special equipment *23 x 30cm (9 x 12in) roasting tin lined with non-stick paper and greased*

1.35kg (3lb) large King Edward potatoes or other floury potatoes

300ml (10fl oz) chicken stock or vegetable stock

150ml (5fl oz) double cream

salt and freshly ground black pepper

25g (scant 1oz) butter

50g (1¾oz) mature Cheddar cheese, grated

1 Preheat the oven to 220°C (200°C fan/425°F/Gas 7). Peel the potatoes and rinse under cold water, then dry and slice very thinly by hand or with the slicer attachment on a processor. Put the stock into a large jug and mix with the cream.

2 Arrange a layer of potato over the base of the tin, season with salt and freshly ground black pepper, then pour over a little of the stock mixture. Continue in the same way until the potato and liquid are used up. Dot the butter over the top and cover tightly with foil.

3 Bake for 30 minutes (45 minutes for 12) or until soft around the edges but still firm in the middle. Remove the foil and cook for a further 25–30 minutes (35–45 minutes for 12) or until golden and tender. Leave to cool, then chill – overnight is best.

4 Choose a lipped board or tray that's bigger than the roasting tin (so it will catch any juices) and place on a worktop. Carefully tip the roasting tin upside down on to it and remove the paper. Cut the potatoes into even-sized servings, arrange on a greased or paper-lined baking sheet, and sprinkle the cheese on top.

5 Reheat in an oven preheated to 200°C (180°C fan/400°F/Gas 6) for 25–30 minutes (35 minutes for 12) or until golden and piping hot.

PREPARE AHEAD AND FREEZE

The dish can be made up to the end of step 3 up to 1 day ahead or up to the end of step 4 up to 8 hours ahead. Freeze for up to 2 months.

IN THE AGA

At step 3, cook on the second set of runners in the roasting oven. At step 5, reheat on the second set of runners in the roasting oven.

These are great all year round, but are especially good in the summer months when the flavour of fresh thyme is at its best. Serve with barbecued meats or fish.

Roast potatoes with chilli and thyme

Serves 6

6 large old potatoes, peeled and cut into 5cm (2in) cubes
salt and freshly ground black pepper
3 tbsp olive oil
juice of ½ lemon
2 tsp freshly chopped thyme leaves

2–3 garlic cloves, crushed
1–2 red chillies (depending on preference), deseeded and finely chopped
2 tbsp freshly chopped parsley

Serves 12

12 large old potatoes, peeled and cut into 5cm (2in) cubes
salt and freshly ground black pepper
6 tbsp olive oil
juice of 1 lemon
4 tsp freshly chopped thyme leaves

5 fat garlic cloves, crushed
2–3 red chillies (depending on preference), deseeded and finely chopped
4 tbsp freshly chopped parsley

1 Preheat the oven to 220°C (200°C fan/425°F/Gas 7). Meanwhile, cook the potatoes in boiling salted water for 4–5 minutes or until they are just soft around the edges but still have a little bite in the middle. Drain and transfer to a bowl.

2 Put all the other ingredients except the parsley into a small bowl and lightly whisk to combine. Pour over the potatoes and season with salt and freshly ground black pepper.

3 Pop a roasting tin (two tins for 12) into the oven for a few minutes to get very hot. Spoon the potatoes and dressing into the tin(s) and roast for 25–30 minutes (45–55 minutes for 12) or until golden and crispy. Garnish with the parsley and serve.

PREPARE AHEAD
The potatoes can be prepared up to the end of step 2 up to 1 day ahead. Not suitable for freezing.

IN THE AGA
Roast on the floor of the roasting oven for 25 minutes (50 minutes for 12).

Roasted vegetables make a wonderful side dish for so many meats and fish. The secret is to cook the vegetables in a single layer, so they chargrill rather than steaming and becoming soggy.

Roasted Mediterranean vegetables

Serves 6

2 tbsp olive oil

1 small aubergine, sliced into 5cm (2in) chunks

2 small courgettes, thickly sliced

1 red pepper, halved, deseeded, and cut into 5cm (2in) chunks

1 onion, quartered

3 garlic cloves (unpeeled)

2 sprigs of fresh rosemary

3 sprigs of fresh thyme

salt and freshly ground black pepper

Serves 12

4 tbsp olive oil

2 small aubergines, sliced into 5cm (2in) chunks

4 small courgettes, thickly sliced

2 red peppers, halved, deseeded, and cut into 5cm (2in) chunks

2 onions, quartered

6 garlic cloves (unpeeled)

4 sprigs of fresh rosemary

6 sprigs of fresh thyme

salt and freshly ground black pepper

1 Preheat the oven to 220°C (200°C fan/425°F/Gas 7). Put the oil into a large roasting tin (two tins for 12) and pop in the oven for a few minutes to get hot.

2 Add the vegetables and toss in the hot oil. Scatter over the garlic and herbs.

3 Roast for 40–45 minutes (1 hour for 12) or until tender and golden. Turn halfway through cooking.

4 Transfer to a serving bowl with a slotted spoon. Squeeze the garlic from their skins and mix in with the vegetables. Discard the herbs if woody. Season with salt and freshly ground black pepper, toss, and serve.

USING LEFTOVERS

If you have any vegetables left over, toss them with a little balsamic vinegar and some olive oil and serve them as a salad.

PREPARE AHEAD

The vegetables can be prepared up to the end of step 4 up to 1 day ahead. Not suitable for freezing.

IN THE AGA

Roast on the floor of the roasting oven for 35 minutes (1 hour for 12), stirring halfway through.

We love recipes that you can do much of the preparation for up to a day ahead and that require little last-minute attention. These carrots can be popped into the oven while you're doing the roast.

Orange-glazed carrots

Serves 6

1kg (2¼lb) carrots, sliced
 thickly diagonally
salt and freshly ground
 black pepper

25g (scant 1oz) butter, melted
½ orange
freshly chopped parsley,
 to garnish

Serves 12

2kg (4½lb) carrots, sliced
 thickly diagonally
salt and freshly ground
 black pepper

50g (1¾oz) butter, melted
1 orange
freshly chopped parsley,
 to garnish

1 Preheat the oven to 200°C (180°C fan/400°F/Gas 6). Immerse the carrots in a pan of boiling salted water for 4 minutes to blanch them, then drain and refresh in cold water.

2 Pour over the melted butter, season with salt and freshly ground black pepper, and stir to coat well.

3 Arrange in a roasting tin or ovenproof dish. Squeeze over the juice from the orange and pop the shell in the tin for extra flavour.

4 Cover with foil and bake for 30 minutes (40 minutes for 12) or until tender.

5 To serve, remove the orange shell and discard. Sprinkle over the parsley and toss lightly.

PREPARE AHEAD
The carrots can be blanched up to 1 day ahead. Coat in the butter and orange juice and roast to serve. Not suitable for freezing.

IN THE AGA
Bake on the lowest set of runners in the roasting oven for 25 minutes (35 minutes for 12).

This is an unusual vegetable dish, best served alongside more conventional vegetables such as broccoli or runner beans. Serve as an accompaniment to meat or fish.

Roasted chicory with garlic butter

Serves 6

salt and freshly ground
  black pepper
12 chicory heads, sliced
  in half lengthways
25g (scant 1oz) butter

2 garlic cloves, crushed
50g (1¾oz) mature Cheddar
  cheese, grated
a little paprika, to dust

Serves 12

salt and freshly ground
  black pepper
24 chicory heads, sliced
  in half lengthways
50g (1¾oz) butter

4 garlic cloves, crushed
100g (3½oz) mature Cheddar
  cheese, grated
a little paprika, to dust

1 Preheat the oven to 220°C (200°C fan/425°F/Gas 7). Bring a pan of cold salted water to the boil, add the chicory, and bring back up to a rolling boil. Cook for 3 minutes, then drain. Arrange the chicory in a single layer in an ovenproof dish.

2 Add the butter and garlic to the empty pan and melt over the heat. Spoon over the chicory in the dish and season with salt and freshly ground black pepper. Sprinkle over the cheese and a light dusting of paprika.

3 Bake for 15–20 minutes (25–30 minutes for 12) or until lightly golden.

PREPARE AHEAD
The chicory can be prepared up to the end of step 1 up to 6 hours ahead. Not suitable for freezing.

IN THE AGA
Bake on the top set of runners in the roasting oven for 15 minutes (30 minutes for 12).

Pot luck parties

Pot luck parties, where various people bring along a contribution, are huge fun and a lot less work than doing it all yourself. The all-in-one dishes in this chapter are portable and ideal for preparing ahead.

Pot luck parties

There are lots of occasions when a pot luck party (sometimes called a safari supper or shared party) fits the bill – a charity event or function at the children's school, a New Year's Eve celebration or family get-together. And though they aren't exactly new, they're all the rage right now because people are leading increasingly busy lives. For a pot luck party to be a success, organization and coordination are called for – you don't want everyone turning up with a fish pie! Here's our guide to organizing or contributing to a pot luck party.

Organizing a pot luck party

● **The occasion** Let people know the reason for the party and what kind of event you'd like it to be – smart or casual? Will guests be able to sit or will they stand, plate in hand?

● **The guests** How many people are you inviting? What sort of age will most people be? Will there be children or teenagers? All these factors can affect what you cook.

● **The venue** Are you hosting the party in your home or will people meet in the village hall or church hall, in someone's garden or on the beach? If you're hosting the party in your home, find out if dishes will require reheating or cooking. And make a note of how many dishes will need to be reheated so you can work out if there'll be enough space in your oven and on your hob. If you're hosting the party at a venue, check what cooking facilities there are – oven, hob, or microwave. Is there enough counter space to lay dishes out on? Find out if there's a fridge or freezer, then let people know so they can plan accordingly.

● **The food** Ask people what dish they'd like to bring along. Listen to their suggestion – some may have strengths they'd like to capitalize on. They might be a dab hand at pastry, for instance. But keep the selection of recipes balanced. It might mean twisting the occasional arm, so someone brings along a dish that wasn't necessarily their first choice.

"For a pot luck party to be a success, organization and coordination are called for – you don't want everyone turning up with a fish pie!"

● **The drink** You might be planning to supply the drink and glasses yourself. Alternatively, you could appoint one person or several people to take care of them. You could even ask everyone to bring what they enjoy themselves.

● **The equipment** If you don't have enough plates and cutlery, make sure you ask people to bring some with them. Will you need to provide platters, baskets, and cooking utensils? Will you need folding chairs? And don't forget the clearing up – pack a few rubbish sacks, as well as some plastic containers or polythene bags for leftovers.

Contributing to a pot luck party

When you're invited to contribute to a pot luck party, your favourite recipe might spring instantly to mind. This might not be ideal, however. These are the points to consider.

● **The time of day** Is it lunch, tea, or supper?

● **The time of year** A casserole would hit the spot in midwinter, but it might be less enthusiastically received on a blisteringly hot summer's day.

● **The occasion** Is the party in honour of a special occasion or is it a more casual affair?

● **The guestlist** How many people are coming and who are they? Check, too, if there are guests with special dietary requirements.

● **The food** Will your dish need reheating? And how? Does it require chilling? Ask about the facilities at the other end.

● **The equipment** Presenting food in the dish it was cooked in is perfectly okay at a casual get-together, and foil containers are ideal when you intend to serve food straight on to plates, but, for a more formal occasion, you might need to take a serving dish. Don't forget any cooking utensils or serving implements you'll need. And stick your name on everything or you may never see them again.

● **Garnishes** Remember to take any last-minute ingredients, garnishes, or decorations.

● **Leftovers** Make provisions for leftovers by taking plastic containers and polythene bags with you. And pack an extra-large bag to bring your dirty cooking dish home in.

This recipe is ideal for preparing the day before. Shelled crayfish tails can be bought in all good supermarkets or fishmongers. They come in tubs of brine. Serve the pie with steamed broccoli or salad.

Salmon and crayfish pie

Serves 6

Special equipment 2.4 litre (4 pint) shallow wide-based ovenproof dish

750g (1lb 10oz) King Edward potatoes or other floury potatoes, cut into 5cm (2in) pieces
salt and freshly ground black pepper
a knob of butter
150ml (5fl oz) milk

For the pie

75g (2½oz) butter
1 onion, finely chopped
2 leeks, finely sliced
50g (1¾oz) plain flour
600ml (1 pint) hot milk
juice of ½ lemon
2 tbsp freshly chopped dill
2 tbsp freshly chopped parsley
2 tbsp capers, drained
500g (1lb 2oz) skinned salmon fillet, cut into 5cm (2in) cubes
250g (9oz) cooked crayfish tails in brine, drained
75g (2½oz) Cheddar cheese, grated
lemon wedges, to serve

Serves 12

Special equipment 2 x 2.4 litre (4 pint) shallow wide-based ovenproof dishes or 1 x 4 litre (7 pint) dish

1.5kg (3lb 3oz) King Edward potatoes or other floury potatoes, cut into 5cm (2in) pieces
salt and freshly ground black pepper
a large knob of butter
300ml (10fl oz) milk

For the pie

175g (6oz) butter
2 onions, finely chopped
4 leeks, finely sliced
100g (3½oz) plain flour
1.2 litres (2 pints) hot milk
juice of 1 lemon
4 tbsp freshly chopped dill
4 tbsp freshly chopped parsley
4 tbsp capers, drained
1kg (2¼lb) skinned salmon fillet, cut into 5cm (2in) cubes
500g (1lb 2oz) cooked crayfish tails in brine, drained
175g (6oz) Cheddar cheese, grated
lemon wedges, to serve

1 Preheat the oven to 220°C (200°C fan/425°F/Gas 7). Put the potatoes in a pan of cold salted water, cover with a lid, bring to the boil, and cook for 15 minutes or until tender. Drain, add the butter and milk, season with salt and freshly ground black pepper, and mash until smooth. You may need a little more milk to get the right consistency.

2 Meanwhile, melt the butter for the pie in a large saucepan. Stir in the onion and leeks, cover with a lid, and cook over a low heat for 15 minutes or until the onion is soft. Stir in the flour and, over a high heat, gradually add the milk, stirring all the time until the sauce is smooth and thick.

3 Remove from the heat, add all the remaining ingredients (except the cheese), and season with salt and freshly ground black pepper. Spoon into the ovenproof dish and level the top. Cover with the mash and fluff up the surface with a fork. Sprinkle over the cheese.

4 Bake for 35 minutes (50 minutes for 12) or until golden brown and piping hot. Serve at once with wedges of lemon.

PREPARE AHEAD
The pie can be made up to the end of step 3 up to 1 day ahead. Not suitable for freezing.

IN THE AGA
Bake on the second set of runners in the roasting oven for 35 minutes (50 minutes for 12).

Named after the area of Scotland famous for its fish and seafood, this pie is quick to make. It's also unusual in that the potatoes are in the bake and not mashed on top. Serve with peas or salad.

Loch Fyne haddock bake

Serves 6

Special equipment *2 litre (3½ pint) shallow wide-based ovenproof dish*

350g (12oz) King Edward potatoes or other floury potatoes, peeled and cut into 2cm (¾in) cubes

salt and freshly ground black pepper

500g (1lb 2oz) baby spinach

1 tbsp olive oil

250g (9oz) small chestnut mushrooms, sliced in half

knob of butter

3 eggs, hardboiled, peeled, and sliced into quarters

500g (1lb 2oz) undyed smoked haddock, skinned and cut into 5cm (2in) pieces

300ml (10fl oz) double cream

2 tsp grainy mustard

75g (2½oz) mature Cheddar cheese, grated

Serves 12

Special equipment *2 x 2 litre (3½ pint) shallow wide-based ovenproof dishes or 1 x 4 litre (7 pint) dish*

750g (1lb 10oz) King Edward potatoes or other floury potatoes, peeled and cut into 2cm (¾in) cubes

salt and freshly ground black pepper

1kg (2¼lb) baby spinach

2 tbsp olive oil

500g (1lb 2oz) small chestnut mushrooms, sliced in half

knob of butter

6 eggs, hardboiled, peeled, and sliced into quarters

1kg (2¼lb) undyed smoked haddock, skinned and cut into 5cm (2in) pieces

600ml (1 pint) double cream

4 tsp grainy mustard

175g (6oz) mature Cheddar cheese, grated

1 Preheat the oven to 200°C (180°C fan/400°F/Gas 6). Meanwhile, put the potatoes into a pan of cold salted water, cover with a lid, bring to the boil, and cook for 10–15 minutes or until just cooked. Drain well and set aside.

2 Heat a large frying pan, add the spinach, and cook for a few minutes or until just wilted but still holding its shape. Drain well in a colander, squeezing to remove excess liquid, then set aside. You may need to do this in batches.

3 Heat the oil in the frying pan, add the mushrooms, and fry for 3 minutes or until just cooked.

4 Grease the ovenproof dish(es) with the butter, then arrange the potatoes, spinach, and mushrooms in the base. Scatter over the eggs and haddock and season with salt and freshly ground black pepper.

5 Mix the cream and mustard in a bowl with some salt and freshly ground black pepper, then pour over the fish mixture, and sprinkle with the cheese.

6 Bake for 20–25 minutes (30–35 minutes for two dishes for 12 or 40–45 minutes for one dish for 12) or until golden on top and cooked through.

SMOKED HADDOCK

Make sure you buy undyed smoked haddock – the dyed fillets are bright yellow and very unnatural-looking.

PREPARE AHEAD

The bake can be made up to the end of step 4 up to 8 hours ahead. Not suitable for freezing.

IN THE AGA

Bake on the top set of runners in the roasting oven for 20 minutes (45 minutes for 12) or until golden and cooked through.

Guests of all ages will enjoy this tasty tuna, macaroni, and cheese bake. And it really is extremely economical to make. Serve with crusty bread or dressed salad.

Macaroni tuna bake

Serves 6

Special equipment 1.5 litre (2¼ pint) shallow wide-based ovenproof dish

350g (12oz) macaroni
salt and freshly ground
    black pepper
150g (5½oz) frozen peas
75g (2½oz) butter
75g (2½oz) plain flour
900ml (1½ pints) hot milk
1 tbsp Dijon mustard

juice of ½ lemon
75g (2½oz) strong Cheddar
    cheese, grated
75g (2½oz) Parmesan cheese,
    freshly grated
2 x 185g cans tuna in
    springwater, drained
4 large tomatoes, cut in
    quarters, deseeded,
    and roughly chopped

Serves 12

Special equipment 2.4 litre (4 pint) shallow wide-based ovenproof dish

750g (1lb 10oz) macaroni
salt and freshly ground
    black pepper
300g (10oz) frozen peas
175g (6oz) butter
175g (6oz) plain flour
1.7 litres (3 pints) hot milk
2 tbsp Dijon mustard

juice of 1 lemon
175g (6oz) strong Cheddar
    cheese, grated
175g (6oz) Parmesan cheese,
    freshly grated
4 x 185g cans tuna in springwater,
    drained
8 large tomatoes, cut in quarters,
    deseeded,
    and roughly chopped

1 Preheat the oven to 200°C (180°C fan/400°F/Gas 6). Cook the macaroni in boiling salted water according to the packet instructions. Add the peas 3 minutes before the end. Drain, refresh in cold water, and set aside.

2 Melt the butter in a saucepan, add the flour, and stir over the heat for 1 minute. Add the hot milk slowly, whisking until the sauce is smooth and thick.

3 Add the mustard, lemon juice, and two-thirds of each cheese. Add the pasta and peas and lots of salt and freshly ground black pepper. Stir in the tuna and mix together. Spoon into the ovenproof dish, scatter over the tomatoes, and sprinkle over the remaining cheese.

4 Bake for 20–25 minutes (30–35 minutes for 12) or until lightly golden and crispy.

PREPARE AHEAD
The dish can be made up to the end of step 3 up to 1 day ahead. Not suitable for freezing.

IN THE AGA
Bake in the middle of the roasting oven for 20–25 minutes (35–40 minutes for 12) or until golden and crispy.

This is an old-fashioned pie, perfect for a winter Sunday lunch. If you're cooking for 12, we think it is easier to make two pies rather than one really large one, but it's up to you.

Traditional chicken, leek, and mushroom pie

Serves 6

Special equipment 2.4 litre (4 pint) *ovenproof pie dish*

75g (2½oz) butter
3 large leeks, sliced
75g (2½oz) plain flour, plus a little extra to dust
300ml (10fl oz) apple juice
450ml (15fl oz) chicken stock
250g (9oz) portabella mushrooms, sliced
1 tbsp Dijon mustard
1 tbsp freshly chopped thyme leaves
3 tbsp full-fat crème fraîche
750g (1lb 10oz) cooked chicken, sliced
salt and freshly ground black pepper
500g packet all-butter puff pastry
1 egg, beaten with a little milk

Serves 12

Special equipment 2 x 2.4 litre (4 pint) *ovenproof pie dishes or 1 x 4 litre (7 pint) dish*

175g (6oz) butter
6 leeks, sliced
175g (6oz) plain flour, plus a little extra to dust
600ml (1 pint) apple juice
900ml (1½ pints) chicken stock
450g (1lb) portabella mushrooms, sliced
2 tbsp Dijon mustard
2 tbsp freshly chopped thyme leaves
6 tbsp full-fat crème fraîche
1.5kg (3lb 3oz) cooked chicken, sliced
salt and freshly ground black pepper
2 x 500g packets all-butter puff pastry
2 eggs, beaten with a little milk

1 Preheat the oven to 200°C (180°C fan/400°F/Gas 6). Meanwhile, melt the butter in a large frying pan, add the leeks, and fry over a high heat for 2 minutes. Cover with a lid, lower the heat, and cook for 10 minutes or until tender.

2 Turn up the heat, stir in the flour, then blend in the apple juice and stock. Bring to the boil, stirring all the time, then add the mushrooms, mustard, thyme, and crème fraîche. Add the chicken, season with salt and freshly ground black pepper, and simmer for 5 minutes. Spoon into the pie dish and set aside to cool.

3 Meanwhile, make the pastry top. On a worktop lightly dusted with flour, roll out the pastry until it is a little bigger than the dish. Cut strips of pastry to the size of the lip of the dish, then wet the lip with water and attach the strips on top. Wet the top of the strips with water, then lay the pastry lid on them and press to seal the edges. Crimp the edges with your fingers.

4 Brush the pastry with the egg and bake in the oven for 35 minutes (1 hour for a large pie for 12 – cover it with foil if it begins to get too brown) or until the pastry is crisp and golden and the filling is piping hot.

PREPARE AHEAD AND FREEZE
The pie can be made up to the end of step 3 up to 1 day ahead. Freeze at the end of step 3 for up to 2 months.

IN THE AGA
Bake on the lowest set of runners in the roasting oven for 30 minutes (50 minutes for 12).

A whole lamb shank can look too filling. Our recipe gives guests the option of having half. Serve with mashed potato and cabbage.

Winter lamb shanks

Serves 6

Special equipment 2.4 litre
(4 pint) shallow ovenproof dish

2 tbsp olive oil
6 lamb shanks, trimmed of
   any excess fat
2 medium onions, thinly sliced
3 garlic cloves, crushed
50g (1¾oz) plain flour
600ml (1 pint) cold
   chicken stock

3 tbsp sun-dried tomato paste
150ml (5fl oz) red wine or Port
3 tbsp soy sauce
1 tbsp freshly chopped
   thyme leaves
salt and freshly ground
   black pepper
1½ tbsp balsamic vinegar

Serves 12

Special equipment 2 x 2.4 litre
(4 pint) shallow ovenproof dishes

4 tbsp olive oil
12 lamb shanks, trimmed of
   any excess fat
4 medium onions, thinly sliced
6 garlic cloves, crushed
100g (3½oz) plain flour
1.2 litres (2 pints) cold
   chicken stock

6 tbsp sun-dried tomato paste
300ml (10fl oz) red wine or Port
6 tbsp soy sauce
2 tbsp freshly chopped
   thyme leaves
salt and freshly ground
   black pepper
3 tbsp balsamic vinegar

1 Preheat the oven to 160°C (140°C fan/325°F/Gas 3). Heat half the oil in a large deep saucepan or casserole. Brown the shanks all over until golden. Remove and set aside. You may need to do this in batches.

2 Add the remaining oil to the pan, add the onions and garlic, and cook over a high heat for 5 minutes or until starting to soften. Put the flour into a jug and slowly whisk in the cold stock until smooth. Add to the pan with the tomato paste and red wine or Port and bring to the boil.

3 Return the lamb to the pan, add the soy sauce and thyme, and season with salt and freshly ground black pepper. Stir well, cover with a lid, and transfer to the oven for 3–4 hours (4 hours for 12) or until the meat is tender and starting to fall off the bone. Stir in the vinegar.

4 Remove the shanks from the sauce, wrap in foil, and set aside to cool. Pour the sauce into a 2.4 litre (4 pint) shallow ovenproof dish (two dishes for 12), cool, and cover with foil. When the sauce and shanks are completely cold, transfer to the fridge overnight.

5 To serve, preheat the oven to 180°C (160°C fan/350°F/Gas 4). Using a spoon, remove the fat from the surface of the sauce and discard. Remove the meat from the bone in one piece, then cut each piece in half. Add to the sauce and cover with foil.

6 Reheat in the oven for 45–50 minutes (1 hour for 12) or until piping hot.

VARIATION
If you don't want to do the second stage of cooking and are happy to present the shanks whole, serve at the end of step 3.

PREPARE AHEAD AND FREEZE
This is best made the day before and reheated. Freeze for up to six weeks.

IN THE AGA
At step 3, transfer to the simmering oven for 4–5 hours or until the meat is tender and falling off the bone. At step 6, slide on to the second set of runners in the roasting oven for 45 minutes (1 hour for 12). Stir from time to time.

This variation on the classic shepherd's pie has a layered topping of potato and cream instead of mash. Serve with a green vegetable.

Shepherd's pie dauphinois

Serves 6

Special equipment *2.4 litre (4 pint) shallow wide-based ovenproof dish*

900g (2lb) raw minced lamb
2 onions, chopped
2 large carrots, finely diced
45g (1½oz) plain flour
300ml (10fl oz) red wine
300ml (10fl oz) beef stock
1 tbsp Worcestershire sauce
1 tbsp tomato purée

dash of gravy browning (optional)
salt and freshly ground black pepper

For the topping

900g (2lb) old King Edward potatoes or other floury potatoes, cut into 3mm (⅛in) slices
150ml (5fl oz) double cream
75g (2½oz) mature Cheddar cheese, grated

Serves 12

Special equipment *2 x 2.4 litre (4 pint) shallow wide-based ovenproof dishes*

1.8kg (4lb) raw minced lamb
4 onions, chopped
4 large carrots, finely diced
75g (2½oz) plain flour
600ml (1 pint) red wine
600ml (1 pint) beef stock
2 tbsp Worcestershire sauce
2 tbsp tomato purée

dash of gravy browning (optional)
salt and freshly ground black pepper

For the topping

1.8kg (4lb) old King Edward potatoes or other floury potatoes, cut into 3mm (⅛in) slices
300ml (10fl oz) double cream
175g (6oz) mature Cheddar cheese, grated

1 Preheat the oven to 160°C (140°C fan/325°F/Gas 3). Meanwhile, put the lamb, onions, and carrots into a deep frying pan or casserole and fry over a high heat, stirring frequently, for 5 minutes or until the meat is brown. Drain away any fat.

2 Stir in the flour and, over a high heat, add the wine, stock, Worcestershire sauce, and tomato purée (add the gravy browning, too, if you want the sauce to be a rich dark colour). Stir until blended, then bring to the boil. Season with salt and freshly ground black pepper, cover with a lid, and transfer to the oven for 1–1½ hours or until the mince is tender.

3 Check the seasoning, then tip the meat into the ovenproof dish(es) and set aside to cool. Increase the oven temperature to 220°C (200°C fan/425°F/Gas 7).

4 Put the potatoes in a pan of boiling salted water for 4–5 minutes to blanch them. Drain, refresh in cold water, and dry well with kitchen paper.

5 Arrange a layer of potato on top of the cold mince, then pour over half the cream and season with salt and freshly ground black pepper. Arrange the remaining potatoes on top, pour over the remaining cream, and sprinkle over the cheese.

6 Bake for 30 minutes (45–50 minutes for 12) or until golden and bubbling.

Great for a crowd... At the end of step 5, brown under the grill before baking so you'll know the pie is already golden on top. Freezes well.

CHEAT

Liquid gravy browning in bottles can be rather hard to track down in the shops these days, but it's well worth the hunt. Not only does it make a sauce or gravy an appetizing rich brown, it saves you time, too, as you don't have to brown the onions for so long. We use it the whole time.

PREPARE AHEAD AND FREEZE

The pie can be prepared up to the end of step 5 up to 1 day ahead. Freeze for up to 2 months.

IN THE AGA

At step 2, transfer to the simmering oven for 2 hours or until the mince is tender. At step 6, bake on the second set of runners in the roasting oven for 30 minutes (45–50 minutes for 12).

Shepherd's pie dauphinois (see overleaf) ▸▸▸

Although there are many trendy new lasagnes out there, we are often asked for a classic lasagne. This is a recipe we've perfected over the years. Leave it to stand for six hours before cooking.

GREAT FOR A CROWD

Classic beef lasagne

Serves 6

Special equipment 2.4 litre (4 pint) shallow wide-based ovenproof dish

1 tbsp sunflower oil
900g (2lb) raw minced beef
2 onions, roughly chopped
4 celery sticks, diced
2 garlic cloves, crushed
2 level tbsp plain flour
2 x 400g cans chopped tomatoes
150ml (5fl oz) beef stock
3 tbsp tomato purée
1 tsp sugar
1 tbsp freshly chopped
  thyme leaves

For the white sauce

50g (1¾oz) butter
50g (1¾oz) plain flour
750ml (1¼ pints) hot milk
2 tsp Dijon mustard
50g (1¾oz) Parmesan cheese,
  freshly grated
salt and freshly ground
  black pepper

6–8 sheets lasagne
85g (3oz) mature Cheddar
  cheese, grated

Serves 12

Special equipment 2 x 2.4 litre (4 pint) shallow wide-based ovenproof dishes or 1 x 4 litre (7 pint) dish

1 tbsp sunflower oil
1.8kg (4lb) raw minced beef
4 onions, roughly chopped
8 celery sticks, diced
4 garlic cloves, crushed
4 level tbsp plain flour
4 x 400g cans chopped tomatoes
300ml (10fl oz) beef stock
6 tbsp tomato purée
2 tsp sugar
2 tbsp freshly chopped
  thyme leaves

For the white sauce

100g (3½oz) butter
100g (3½oz) plain flour
1.5 litres (2¾ pints) hot milk
1 heaped tbsp Dijon mustard
100g (3½oz) Parmesan cheese,
  freshly grated
salt and freshly ground
  black pepper

12–16 sheets lasagne
175g (6oz) mature Cheddar
  cheese, grated

1 Preheat the oven to 160°C (140°C fan/325°F/Gas 3). Heat the oil in a large frying pan until hot, then add the mince and cook until brown all over. Stir in the onions, celery, and garlic.

2 Add the flour and stir to coat the vegetables and beef, then blend in the tomatoes, stock, tomato purée, sugar, and thyme. Bring to the boil, cover with a lid, then transfer to the oven for 1–1½ hours or until the beef is tender.

3 Meanwhile, make the white sauce (see opposite). Melt the butter in a saucepan, add the flour, and cook over the heat for 1 minute. Slowly add the hot milk, whisking until the sauce is thick and smooth. Add the mustard and Parmesan cheese and season well with salt and freshly ground black pepper.

4 Remove the meat sauce from the oven and put one-third into the base of the ovenproof dish (two dishes for 12). Spoon one-third of the white sauce on top and arrange a layer of lasagne on top of that. Season with salt and freshly ground black pepper.

5 Spoon half the remaining meat sauce on top, then half the remaining white sauce. Put another layer of lasagne on top and season with salt and freshly ground black pepper. Add the rest of the meat sauce followed by the rest of the white sauce.

6 Sprinkle over the Cheddar cheese, then transfer to the fridge for a minimum of 6 hours before cooking so the pasta has chance to soften.

7 To serve, preheat the oven to 200°C (180°C fan/400°F/Gas 6), then cook the lasagne in the middle of the oven for 45 minutes (1 hour for 12) or until golden brown on top, bubbling around the edges, and the pasta is soft.

Great for a crowd... Make a batch of meat sauce, using just enough oil to coat the bottom of the pan. Make a batch of white sauce, then assemble the lasagnes. Freezes well.

PREPARE AHEAD AND FREEZE
The lasagne can be made up to the end of step 6 up to 2 days ahead. Freeze the lasagne at the end of step 6 for up to 2 months.

IN THE AGA
Cook the meat sauce in the simmering oven for 1–1½ hours or until the beef is tender. Cook the assembled lasagne in the middle of the roasting oven for 40–45 minutes (1 hour for 12), using the cold sheet if it is getting too brown.

"It's good to have a few of these lasagnes ready and waiting in the freezer. They are wonderful for big events like buffets and pot luck parties and are always a huge success."

MAKING THE WHITE SAUCE

STEP 1 Melt the butter in a fairly large saucepan, add the flour, and cook for 1 minute, stirring.

STEP 2 Gradually blend in the hot milk, whisking all the time until the mixture bubbles and thickens.

A lasagne with wow factor. The secret ingredient is butternut squash. Prepare the dish the day before if you can, so the lasagne sheets have time to soften in the sauce. Serve with salad and crusty bread.

Butternut squash lasagne

Serves 6

Special equipment 2.4 litre (4 pint) shallow wide-based ovenproof dish

1 tbsp olive oil
225g (8oz) butternut squash (peeled weight), chopped into small cubes (see page 229)
1 red pepper, halved, deseeded, and diced
1 onion, roughly chopped
2 garlic cloves, crushed
225g (8oz) chestnut mushrooms, sliced
2 x 400g cans chopped tomatoes
1 tbsp tomato purée
2 tsp sugar
1 tbsp freshly chopped thyme
salt and freshly ground black pepper
100g (3½oz) spinach, chopped
6–8 sheets lasagne

For the white sauce

75g (2½oz) butter
75g (2½oz) plain flour
900ml (1½ pints) hot milk
2 tsp Dijon mustard
100g (3½oz) Gruyère cheese, grated
250g (9oz) mozzarella, chopped into small cubes

Serves 12

Special equipment 2 x 2.4 litre (4 pint) shallow wide-based ovenproof dishes or 1 x 4 litre (7 pint) shallow wide-based ovenproof dish

2 tbsp olive oil
500g (1lb 2oz) butternut squash (peeled weight), chopped into small cubes (see page 229)
2 red peppers, halved, deseeded, and diced
2 onions, roughly chopped
4 garlic cloves, crushed
500g (1lb 2oz) chestnut mushrooms, sliced
4 x 400g cans chopped tomatoes
2 tbsp tomato purée
1 heaped tbsp sugar
2 tbsp freshly chopped thyme
salt and freshly ground black pepper
200g (7oz) spinach, chopped
12–16 sheets lasagne

For the white sauce

175g (6oz) butter
175g (6oz) plain flour
1.7 litres (3 pints) hot milk
1 heaped tbsp Dijon mustard
200g (7oz) Gruyère cheese, grated
500g (1lb 2oz) mozzarella, chopped into small cubes

1 Heat the oil in a large deep frying pan. Add the squash, pepper, onion, and garlic and fry over a moderate heat for 4–5 minutes or until the onion is starting to soften. Add the mushrooms, tomatoes, tomato purée, sugar, thyme, and some salt and freshly ground black pepper. Cover with a lid and simmer over a low heat for 20–30 minutes (35–40 minutes for 12) or until the vegetables are tender. Add the spinach and toss together until just wilted.

2 Meanwhile, make the white sauce. Melt the butter in a saucepan, add the flour, and stir over the heat for 1 minute. Slowly whisk in the hot milk until the sauce is smooth and thick. Season with salt and freshly ground black pepper, then stir in the mustard and half the Gruyère.

3 Spoon one-third of the tomato sauce over the base of the ovenproof dish, then spoon one-third of the white sauce on top. Arrange a single layer of lasagne over the white sauce and scatter over half the mozzarella. Spoon half the remaining tomato sauce on top, followed by half the remaining white sauce. Arrange another layer of lasagne on top and scatter over the remaining mozzarella. Spread the rest of the tomato sauce on top, followed by the rest of the white sauce, then sprinkle with the remaining Gruyère.

4 Transfer to the fridge for at least 6 hours or overnight so the lasagne starts to soften.

5 To serve, preheat the oven to 200°C (180°C fan/400°F/Gas 6), then bake the lasagne for 45 minutes (1–1¼ hours for 12) or until golden brown and bubbling around the edges.

PREPARE AHEAD AND FREEZE
The lasagne can be made up to the end of step 3 up to 2 days ahead. Freeze for up to 2 months.

IN THE AGA
Cook the tomato sauce in the simmering oven for 20–30 minutes. Bake the lasagne in the middle of the roasting oven for 40–45 minutes (1 hour for 12).

Buy mozzarella in a log rather than a ball for this – it is far easier to cut into small pieces. You can use rigatoni or penne if you can't get hold of elicoidali. Serve with dressed salad.

GREAT FOR A CROWD

Pasta and meatball bake with tomato and basil sauce

Serves 6

Special equipment 2 litre (3½ pint) shallow wide-based ovenproof dish

For the sauce

1 tbsp olive oil

1 large onion, finely chopped

1 red chilli, halved, deseeded, and finely chopped

2 garlic cloves, crushed

800g can chopped tomatoes

2 tbsp tomato purée

salt and freshly ground black pepper

2 tbsp coarsely chopped fresh basil

a dash of caster sugar (optional)

For the meatballs

450g (1lb) good-quality sausagemeat

25g (scant 1oz) fresh fine breadcrumbs

50g (1¾oz) freshly grated Parmesan cheese

2 tbsp finely chopped fresh basil

50g (1¾oz) mozzarella, cut into about 30 cubes

1 tbsp olive oil

225g (8oz) elicoidali pasta

50g (1¾oz) Parmesan cheese, freshly grated

50g (1¾oz) mozzarella, chopped into small pieces

Serves 12

Special equipment 2 x 2 litre (3½ pint) shallow wide-based ovenproof dishes or 1 x 4 litre (7 pint) dish

For the sauce

2 tbsp olive oil

2 large onions, finely chopped

2 red chillies, halved, deseeded, and finely chopped

4 garlic cloves, crushed

2 x 800g cans chopped tomatoes

3 tbsp tomato purée

salt and freshly ground black pepper

3 tbsp coarsely chopped fresh basil

a dash of caster sugar (optional)

For the meatballs

900g (2lb) good-quality sausagemeat

50g (1¾oz) fresh fine breadcrumbs

100g (3½oz) freshly grated Parmesan cheese

4 tbsp finely chopped fresh basil

100g (3½oz) mozzarella, cut into about 60 cubes

1 tbsp olive oil

450g (1lb) elicoidali pasta

100g (3½oz) Parmesan cheese, freshly grated

100g (3½oz) mozzarella, chopped into small pieces

1 Preheat the oven to 200°C (180°C fan/400°F/Gas 6). Meanwhile, put the oil for the sauce into a deep saucepan, add the onion, and fry over a high heat for a few minutes or until softened slightly but not coloured.

2 Add the chilli and garlic and fry over a high heat for a few minutes. Add the tomatoes and tomato purée, then season with salt and freshly ground black pepper. Bring to the boil, cover with a lid, then lower the heat and simmer for 15 minutes. Add the basil and taste – if it is a little sharp, add a dash of caster sugar.

3 Meanwhile, make the meatballs. Put the sausagement, breadcrumbs, Parmesan, and basil into a mixing bowl. Mix together with your hands, season with salt and freshly ground black pepper, and shape into 30 balls (60 for 12). Using your finger, make a hole in the middle of each meatball, then push a cube of mozzarella into the centre and reshape so the mozzarella is hidden inside.

4 Heat the oil in a large frying pan and fry the meatballs for 4 minutes or until they are golden brown all over and just cooked through. You may need to do this in batches.

5 Meanwhile, cook the pasta in boiling salted water according to the packet instructions until just tender. Drain, refresh in cold water, and dry well with kitchen paper.

6 Stir the pasta into the sauce and season with salt and freshly ground black pepper. Stir in the meatballs, then spoon into the ovenproof dish and sprinkle the Parmesan cheese and mozzarella on top.

7 Bake for 20–25 minutes (45 minutes for 12) or until golden brown on top and piping hot in the centre.

Great for a crowd... Make a batch of tomato sauce. Make the meatballs, but leave out the mozzarella in the centre, as it will take too long to do. Cook the pasta, then assemble the bakes.

PREPARE AHEAD
You can make the bake up to the end of step 6 up to 8 hours ahead. Not suitable for freezing.

IN THE AGA
Bake on the second set of runners in the roasting oven for 20 minutes (45 minutes for 12).

"This is a perfect all-in-one dish of pasta, meatballs, and tomato sauce. Each meatball is stuffed with mozzarella to give a lovely surprise when you bite into it. Enjoy!"

CHOPPING BASIL LEAVES

STEP 1 Gather the basil leaves together in two small piles. Roll one pile of leaves up tightly into a ball.

STEP 2 Slice across to make shreds. Gather together, turn 90° and chop small. Repeat with the other pile.

Half a small butternut squash per person is ideal at lunchtime or even as a main meal. Serve with dressed salad and bread.

Butternut squash with spinach and bacon

Serves 6

3 x 400g (14oz) butternut squash, halved lengthways through the stalk and seeds and fibres discarded (see page 229)

2 tbsp olive oil

150ml (5fl oz) water

salt and freshly ground black pepper

200g (7oz) smoked bacon lardons

2 leeks, sliced

250g (9oz) chestnut mushrooms, quartered

100g (3½oz) baby spinach

100ml (3½fl oz) double cream

75g (2½oz) Parmesan cheese, freshly grated

freshly chopped parsley, to garnish

Serves 12

6 x 400g (14oz) butternut squash, halved lengthways through the stalk and seeds and fibres discarded (see page 229)

4 tbsp olive oil

150ml (5fl oz) water

salt and freshly ground black pepper

400g (14oz) smoked bacon lardons

4 leeks, sliced

500g (1lb 2oz) chestnut mushrooms, quartered

200g (7oz) baby spinach

200ml (7fl oz) double cream

175g (6oz) Parmesan cheese, freshly grated

freshly chopped parsley, to garnish

1 Preheat the oven to 200°C (180°C fan/400°F/Gas 6). Put the squash cut side up in a large roasting tin (two tins for 12) and drizzle over the oil. Pour the water around them, season with salt and freshly ground black pepper, and roast in the oven for 45 minutes (1 hour for 12) or until the flesh is soft. Set aside and allow to cool slightly.

2 Meanwhile, put the lardons into a dry frying pan and stir over a medium heat until the fat comes out. Add the leeks and cook slowly for 10 minutes or until soft. Add the mushrooms and spinach and stir together over a high heat for 10 minutes or until the spinach has wilted and the mushrooms are nearly cooked.

3 Remove the pan from the heat and stir in the cream, some salt and freshly ground black pepper, and half the cheese. Scoop out some of the cooked squash, leaving a 2cm (¾in) border inside each squash case, and stir into the spinach mixture. Spoon the mixture into the squash cases and sprinkle over the remaining cheese.

4 Bake for 20–25 minutes (55 minutes for 12) or until golden on top and heated through. Garnish with a sprinkle of parsley and serve.

PREPARE AHEAD
The squash can be prepared up to the end of step 3 up to 1 day ahead. Not suitable for freezing.

IN THE AGA
Roast the squash on the grid shelf on the floor of the roasting oven for 40–45 minutes. At step 4, bake on the highest set of runners in the roasting oven for 20–25 minutes (55 minutes for 12).

This is a winning recipe for vegetarians and perfect for a summer lunch with a green salad and crusty bread.

Aubergines baked with feta and chickpeas

Serves 6

3 medium aubergines, sliced
  in half lengthways
2 tbsp olive oil
salt and freshly ground
  black pepper
1 large onion, roughly chopped
2 garlic cloves, crushed
400g can chopped tomatoes
400g can chickpeas, drained
  and rinsed

2 tbsp sun-dried tomato paste
50g (1¾oz) pitted black or green
  olives, sliced in half
small bunch of fresh mint,
  chopped
100g (3½oz) feta cheese,
  crumbled

Serves 12

6 medium aubergines, sliced
  in half lengthways
4 tbsp olive oil
salt and freshly ground
  black pepper
2 large onions, roughly chopped
4 garlic cloves, crushed
2 x 400g cans chopped tomatoes
2 x 400g cans chickpeas, drained
  and rinsed

4 tbsp sun-dried tomato paste
100g (3½oz) pitted black or green
  olives, sliced in half
large bunch of fresh mint,
  chopped
200g (7oz) feta cheese, crumbled

1 Preheat the oven to 200°C (180°C fan/400°F/Gas 6). Put the aubergines cut side up in a roasting tin. Drizzle over half the oil, season with salt and freshly ground black pepper, and bake for 25 minutes (40 minutes for 12) or until the flesh is tender. Remove from the oven and leave to cool.

2 Heat the remaining oil in a frying pan. Add the onion and garlic and cook for 10 minutes or until soft. Add the tomatoes, chickpeas, tomato paste, and olives, and simmer for 5 minutes.

3 Meanwhile, scoop out a little of the flesh from the aubergine halves, leaving a 1cm (½in) border inside the aubergine cases. Add the flesh to the chickpea mixture and mix together. Add the mint and half the feta and season with salt and freshly ground black pepper. Spoon the mixture into the aubergine cases and top with the remaining feta.

4 Bake in the oven for 20 minutes (35 minutes for 12) or until the feta is tinged brown and the aubergines are hot.

PREPARE AHEAD
The dish can be assembled up to the end of step 3 up to 1 day ahead. Not suitable for freezing.

IN THE AGA
Bake the aubergines on the grid shelf on the floor of the roasting oven for 20–25 minutes. To serve, slide the roasting tin on the highest set of runners in the roasting oven and cook for 20–35 minutes or until golden.

Use your favourite sausages for this smoky casserole. We like Cumberland or pork and leek. Serve with a green vegetable.

Smoky sausage cassoulet

Serves 6

3 tbsp olive oil

12 sausages

4 large onions, sliced

2 tsp paprika

50g (1¾oz) chorizo, very
  finely chopped

2 x 400g cans chopped tomatoes

2 tbsp tomato purée

2 tbsp Worcestershire sauce

2 tsp balsamic vinegar

salt and freshly ground
  black pepper

400g can butter beans, drained
  and rinsed

Serves 12

5 tbsp olive oil

24 sausages

7 large onions, sliced

4 tsp paprika

100g (3½oz) chorizo, very
  finely chopped

4 x 400g cans chopped tomatoes

4 tbsp tomato purée

4 tbsp Worcestershire sauce

1 tbsp balsamic vinegar

salt and freshly ground
  black pepper

2 x 400g cans butter beans,
  drained and rinsed

1 Heat 1 tablespoon of the oil in a large non-stick frying pan or casserole dish over a high heat, then brown the sausages until golden on all sides. Remove with a slotted spoon and set aside. You may need to do this in batches.

2 Add the remaining oil to the pan and fry the onions for a few minutes or until lightly golden. Add the remaining ingredients (except the butter beans and sausages) and season with salt and freshly ground black pepper.

3 Simmer over a gentle heat for 20–25 minutes or until the onions are nearly soft. Add the butter beans and stir.

4 Arrange the sausages on top, cover with a lid, and cook for 20 minutes (35–40 minutes for 12) or until the sausages are completely cooked.

VARIATION

The dish is especially popular with the young. If you know they like baked beans, you can substitute them for the butter beans.

PREPARE AHEAD

The cassoulet can be made up to the end of step 3 up to 1 day ahead. Alternatively, cook it completely and reheat to serve. Not suitable for freezing.

IN THE AGA

At step 3, cover with a lid and transfer to the simmering oven for 30 minutes. Add the beans and sausages, cover again, and return to the simmering oven for a further 25 minutes.

All Italian

In Italy, eating is such a relaxed communal affair, centred around family and friends. Here, we've brought together some of the best-loved dishes Italians serve when they're cooking for a crowd.

All Italian

There's something so wonderful about Italian cooking. Maybe it's because the dishes are so simple, honest, and straightforward. Or perhaps it's because the Italians use only the finest ingredients and never overload them with fussy sauces.

Lunch is the most important meal of the day – so much so that at noon the country almost comes to a standstill. Pasta or risotto is eaten as a first course, followed by a second course of meat or fish served with salad or vegetables.

We are less traditional about this and offer one of these courses as a main meal – either in the evening or at lunchtime. Served in slightly larger portions, an Italian "first course" of pasta or risotto makes an elegant and crowd-pleasing dish – likewise a "second course" of chicken stuffed with pork sausagemeat or chicken casseroled in a gutsy tomato sauce.

Dried pasta v fresh pasta

Pasta is so endlessly versatile, teaming well with almost every ingredient under the sun. In the recipes in this chapter, we serve it with fish, seafood, cheese, and tomatoes, as well as with a classic bolognese sauce.

We always use dried pasta – as the Italians do – it's so convenient to have in the house. But you can use fresh pasta if you prefer, although its texture is not always so good. Our pasta of choice is a trusted Italian brand, made from 100 per cent durum wheat ("semola di grano duro"). It keeps for several months in a tightly closed packet.

"Pasta is so endlessly versatile, teaming well with almost every ingredient in the sun. In this chapter, we serve it with fish, seafood, cheese, and tomatoes."

Perfect pasta every time

The golden rule when cooking pasta is to use a very large pan and plenty of water and salt – at least 2 litres (3½ pints) water and 2 tsp salt for every 225g (8oz) pasta. It's important to get it right at this stage because you can't season pasta once it's cooked. Some people also swear by a splash of oil to stop the pasta sticking, but in our experience it makes no difference at all because it simply makes its way to the surface, where it floats.

● Start by bringing the salted water to the boil. Add the pasta and stir to separate. If you are cooking spaghetti, let the ends soften, then push the strands slowly against the side of the pan, twisting and lowering them into the water as you do so.

● Cover the pan with a lid so the water returns to the boil as quickly as possible, then reduce the heat so it is bubbling briskly. Remove the lid and cook, uncovered, according to the timings on the packet.

● To test if the pasta is cooked, lift a piece out and bite it – it should be tender but still a little firm. The Italians call this "al dente".

● Pour the contents of the pan into a large colander and shake it to drain the pasta well. It is now ready to serve, with or without a sauce.

● If you're preparing the pasta ahead of time, cook it until "al dente", then drain and refresh first under running warm water and then under cold water. Don't leave it sitting in the water in the pan or it will disintegrate. To reheat, plunge it into boiling water for a minute or until heated through, then drain.

Adding the sauce

● If you're serving the pasta with a sauce, make sure the frying pan or saucepan you're making the sauce in is large enough to accommodate the pasta as well.

● Add the pasta to the sauce and not the sauce to the pasta. That way, you can work it in gradually without it sticking.

Risottos are popular with everyone, and this version, full of flavour and bright healthy vegetables, is great for vegetarians. Serve hot with fresh salad leaves.

Roasted vegetable risotto

Serves 6

225g (8oz) butternut squash, peeled and cut into 2cm (¾in) cubes (see page 229)

1 onion, coarsely chopped

1 small aubergine, cut into 1cm (½in) cubes

1 small red pepper, halved, deseeded, and cut into 1cm (½in) cubes

3 tbsp olive oil

salt and freshly ground black pepper

2 tsp freshly chopped thyme leaves

300g (11oz) risotto rice

225g (8oz) chestnut mushrooms, sliced

1.2 litres (2 pints) hot vegetable stock

50g (1¾oz) Parmesan cheese, made into small shavings with a vegetable peeler

2 tbsp freshly snipped chives

Serves 12

450g (1lb) butternut squash, peeled and cut into 2cm (¾in) cubes (see page 229)

2 onions, coarsely chopped

2 small aubergines, cut into 1cm (½in) cubes

2 small red peppers, halved, deseeded, and cut into 1cm (½in) cubes

6 tbsp olive oil

salt and freshly ground black pepper

1 heaped tbsp freshly chopped thyme leaves

600g (1lb 5oz) risotto rice

450g (1lb) chestnut mushrooms, sliced

2.4 litres (4 pints) hot vegetable stock

100g (3½oz) Parmesan cheese, made into small shavings with a vegetable peeler

4 tbsp freshly snipped chives

1 Preheat the oven to 200°C (180°C fan/400°F/Gas 6). Put the squash, onion, aubergine, and pepper into a large roasting tin (two tins for 12) in a single layer.

2 Pour over a third of the oil and toss well with your hands. Season with salt and freshly ground black pepper, then sprinkle over the thyme.

3 Roast for 30 minutes (35 minutes for 12) or until tender and golden.

4 Heat the remaining oil in a deep saucepan, add the rice, then stir in the mushrooms and gradually add the stock (see right).

5 When all the stock has been absorbed and the rice is cooked, stir in the roasted vegetables and half the Parmesan. Transfer to a serving dish and sprinkle with the remaining Parmesan and the chives.

PREPARE AHEAD
The vegetables can be roasted up to 8 hours ahead. Not suitable for freezing.

IN THE AGA
At step 3, roast on the floor of the roasting oven for 20–30 minutes.

MAKING A RISOTTO

STEP 1 Heat the oil in a deep pan over a high heat, add the rice, and stir to coat. Add the mushrooms.

STEP 2 Add the hot stock a ladleful at a time. Stir continuously and only add more when it's been absorbed.

Mary's sister-in-law, Margaret, made this for 90 people for a charity lunch recently and it was a triumph. Serve with new potatoes.

GREAT FOR A CROWD

Sardinian chicken

Serves 6

2 tbsp olive oil

75g (2½oz) pancetta, cut into strips

6 large chicken thighs (bone in), skinned

1 large onion, chopped

1 small red pepper, halved, deseeded, and diced

3 garlic cloves, crushed

225g (8oz) button mushrooms, quartered

120ml (4fl oz) red wine

1 level tbsp plain flour

400g can chopped tomatoes

5 tbsp tomato purée

salt and freshly ground black pepper

1 tsp freshly chopped thyme leaves

grated zest of 1 lemon

2 tbsp capers, drained and chopped

Serves 12

4 tbsp olive oil

175g (6oz) pancetta, cut into strips

12 large chicken thighs (bone in), skinned

2 large onions, chopped

1 large red pepper, halved, deseeded and diced

6 garlic cloves, crushed

450g (1lb) button mushrooms, quartered

250ml (8fl oz) red wine

1 heaped tbsp plain flour

2 x 400g cans chopped tomatoes

150ml (5fl oz) tomato purée

salt and freshly ground black pepper

2 tsp freshly chopped thyme leaves

grated zest of 2 lemons

4 tbsp capers, drained and chopped

1 Preheat the oven to 180°C (160°C fan/350°F/Gas 4). Heat half the oil in a large deep frying pan or casserole, add the pancetta and chicken, and cook over a high heat for a few minutes or until the pancetta is crisp and the chicken golden all over. You may need to do this in batches. Remove with a slotted spoon and set aside.

2 Add the remaining oil to the pan, followed by the onion, pepper, garlic, and mushrooms, and fry for a few minutes or until starting to soften.

3 Put the wine into a jug and blend to a smooth paste with the flour.

4 Add the tomatoes and tomato purée to the pan, then blend in the wine mixture, season with salt and freshly ground black pepper, and bring to the boil. Return the chicken and pancetta to the pan, add the thyme, lemon zest, and capers, and bring to the boil.

5 Cover with a lid and transfer to the oven for 1 hour (1¼ hours for 12) or until the chicken is tender. Serve piping hot.

Great for a crowd... This is perfect for making in one large batch if you have a pan or casserole big enough. Brown the chicken in batches beforehand. And make sure it is completely tender when you take it out of the oven.

VARIATION

You can use boned thighs if you prefer. They'll take about 30 minutes less to cook.

PREPARE AHEAD AND FREEZE

The casserole can be made up to 2 days ahead. Freeze for up to 2 months.

IN THE AGA

Cook in the simmering oven for 1–1¼ hours or until the chicken is tender.

If time is short, you can use peppers from a jar for this. Serve with rice or mashed potatoes and a green vegetable.

Italian farmhouse chicken

Serves 6

1 tbsp olive oil

1 large onion, coarsely chopped

2 garlic cloves, crushed

2 x 400g cans chopped tomatoes

2 tbsp tomato purée

1 tsp caster sugar

salt and freshly ground
   black pepper

3 red peppers, cut in half
   and deseeded

For the stuffing

450g (1lb) pork sausagemeat

finely grated zest of ½ lemon

small bunch of basil leaves, torn

1 tbsp Dijon mustard

12 boneless skinless
   chicken thighs

Serves 12

2 tbsp olive oil

2 large onions, coarsely chopped

4 garlic cloves, crushed

4 x 400g cans chopped tomatoes

4 tbsp tomato purée

2 tsp caster sugar

salt and freshly ground
   black pepper

6 red peppers, cut in half
   and deseeded

For the stuffing

900g (2lb) pork sausagemeat

finely grated zest of 1 lemon

large bunch of basil leaves, torn

2 tbsp Dijon mustard

24 boneless skinless
   chicken thighs

1 Preheat the oven to 200°C (180°C fan/400°F/Gas 6). Heat the oil in a frying pan, add the onion and garlic, and fry over a high heat for a few minutes or until lightly golden. Stir in the tomatoes, tomato purée, and sugar, season with salt and freshly ground black pepper, and bring to the boil. Cover with a lid and simmer for 25 minutes or until the onion is tender.

2 Meanwhile, arrange the peppers cut side down on a baking sheet and bake for 20 minutes or until the skin has started to blacken. Transfer to a polythene bag, seal the top, and set aside (this makes it easier to remove the skin). Once cool, peel and cut each half in two.

3 To make the stuffing, put the sausagemeat into a mixing bowl, add the lemon zest, basil, and mustard, season with salt and freshly ground black pepper, and mix well. Divide the mixture into 12 (24 for 12) and shape into little sausages.

4 Place the chicken thighs skinned side down on a board, open them up flat, and bash with a rolling pin to make them a little thinner (see right). Make sure each thigh is the same thickness. Season with salt and freshly ground black pepper.

5 Place a slice of pepper on each thigh, add one of the sausages, and roll the thigh up. Repeat with the other thighs. Arrange join side down in a single layer in a shallow ovenproof dish and pour over the tomato sauce.

6 Bake for 40–45 minutes (45–50 minutes for 12) or until bubbling and the chicken is cooked.

PREPARING THE THIGHS

Place the chicken thigh on a cutting board between sheets of cling film and flatten with a rolling pin.

PREPARE AHEAD AND FREEZE

The chicken thighs can be prepared up to the end of step 5 up to 12 hours ahead. Freeze the uncooked stuffed rolled chicken thighs for up to 2 months.

IN THE AGA

Roast the peppers at the top of the roasting oven for 12 minutes. Bake the thighs on the grid shelf on the floor of the roasting oven for 40–45 minutes (45–55 minutes for 12).

These look so lovely and the soft-yolked quail's eggs on top are an extra treat. Marinated and grilled aubergines are available from the deli counter of the supermarket.

Mini aubergine and rocket pizzas

Serves 6

Special equipment 10cm (4in) scone cutter

2 x 150g (5½oz) pizza bases
100ml (3½fl oz) passata
2 tbsp sun-dried tomato paste
salt and freshly ground
    black pepper

200g tub marinated and grilled aubergines, drained (oil reserved) and sliced
100g (3½oz) Gruyère cheese, grated
6 quail's eggs
50g (1¾oz) rocket

Serves 12

Special equipment 10cm (4in) scone cutter

4 x 150g (5½oz) pizza bases
200ml (7fl oz) passata
4 tbsp sun-dried tomato paste
salt and freshly ground
    black pepper

2 x 200g tubs marinated and grilled aubergines, drained (oil reserved) and sliced
225g (8oz) Gruyère cheese, grated
12 quail's eggs
100g (3½oz) rocket

1 Preheat the oven to 200°C (180°C fan/400°F/Gas 6). Using a 10cm (4in) scone cutter, cut three circles from each pizza base and arrange on a baking sheet (two baking sheets for 12).

2 Put the passata into a bowl, add the sun-dried tomato paste, season with salt and freshly ground black pepper, and mix well. Spread over the base of each dough circle.

3 Arrange the aubergine slices over the tomato and sprinkle with the cheese. Using the back of a tablespoon, make a well in the centre of each pizza, ready for the egg to sit in.

4 Bake for 8 minutes (10 minutes for 12) or until the pizzas are very hot, then carefully crack an egg into the well in each one, keeping the yolk intact. Return to the oven for 3 minutes or until the pizza is lightly golden, the egg white completely cooked, and the yolk just set.

5 Transfer to serving plates, arrange some rocket on top of each pizza, and drizzle with a little of the reserved aubergine oil. Serve at once.

PIZZA BASES

You'll find pizza bases in most supermarkets. The uncooked dough comes in packets ready for you to add your choice of topping.

PREPARE AHEAD AND FREEZE

The pizzas can be made up to the end of step 3 up to 8 hours ahead. Freeze at the end of step 3 for up to 2 months.

IN THE AGA

Bake on the grid shelf on the floor of the roasting oven for 8 minutes (8–10 minutes for 12), add the eggs, then bake for a further 3 minutes.

This is a traditional bolognese sauce, with chicken livers for a lovely depth of flavour. It's well worth making double the quantity, so you can freeze a batch for another day.

Classic spaghetti bolognese

Serves 6

1 tbsp sunflower oil

200g (7oz) fresh chicken livers, trimmed of any sinew and cut into small pieces

900g (2lb) raw lean minced beef

2 onions, finely chopped

2 garlic cloves, crushed

100ml (3½fl oz) Port

2 x 400g cans chopped tomatoes

3 tbsp tomato purée

1 tsp caster sugar

salt and freshly ground black pepper

300g (11oz) spaghetti

Serves 12

2 tbsp sunflower oil

450g (1lb) fresh chicken livers, trimmed of any sinew and cut into small pieces

1.8kg (4lb) raw lean minced beef

4 onions, finely chopped

4 garlic cloves, crushed

200ml (7fl oz) Port

4 x 400g cans chopped tomatoes

6 tbsp tomato purée

2 tsp caster sugar

salt and freshly ground black pepper

600g (1lb 5oz) spaghetti

1 Preheat the oven to 160°C (140°C fan/325°F/Gas 3). Heat the oil in a large non-stick frying pan over a high heat, add the chicken livers, and brown quickly all over. Remove with a slotted spoon and set aside.

2 Add the minced beef in batches and brown all over, adding a little more oil if the pan's getting dry. Return the chicken livers to the pan along with all the beef.

3 Add the onions and garlic and fry for 2 minutes. Stir in the Port, tomatoes, tomato purée, and sugar and bring to the boil. Season with salt and freshly ground black pepper, cover with a lid, and transfer to the oven for 1–1¼ hours or until tender.

4 To serve, cook the spaghetti in boiling salted water according to the packet instructions. Drain well, transfer to a serving bowl, and top with the bolognese sauce.

PREPARE AHEAD AND FREEZE

The sauce can be made up to 2 days ahead. Freeze for up to 3 months.

IN THE AGA

Cook in the simmering oven for 1–1½ hours or until tender.

We usually buy ready-peeled prawns for this, but if you can only find them with their shells on, buy a few extra and do it yourself – they're very easy to shell. Serve with dressed salad.

Seafood linguine

Serves 6

225g (8oz) dried linguine
salt and freshly ground
  black pepper
small knob of butter
150g (5½oz) (shelled weight)
  raw tiger prawns
150g (5½oz) raw squid, sliced

150g (5½oz) raw queen scallops,
  sliced in half horizontally
1 large shallot, finely chopped
250ml (8fl oz) dry white wine
200ml (7fl oz) double cream
juice of 1 large lemon
small bunch of dill, chopped

Serves 12

450g (1lb) dried linguine
salt and freshly ground
  black pepper
large knob of butter
300g (11oz) (shelled weight)
  raw tiger prawns
300g (11oz) raw squid, sliced

300g (11oz) raw queen scallops,
  sliced in half horizontally
2 large shallots, finely chopped
600ml (1 pint) dry white wine
450ml (15fl oz) double cream
juice of 2 large lemons
large bunch of dill, chopped

1 Cook the linguine in boiling salted water according to the packet instructions. Drain well.

2 Heat the butter in a large frying pan, add the prawns, squid, and scallops, and fry for 3–4 minutes or until the prawns have turned pink and the squid and scallops are just cooked. Remove with a slotted spoon and set aside.

3 Add the shallot and wine to the pan, bring to the boil, and allow to bubble over a high heat until the wine has reduced by half. Add the cream and return to the boil.

4 Add the cooked seafood and toss together. Season with salt and freshly ground black pepper, stir in the pasta, lemon juice, and dill, heat through thoroughly, and serve.

PREPARE AHEAD
The dish is best prepared and served straightaway.
Not suitable for freezing.

SHELLING PRAWNS

STEP 1 Start by pulling off the head of the prawn, then peel off the shell and legs with your fingers.

STEP 2 If the prawns are large, slice along the back and remove the dark intestinal vein. This step is optional.

This is a budget recipe. A sort of upmarket macaroni cheese – perfect for a crowd of hungry teenagers – and one they could very easily cook for themselves. Serve with dressed salad.

Penne alla parmigiana

Serves 6

Special equipment *1.5 litre (2¾ pint) shallow ovenproof dish*

350g (12oz) penne
salt and freshly ground black pepper
50g (1¾oz) butter
50g (1¾oz) plain flour
1.2 litres (2 pints) hot milk

1 tbsp Dijon mustard
100g (3½oz) strong Cheddar cheese, grated
100g (3½oz) Parmesan cheese, freshly grated
6 tomatoes, halved, deseeded, and roughly chopped

Serves 12

Special equipment *2.4 litre (4 pint) shallow ovenproof dish*

600g (1lb 5oz) penne
salt and freshly ground black pepper
100g (3½oz) butter
100g (3½oz) plain flour
1.7 litres (3 pints) hot milk

2 tbsp Dijon mustard
175g (6oz) strong Cheddar cheese, grated
175g (6oz) Parmesan cheese, freshly grated
8 large tomatoes, halved, deseeded, and roughly chopped

1 Preheat the oven to 200°C (180°C fan/400°F/Gas 6). Cook the penne in boiling salted water according to the packet instructions. Drain and refresh in cold water.

2 Melt the butter in a large saucepan, add the flour, and stir over the heat for 1 minute. Gradually add the milk, whisking all the time, until the sauce is smooth and thick.

3 Add the mustard and two-thirds of the Cheddar and Parmesan, then add the penne and some salt and freshly ground black pepper.

4 Spoon into the ovenproof dish, arrange the tomatoes on top, and sprinkle over the remaining cheese.

5 Bake for 20–25 minutes (35–40 minutes for 12) or until lightly golden and crispy.

PREPARE AHEAD
The dish can be made up to the end of step 4 up to 1 day ahead. Not suitable for freezing.

IN THE AGA
Bake in the middle of the roasting oven for 20–25 minutes (30–35 minutes for 12) or until golden and crispy.

PREPARING TOMATOES

STEP 1 Halve the tomato, loosen the seeds with a teaspoon, then gently squeeze them out into a bowl.

STEP 2 Place cut side down on a board and slice into strips. Cut across the strips if you want dice.

This full-flavoured tomato and garlic sauce with a hint of chilli is excellent with spaghetti. The breadcrumbs give a lovely crispy texture – make sure they are very fine. Serve with dressed salad.

Spaghetti with king prawns and tomatoes

Serves 6

300g (11oz) spaghetti

salt and freshly ground black pepper

4 tbsp olive oil

50g (1¾oz) very fine fresh brown breadcrumbs

finely grated zest and juice of 1 lemon

1 large shallot, finely chopped

4 garlic cloves, crushed

1 red chilli, halved, deseeded, and finely diced

300g (11oz) shelled cooked king prawns

6 large ripe tomatoes, halved, deseeded, and roughly chopped

1 large bunch of flat-leaf parsley, chopped

freshly grated Parmesan cheese, to serve

Serves 12

600g (1lb 5oz) spaghetti

salt and freshly ground black pepper

7 tbsp olive oil

100g (3½oz) very fine fresh brown breadcrumbs

finely grated zest and juice of 2 lemons

2 large shallots, finely chopped

8 garlic cloves, crushed

2 red chillies, halved, deseeded, and finely diced

600g (1lb 5oz) shelled cooked king prawns

12 large ripe tomatoes, halved, deseeded, and roughly chopped

1 very large bunch of flat-leaf parsley, chopped

freshly grated Parmesan cheese, to serve

1 Cook the spaghetti in boiling salted water according to the packet instructions. Drain well.

2 Heat 1 tablespoon of the oil (1½ tablespoons for 12) in a deep frying pan, add the breadcrumbs and lemon zest, and fry for 1 minute or until crispy. Remove with a slotted spoon and set aside.

3 Add the remaining oil to the pan, stir in the shallot, garlic, and chilli and fry for 3–4 minutes or until starting to soften.

4 Stir in the prawns and tomatoes, then add the parsley and lemon juice.

5 Stir in the spaghetti, season with salt and freshly ground black pepper, and heat through thoroughly. Stir in the breadcrumbs and serve immediately with the Parmesan.

PREPARE AHEAD

This is best prepared and served immediately.
Not suitable for freezing.

Spaghetti with king prawns and tomatoes (see overleaf) ●●●>

Penne are one of our favourite kinds of pasta because sauces cling really well to the quill shape. But you can use spaghetti if you prefer. Serve with dressed salad.

Penne with asparagus and dolcelatte

Serves 6

350g (12oz) asparagus spears

350g (12oz) penne

salt and freshly ground
    black pepper

1 tbsp olive oil

250g (9oz) small portabella
    mushrooms, sliced

1 garlic clove, crushed

150ml (5fl oz) double cream

100g (3½oz) dolcelatte cheese,
    cut into small cubes

small bunch of basil, chopped

Serves 12

600g (1lb 5oz) asparagus spears

600g (1lb 5oz) penne

salt and freshly ground
    black pepper

2 tbsp olive oil

500g (1lb 2oz) small portabella
    mushrooms, sliced

2 garlic cloves, crushed

300ml (10fl oz) double cream

225g (8oz) dolcelatte cheese,
    cut into small cubes

large bunch of basil, chopped

1 Cut off the tips of the asparagus about 5cm (2in) from the top and set aside. Cut the rest of the spears into small slices.

2 Cook the penne in boiling salted water according to the packet instructions. Add the sliced asparagus 5 minutes before the end of cooking. Add the asparagus tips 3 minutes before the end of cooking. Drain and refresh in cold water.

3 Heat the oil in a large frying pan, add the mushrooms and garlic, and fry for 2 minutes. Add the cream and cheese, season with salt and freshly ground black pepper, and stir well.

4 Add the pasta and asparagus to the pan, bring to the boil, and reheat until piping hot. Stir in half the basil and transfer to a serving bowl.

5 Garnish with the remaining basil and serve at once.

PREPARE AHEAD

The penne and asparagus can be cooked up to the end of step 2 up to 6 hours ahead and kept in a colander covered in cling film. Not suitable for freezing.

A delicious creamy pasta dish that's also quick to cook – it takes barely 15 minutes once you've prepared the ingredients. You can use bacon instead of pancetta if you prefer. Serve with salad.

Pasta with pancetta, broad beans, and mascarpone

Serves 6

300g (11oz) conchiglie shell pasta
salt and freshly ground
  black pepper
150g (5½oz) frozen small
  broad beans
200g (7oz) French beans,
  trimmed and sliced into three
140g packet pancetta cubes

250g tub full-fat
  mascarpone cheese
75g (2½oz) freshly grated
  Parmesan cheese
juice of 1 small lemon
small bunch of basil,
  roughly chopped

Serves 12

600g (1lb 5oz) conchiglie
  shell pasta
salt and freshly ground
  black pepper
300g (11oz) frozen small
  broad beans
400g (14oz) French beans,
  trimmed and sliced into three
2 x 140g packets pancetta cubes

2 x 250g tubs full-fat
  mascarpone cheese
175g (6oz) freshly grated
  Parmesan cheese
juice of 1 large lemon
large bunch of basil,
  roughly chopped

1 Cook the pasta in boiling salted water according to the packet instructions. Add the broad beans and French beans 5 minutes before the end of cooking.

2 Meanwhile, heat a large frying pan, add the pancetta, and fry until crisp. Stir in the mascarpone and two-thirds of the Parmesan and stir until melted.

3 Drain the pasta and beans, leaving a little of the cooking water in the saucepan. Add the pasta and beans to the frying pan along with 6 tablespoons of the cooking water (10 tablespoons for 12). Add the lemon juice and basil, toss together well, and season with salt and freshly ground black pepper.

4 Sprinkle with the remaining Parmesan and serve at once.

PREPARE AHEAD
The pasta and beans can be cooked, drained, and refreshed in cold water up to 6 hours ahead. Remember to reserve a little of the cooking water. Not suitable for freezing.

To make the cannelloni easier to serve, arrange them in neat rows in a rectangular dish. Serve with dressed salad and crusty bread.

Mushroom and spinach cannelloni

Serves 6

Special equipment *1.7 litre (3 pint) wide-based ovenproof dish*

1 tbsp olive oil

500g (1lb 2oz) mixed mushrooms, such as shiitake, chestnut, and button, roughly chopped

3 garlic cloves, crushed

225g (8oz) baby spinach, roughly chopped

salt and freshly ground black pepper

400g can tomatoes, drained and juice discarded

2 tbsp pesto

75g (2½oz) freshly grated Parmesan cheese

12 cannelloni tubes

For the sauce

75g (2½oz) butter

75g (2½oz) plain flour

900ml (1½ pints) hot milk

100ml (3½fl oz) double cream

2 heaped tbsp pesto

Serves 12

Special equipment *2 x 1.7 litre (3 pint) wide-based ovenproof dishes or 1 x 3 litre (5¼ pint) dish*

2 tbsp olive oil

1kg (2¼lb) mixed mushrooms, such as shiitake, chestnut, and button, roughly chopped

6 garlic cloves, crushed

500g (1lb 2oz) baby spinach, roughly chopped

salt and freshly ground black pepper

2 x 400g cans tomatoes, drained and juice discarded

4 tbsp pesto

175g (6oz) freshly grated Parmesan cheese

24 cannelloni tubes

For the sauce

175g (6oz) butter

175g (6oz) plain flour

1.7 litres (3 pints) hot milk

200ml (7fl oz) double cream

4 heaped tbsp pesto

1 Heat the oil in a frying pan, add the mushrooms, and fry over a high heat for 2 minutes or until just cooked. Add the garlic and spinach and toss together until the spinach is just wilted. Season with salt and freshly ground black pepper and set aside to cool.

2 To make the sauce, melt the butter in a saucepan, whisk in the flour, and cook for 1 minute. Whisking all the time, gradually blend in the hot milk and the cream and bring to the boil. Season with salt and freshly ground black pepper, remove from the heat, and stir in the pesto.

3 Put the tomatoes into a mixing bowl, add the cooled mushroom mixture, the pesto, and one-third of the Parmesan. Stir to combine.

4 Preheat the oven to 200°C (180°C fan/400°F/Gas 6). Meanwhile, fill the cannelloni tubes with the mushroom and spinach filling, dividing it equally among them.

5 Spoon one-third of the sauce into the base of the ovenproof dish and arrange the filled cannelloni on top in neat rows. Pour the remaining sauce over the top and sprinkle with the rest of the Parmesan.

6 Bake for 30–35 minutes (45 minutes for 12) or until golden brown and bubbling.

PREPARE AHEAD

The cannelloni can be made up to the end of step 5 up to 8 hours ahead. Not suitable for freezing.

IN THE AGA

Bake the cannelloni on the grid shelf on the floor of the roasting oven for 15 minutes (25 minutes for 12), transfer to the top set of runners, and cook for a further 20 minutes (30 minutes for 12).

Buffets
and bowls

Buffets probably need no introduction, but "bowls" might. Bowl food is 21st-century party fare, as substantial as lunch or supper, but served in a bowl and designed to be eaten standing up.

Buffets and bowls

When it comes to informal gatherings, the two of us have rather different ideas – it's probably a generation thing. Mary likes buffets because guests can help themselves and sit down at the table or perch somewhere to chat and eat. For Lucy, buffets are still way too formal. Space is also at a premium in her house, so her guests have to cram together and pitch in. The ideal way for her to entertain her family and friends is with one choice of main course presented in bowls, which people eat standing up.

Buffet or bowls?

For Mary, the advantages of buffets are simple.

● You can invite more people than for a sit-down meal. Some can stand and some can sit and everyone is free to mix and chat.

● Your guests can see what's on offer and choose their favourites, serving themselves as much or as little as they like.

● Less help is needed when serving.

While for Lucy the plus points of bowl food are:

● Just a bowl and fork are needed, so it's easy for guests to stand and eat.

● You don't need to worry about not having enough chairs, and there's no need to bother with laying the table, either.

● You can offer just one dish – unlike at a buffet.

● So long as the food is easy to eat from a bowl with a fork, you can serve almost anything – a curry, casserole and dumplings, lasagne, or a hearty stew.

● You have the option of serving food straight into the bowls or putting it out for people to help themselves.

So, that's us. But the choice of styles is entirely yours.

"The beauty of bowl parties is that you can cram all your friends into one room and don't have to worry about where they'll sit."

Bowl food

● Avoid anything you need to eat with a knife and fork.

● If you decide to offer a choice, make life easier for yourself by mixing cold dishes with hot. That way, you only have to worry about serving one dish hot, rather than several.

● Serve accompaniments such as sauces, raita, and chutneys on a side table. Put them in bowls with a teaspoon for guests to help themselves.

● Deep white bowls are ideal for serving bowl food, but you could also use cereal bowls or dessert bowls with a large rim. It doesn't matter if you mix and match.

● For an oriental theme, use oriental food boxes – they're made of cardboard and are foldable. You can buy them online and in specialist stores.

Buffets

A buffet usually consists of one or two main courses, with a selection of side dishes and a choice of puddings.

● Cold buffets are easier because almost everything can be prepared ahead. However, we always serve warm new potatoes or jacket potatoes, even at a cold buffet.

● Prepare all the dishes to serve the number of people you have coming. If you make them any smaller, there's the risk that some will run out. People will go back for second helpings, and any leftovers can be kept in the fridge for a few days or frozen.

● Make portions attractive and small. With guests tucking into more than one dish, you don't want to overwhelm them. We score suggested serving portions on the top of large dishes such as pies and lasagnes.

● Take care what dishes you serve together – most guests will want to sample everything, and poached salmon might not be the perfect partner for chicken tikka masala.

● If you're serving a whole ham, carve a few slices to get people going.

● If you're offering a first course at a formal meal, serve it at the tables where guests will sit.

For our guide to laying a buffet table, turn the page.

How to lay a buffet table

Put the table against a wall, with just enough room behind it for you to squeeze in and replace the dishes at the back or carve a ham. Depending on the layout of your room, display the food from right to left (as here) or left to right, and in the order guests will put it on their plates, so main dishes should come before sauces or side dishes. Keep any meat dishes together and any fish dishes together. Presenting food in a logical order like this makes it quicker and easier for your guests. Here, we've shown you how to lay a buffet table for a bowl party.

Side dish
Place side dishes of potatoes, pasta, or rice after the sauces.

Salad
Have the bowl of salad at the end.

Sauces
Place any sauces after the main dishes.

Bread basket
Cut the bread into even-sized pieces and place it next to the side dishes.

Butter
Put cubes of butter in a small dish near the bread.

Napkins
Place a pile of paper or fabric napkins at the end.

Cutlery
Arrange forks in a jug. If your guests need knives and forks, wrap them in napkins and place at the end of the table.

Seasonings
Serve salt and ready-ground black pepper in shallow dishes that guests can take a pinch from.

Finish <·········   <·········

"Indoors or out, a buffet is such an easy way to entertain a crowd. If you've invited more than 30 people and have enough room, lay two buffet tables, with the same food on each."

Serving platters
Position the main dish(es) up front and make sure there are serving implements next to each one.

Bowls or plates
These are the very first thing your guests will need. Place them in a pile at the start.

The traditional Italian salsa verde sauce gives an amazing flavour and a wonderful green layer. Pastry aside, this is a very healthy recipe.

Salmon salsa verde en croûte

Serves 6

For the salsa verde

3 tbsp flat-leaf parsley
2 tbsp fresh basil leaves
2 tbsp fresh mint leaves
1 garlic clove, halved
3 anchovy fillets
2 tbsp Dijon mustard
1 egg yolk
freshly ground black pepper

2 x 350g (12oz) salmon fillets, skinned and bones removed
375g packet all-butter puff pastry

a little plain flour, to dust
1 egg beaten with 1 tbsp milk

For the dressing

2 large firm but ripe tomatoes
salt
2 spring onions, finely chopped
2 tsp caster sugar
2 tbsp white wine vinegar
4 tbsp olive oil
½ tsp Dijon mustard
1 tbsp freshly chopped parsley

Serves 12

For the salsa verde

75g (2½oz) flat-leaf parsley
25g (scant 1oz) fresh basil leaves
25g (scant 1oz) fresh mint leaves
2 garlic cloves, halved
6 anchovy fillets
4 tbsp Dijon mustard
1 egg
freshly ground black pepper

2 x 750g (1lb 10oz) salmon fillets, skinned and bones removed
500g packet all-butter puff pastry

a little plain flour, to dust
1 egg beaten with 1 tbsp milk

For the dressing

4 large firm but ripe tomatoes
salt
3 spring onions, finely chopped
1 tbsp caster sugar
4 tbsp white wine vinegar
8 tbsp olive oil
1 tsp Dijon mustard
2 tbsp freshly chopped parsley

1 To make the salsa verde, put the herbs into a processor and whiz until smooth. Add the garlic, anchovies, mustard, egg yolk (egg for 12), and some freshly ground black pepper (but no salt) and whiz again until smooth.

2 Arrange one fillet on a chopping board and spread the salsa verde over the top in an even layer. Sit the other fillet on top so it looks like a whole fish.

3 Cut two-thirds of the pastry from the block (freeze the rest for later) and place on a piece of lightly floured baking parchment. Roll it out so it is long enough and wide enough to enclose the fillets completely. Sit the fillets in the centre and brush the pastry with the beaten egg (reserving some for later). Fold the ends of the pastry over the fillet and bring the sides up to meet at the top. Pinch the edges together with your fingers. Chill for a minimum of 30 minutes.

4 Preheat the oven to 220°C (200°C fan/425°F/Gas 7) and put a baking sheet in to get hot. Brush the en croûte with beaten egg, then coarsely grate the frozen pastry and scatter on top.

5 Transfer the en croûte (still on the baking parchment) to the hot baking sheet and bake for 25–30 minutes (35–40 minutes for 12) or until the pastry is golden and cooked at the top and bottom. Allow to rest at room temperature for about 15 minutes.

6 Meanwhile, make the dressing. Plunge the tomatoes into boiling salted water for 1 minute, then remove with a slotted spoon, plunge into cold water, and drain. Remove the skins, then deseed, cut into dice (see page 166), and tip into a bowl. Add the remaining ingredients, season with salt and freshly ground black pepper, and stir to combine.

7 Carve the en croûte into thick slices and serve the dressing alongside in a bowl.

PREPARE AHEAD AND FREEZE

The en croûte can be made up to 12 hours ahead. The dressing can be made up to 2 days ahead. Freeze the uncooked en croûte for up to 2 months.

IN THE AGA

Bake on a cold baking sheet on the floor of the roasting oven for 25–30 minutes (35–40 minutes for 12). Check after 20 minutes to see if the pastry underneath is getting too brown. If it is, lift the baking sheet on to the grid shelf on the floor of the roasting oven for the remaining time.

We find this the best way to poach salmon and over the years we have perfected the method so it's foolproof. We do it in a fish kettle, which you can usually borrow from the fishmonger or supermarket.

Classic poached salmon

Serves 12

2.7–3kg (6–6½lb) salmon (head on), gutted
small handful of salt
12 black peppercorns
cucumber, very thinly sliced, to garnish
24 cooked North Atlantic prawns, shelled but heads left on, to garnish
parsley or dill, to garnish

For the sauce

2 tbsp fresh dill
2 tbsp fresh chives
2 tbsp fresh mint
2 tbsp fresh flat-leaf parsley
200ml tub full-fat crème fraîche
200g tub full-fat Greek yogurt
300ml (10fl oz) good mayonnaise
1 tbsp caster sugar
juice of 1 lemon

Serves 20

5–5.5kg (11–12lb) salmon (head on), gutted
small handful of salt
12 peppercorns
cucumber, very thinly sliced, to garnish
40 cooked North Atlantic prawns, shelled but heads left on, to garnish
parsley or dill, to garnish

For the sauce

4 tbsp fresh dill
4 tbsp fresh chives
4 tbsp fresh mint
4 tbsp fresh flat-leaf parsley
400ml tub full-fat crème fraîche
400g tub full-fat Greek yogurt
600ml (1 pint) good mayonnaise
2 tbsp caster sugar
juice of 2 lemons

1 Put the salmon in the fish kettle and pour in enough cold water from the tap to cover it completely. Remove the fish.

2 Add the salt and peppercorns to the water, then bring to a full rolling boil. Carefully lower the salmon into the water, bring back to the boil, and boil for 2 minutes per kilo (1 minute per pound) and no more. Do not cover with a lid.

3 Remove from the heat and cover with a tight-fitting lid. Set in a cool place (not the fridge) and leave undisturbed for about 8 hours – the salmon will continue to cook as it cools.

4 Transfer the salmon to a chopping board or work surface and carefully peel off the skin while it is still lukewarm. Using two fish slices and taking care not to damage the flesh, turn the fish over and peel the skin from the other side, leaving a little over the end of the tail and the head. Cut off the fins with scissors and cut a neat "V" in the tail.

5 To make the sauce, put the herbs into a processor and whiz until chopped. Add the rest of the ingredients and season well with salt and freshly ground black pepper. Spoon into a serving dish (not silver as the sauce will discolour), cover, and chill until required.

6 To serve, arrange the salmon on a platter and overlap cucumber slices along the spine. Take pairs of the prawns and interlock the tails, then arrange them around the fish. Finish with the sprigs of parsley or dill. Serve cold with the lemon and herb sauce.

Great for a crowd... Buy extra salmon and poach separately. Don't be tempted to buy one really huge salmon – you may have trouble fitting it in the fish kettle.

BIG FISH

If you are cooking a very large salmon and it is too big for the fish kettle, cut off the head before poaching. The timing will be the same.

PREPARE AHEAD

The salmon can be poached up to 1 day ahead, then skinned and wrapped tightly in cling film to keep it moist. Garnish to serve. The herb sauce is better made 1 day ahead and can be made up to 3 days ahead. Not suitable for freezing.

Served with rice, this Hungarian classic is perfect bowl food. We like it made with pork shoulder, but you could also use pork fillet if you prefer. Reduce the cooking time by half for fillet.

Paprika pork goulash

Serves 6

2 tbsp olive oil

900g (2lb) boneless pork shoulder, cut into 4cm (1½in) pieces

2 medium onions, sliced

2 garlic cloves, crushed

2 tbsp paprika

3 tbsp tomato purée

300ml (10fl oz) chicken stock or beef stock

salt and freshly ground black pepper

2 red peppers, peeled, deseeded, and thinly sliced

1 tbsp balsamic vinegar

1 tsp brown sugar

2–3 tbsp soured cream or crème fraîche (depending on taste)

2 tbsp freshly chopped flat-leaf parsley

Serves 12

4 tbsp olive oil

1.8kg (4lb) boneless pork shoulder, cut into 4cm (1½in) pieces

3 large onions, sliced

4 garlic cloves, crushed

3 heaped tbsp paprika

5 heaped tbsp tomato purée

600ml (1 pint) chicken stock or beef stock

salt and freshly ground black pepper

4 red peppers, peeled, deseeded, and thinly sliced

2 tbsp balsamic vinegar

2 tsp brown sugar

6 tbsp soured cream or crème fraîche

4 tbsp freshly chopped flat-leaf parsley

1 Preheat the oven to 160°C (140°C fan/325°F/Gas 3). Meanwhile, heat the oil in a deep frying pan or casserole. Add the pork and brown quickly on all sides. You may need to do this in batches. Remove with a slotted spoon and set aside.

2 Add the onions to the pan and fry for 3 minutes or until starting to soften. Stir in the garlic and paprika and fry for 1 minute. Add the tomato purée and stock and return the meat to the pan. Bring to the boil, season with salt and freshly ground black pepper, cover with a lid, and transfer to the oven for 1¼–1½ hours (2 hours for 12) or until the pork is tender.

3 Add the peppers, vinegar, and sugar, bring to the boil, then check the seasoning. Stir in the soured cream or crème fraîche to taste and serve garnished with the parsley.

PREPARE AHEAD AND FREEZE
You can make the goulash up to 1 day ahead. The flavour will improve, in fact. Freeze without the cream for up to 2 months.

IN THE AGA
Cook in the simmering oven for 2 hours or until tender.

PREPARING RED PEPPERS

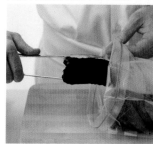

STEP 1 Blacken the skin of the pepper under the grill, then pop it into a polythene bag and seal.

STEP 2 When cold, peel off the charred skin with your fingers, then pull out the core and seeds.

Hot or cold, ham is irresistible and perfect for any buffet table. We like to serve it with Cumberland sauce (see facing page). It feeds twice the number when cold because it's easier to slice thinly.

Watercroft glazed ham

Serves 6–12

1.35kg (3lb) joint smoked or unsmoked gammon
½ onion, cut in half
1 small celery stick, cut into three
1 small bay leaf

50g (1¾oz) light or dark muscovado sugar
2 tbsp redcurrant jelly
2 tsp grainy mustard

Serves 12–20

3kg (6½lb) joint smoked or unsmoked gammon
1 onion, quartered
1 celery stick, cut into four
1 bay leaf

100g (3½oz) light or dark muscovado sugar
4 tbsp redcurrant jelly
1 tbsp grainy mustard

1 Weigh the joint and calculate the cooking time based on 20 minutes per 450g (1lb). A 1.35kg (3lb) joint will take 1 hour. A 3kg (6½lb) joint will take 2 hours 10 minutes.

2 Place it skin side down in a large deep saucepan. Add the vegetables, bay leaf, and sugar, then cover with cold water and a lid.

3 Bring to the boil (this takes longer than you may imagine) and, once boiling, start the timing. Simmer very gently until cooked. Check from time to time and top up with boiling water, if needed, to ensure the gammon is covered.

4 Once the ham is cooked through, carefully lift it out of the pan and, using a small sharp knife, remove the skin, leaving a very thin layer of fat on the joint. Preheat the oven to 200°C (180°C fan/400°F/Gas 6).

5 Meanwhile, put the redcurrant jelly and mustard into a bowl and stir until combined. Spread the mixture over the layer of fat, then score it in a lattice pattern with a knife.

6 Line a large roasting tin with foil and sit the ham in the centre with the glaze at the top. Bring the foil up so the flesh is completely covered and only the glaze is exposed – this prevents the ham drying out.

7 Bake for 15–20 minutes or until the glaze has melted and started to caramelize. If serving hot, rest for a good 10 minutes before carving. If serving cold, set aside until needed.

Great for a crowd... Cook one large gammon – it looks more impressive than two smaller ones. In an emergency, you could even buy a cooked ham. Cut off the crumb topping, add your own glaze, and brown as in the recipe.

BUYING GAMMON

When you're buying the gammon, ask the butcher if it needs soaking to remove any excess saltiness. If you get it from supermarkets, it is usually presoaked, but always check the label.

PREPARE AHEAD

The ham can be prepared up to 5 days ahead. To serve warm, it can be boiled up to 5 days ahead and then glazed on the day. Not suitable for freezing.

IN THE AGA

Bring to the boil on the boiling plate, then, with the lid still on, transfer to the simmering oven and start the timing. At step 7, bake at the top of the roasting oven for 10–15 minutes.

This is a wonderfully rich vibrantly coloured sauce. We suggest serving it with our baked ham (see facing page), but it is also very good with cold meats, turkey at Christmas, and game pie.

Cumberland sauce

Serves 6

1 orange
340g jar redcurrant jelly
75ml (2½fl oz) Port
1 tsp Dijon mustard
a dash of Worcestershire sauce
salt and freshly ground black pepper
juice of ½ lemon

Serves 12

2 oranges
2 x 340g jars redcurrant jelly
150ml (5fl oz) Port
2 tsp Dijon mustard
a dash of Worcestershire sauce
salt and freshly ground black pepper
juice of 1 lemon

1 Using a potato peeler, remove very thin strips of peel from the orange. Scrape off any white pith from the underside. Cut into needle-thin strips and transfer to a pan. Cover with water, bring to the boil, and simmer over a low heat for 3–4 minutes or until soft. Drain, refresh in cold water, then dry well with kitchen paper and set aside.

2 Put the redcurrant jelly and Port into a saucepan. Squeeze the orange and add the juice to the pan with the mustard and Worcestershire sauce. Whisk over a high heat until the jelly has melted, then boil rapidly for 4–5 minutes or until reduced by half.

3 Season with salt and freshly ground black pepper, add lemon juice to taste, then spoon into a serving dish and sprinkle with the orange strips. Serve warm or cold.

PREPARE AHEAD
The sauce can be made up to 1 week ahead.
To serve warm, reheat gently in a pan. Not suitable for freezing.

No buffet would be complete without coronation chicken. It's also delicious made with cooked turkey – ideal for a Boxing Day bowl party. Serve with baby new potatoes and dressed salad.

21st-century coronation chicken

Serves 6

2 tbsp apricot jam

1 tbsp curry powder

300ml (10fl oz) mayonnaise

150ml (5fl oz) half-fat crème fraîche

1 tbsp tomato purée

finely grated zest and juice of 1 lemon

450g (1lb) cooked chicken, cut into bite-sized pieces

2 spring onions, finely chopped

salt and freshly ground black pepper

175g (6oz) black and green seedless grapes, cut in half lengthways

rocket, to garnish

Serves 12

4 tbsp apricot jam

2 tbsp curry powder

600ml (1 pint) mayonnaise

300ml (10fl oz) half-fat crème fraîche

2 tbsp tomato purée

finely grated zest and juice of 2 lemons

900g (2lb) cooked chicken, cut into bite-sized pieces

4 spring onions, finely chopped

salt and freshly ground black pepper

300g (11oz) black and green seedless grapes, cut in half lengthways

rocket, to garnish

1 Put the jam and curry powder in a small saucepan and heat gently, stirring until the jam has melted. Set aside to cool a little.

2 Meanwhile, put the mayonnaise, crème fraîche, and tomato purée in a mixing bowl with the lemon zest and lemon juice and mix together until combined.

3 Stir in the jam mixture, then add the chicken and spring onions. Season with salt and freshly ground black pepper, add half the grapes, and stir until combined.

4 Spoon on to a serving platter and garnish with the remaining grapes and the rocket.

Great for a crowd... Make the sauce up to three days ahead so the flavours have time to infuse.

BACK IN THE DAY

The original recipe for Coronation chicken – created for the Queen's coronation in 1953 – was made with red wine and apricots and took ages to prepare. This is considerably simpler, but every bit as good.

PREPARE AHEAD

The dish can be made up to 1 day ahead.

The sauce can be made up to 3 days ahead.

Not suitable for freezing.

You can buy packets of mixed boneless game in supermarkets or at the butcher's. If you don't have quite enough, make up the weight with stewing beef. Served with creamy mashed potatoes.

Game casserole with thyme and mustard dumplings

Serves 6

900g (2lb) mixed game, sliced into large pieces
150ml (5fl oz) Port
2 tbsp sunflower oil
30g (1oz) butter
2 large leeks, sliced
4 celery sticks, sliced
1 apple, peeled, cored, and chopped into small cubes
1 tbsp brown sugar
45g (1½oz) plain flour
450ml (15fl oz) chicken stock or game stock
1 tbsp Worcestershire sauce
2 tsp Dijon mustard
1 tbsp balsamic vinegar
salt and freshly ground black pepper

For the dumplings

175g (6oz) self-raising flour
85g (3oz) suet
2 tbsp grainy mustard
1 tsp freshly chopped thyme leaves, plus extra to garnish (see opposite)

Serves 12

1.8kg (4lb) mixed game, sliced into large pieces
300ml (10fl oz) Port
4 tbsp sunflower oil
50g (1¾oz) butter
4 large leeks, sliced
8 celery sticks, sliced
2 apples, peeled, cored, and chopped into small cubes
2 tbsp brown sugar
85g (3oz) plain flour
900ml (1½ pints) chicken stock or game stock
2 tbsp Worcestershire sauce
1 heaped tbsp Dijon mustard
2 tbsp balsamic vinegar
salt and freshly ground black pepper

For the dumplings

350g (12oz) self-raising flour
175g (6oz) suet
4 tbsp grainy mustard
2 tsp freshly chopped thyme leaves, plus extra to garnish (see opposite)

1 Put the game and Port into a bowl and leave to marinate for a few hours or overnight.

2 Preheat the oven to 160°C (140°C fan/325°F/Gas 3). Meanwhile, heat the oil in a large frying pan or casserole. Drain the meat from the marinade (reserving the marinade) and brown quickly over a high heat. Remove with a slotted spoon and set aside. You may need to do this in batches.

3 Melt the butter in the frying pan, add the leeks, celery, and apple, and fry for 2 minutes. Add the brown sugar and fry for 2 minutes more or until the leeks are starting to soften.

4 Add the flour, then blend in the reserved marinade and stock. Return the meat to the pan and add the Worcestershire sauce, mustard, balsamic vinegar, and some salt and freshly ground black pepper.

5 Bring to the boil, cover with a lid, then transfer to the oven for 1–1½ hours (1½–2 hours for 12) or until the meat is tender.

6 Remove from the oven and increase the temperature to 200°C (180°C fan/400°F/Gas 6).

7 To make the dumplings, mix all the ingredients together in a large mixing bowl. Add about 150ml (5fl oz) cold water (300ml/10fl oz for 12) to make a sticky but manageable dough. Lightly knead the dough in the bowl, then shape into 12 small balls (24 for 12).

8 Put the dumplings on top of the casserole and bake without a lid near the top of the oven for 20 minutes or until the dumplings have risen and are golden brown on top. Garnish with chopped thyme.

STRIPPING THYME LEAVES

Hold each sprig in one hand, then run the forefinger and thumb of your other hand along the stalk.

PREPARE AHEAD AND FREEZE

The casserole can be made up to the end of step 5 up to 2 days ahead. The dumplings are best freshly made. Freeze without the dumplings for up to 2 months.

IN THE AGA

Cook the casserole in the simmering oven for 1½–2 hours or until tender. Add the dumplings and cook near the top of the roasting oven for 20 minutes or until risen and golden brown.

"This is the perfect casserole for a winter buffet or bowl party. Start it the day before so that the game has chance to absorb all the flavours of the Port."

Game casserole with thyme and mustard dumplings (see overleaf) ●●●>

The hotness of chilli con carne is a personal choice. Taste it at the end and, if you like yours hot, add more chilli powder, then bring to the boil to cook it through. The chutney adds a touch of sweetness.

Chilli con carne

Serves 6

1 tbsp olive oil

900g (2lb) raw minced beef

2 medium onions, coarsely chopped

2 garlic cloves, crushed

2 red chillies, halved, deseeded, and finely chopped

2 tbsp paprika

2 tsp cumin powder

½–1 tsp hot chilli powder (depending on taste)

200ml (7fl oz) red wine

2 x 400g cans chopped tomatoes

2 tbsp tomato purée

salt and freshly ground black pepper

2 x 400g cans kidney beans in water, drained and rinsed

1–2 tbsp mango chutney (depending on taste)

Serves 12

2 tbsp olive oil

1.8kg (4lb) raw minced beef

3 large onions, coarsely chopped

4 garlic cloves, crushed

4 red chillies, halved, deseeded, and finely chopped

4 tbsp paprika

1 heaped tbsp cumin powder

1–2 tsp hot chilli powder (depending on taste)

400ml (14fl oz) red wine

4 x 400g cans chopped tomatoes

4 tbsp tomato purée

salt and freshly ground black pepper

4 x 400g cans kidney beans in water, drained and rinsed

2–3 tbsp mango chutney (depending on taste)

1 Preheat the oven to 180°C (160°C fan/350°F/Gas 4). Meanwhile, heat the oil in a deep, non-stick frying pan or casserole, add the mince, and fry over a high heat for 5 minutes or until brown all over. You may need to do this in batches.

2 Add the onions, garlic, and chillies and fry with the mince for a few minutes.

3 Sprinkle in the paprika, cumin, and chilli powder and fry for a few minutes more. Blend in the wine, tomatoes, and tomato purée and stir as you bring to the boil. Season with salt and freshly ground black pepper, cover with a lid, and transfer to the oven for about an hour.

4 Add the kidney beans and chutney, return to the oven, and continue to cook for a further 30 minutes (1 hour for 12) or until the meat is completely tender. Serve straightaway.

Great for a crowd... This is perfect for making in one large batch if you have a saucepan big enough. Remember to stir often. If the mixture gets too thick, add a little stock. Freezes well.

SERVING SUGGESTIONS

Serve with long-grain rice, grated Cheddar or Red Leicester cheese, and a dollop of soured cream. Teenagers love it with tortilla chips or served in taco shells.

PREPARE AHEAD AND FREEZE

The chilli can be made up to 2 days ahead. Freeze for up to 2 months.

IN THE AGA

Cook in the simmering oven for 1½ hours. Add the beans and chutney after 1 hour.

This traditional stew has lots of flavour and is a favourite of Lucy's family, especially at holiday times when everyone is gathered together. Serve with creamy mashed potatoes and green vegetables.

Good old-fashioned beef stew

Serves 6

2 tbsp sunflower oil

900g (2lb) stewing beef, cut into bite-sized pieces

12 small shallots, peeled

2 medium carrots, diced

4 level tbsp plain flour

300ml (10fl oz) red wine

450ml (15fl oz) beef stock

1 tbsp redcurrant jelly

1 tbsp Worcestershire sauce

5 thyme sprigs

salt and freshly ground black pepper

250g (9oz) button mushrooms

Serves 12

2 tbsp sunflower oil

1.8kg (4lb) stewing beef, cut into bite-sized pieces

24 small shallots, peeled

4 medium carrots, diced

100g (3½oz) plain flour

600ml (1 pint) red wine

900ml (1½ pints) beef stock

2 tbsp redcurrant jelly

2 tbsp Worcestershire sauce

small bunch of thyme sprigs

salt and freshly ground black pepper

500g (1lb 2oz) button mushrooms

1 Preheat the oven to 160°C (140°C fan/325°F/Gas 3). Meanwhile, heat the oil in a large frying pan or casserole and quickly brown the beef all over. Remove with a slotted spoon and set aside. You may need to do this in batches.

2 Add the shallots and carrots to the pan and brown over a high heat. Add the flour and stir to coat the vegetables, then blend in the wine and stock. Add the redcurrant jelly, Worcestershire sauce, thyme, and some salt and freshly ground black pepper. Add the mushrooms and return the beef to the pan.

3 Bring to the boil, cover with a lid, and cook in the oven for 2–2½ hours (2½–3 hours for 12) or until the beef is tender. Serve piping hot.

PREPARE AHEAD AND FREEZE
The stew can be made up to 1 day ahead. Freeze for up to 2 months.

IN THE AGA
Cook in the simmering oven for 2–2½ hours or until tender.

A wonderful untemperamental casserole – warming and spicy. Serve with Cheese-topped dauphinois potatoes (page 125) and peas.

GREAT FOR A CROWD

Hot mustard spiced beef

Serves 6

1 tbsp sunflower oil

900g (2lb) chuck steak, cut into 2cm (¾in) cubes

2 large onions, chopped

100g (3½oz) button mushrooms, cut into quarters

1 tbsp Dijon mustard

2 tsp medium curry powder

1 tbsp muscovado sugar

2 tbsp Worcestershire sauce

25g (scant 1oz) plain flour

600ml (1 pint) beef stock or 2 beef stock cubes dissolved in 600ml (1 pint) water

salt and freshly ground black pepper

450g (1lb) Chantenay carrots

freshly chopped parsley, to garnish (optional)

Serves 12

2 tbsp sunflower oil

1.8kg (4lb) chuck steak, cut into 2cm (¾in) cubes

4 large onions, chopped

225g (8oz) button mushrooms, cut into quarters

2 tbsp Dijon mustard

4 tsp medium curry powder

2 tbsp muscovado sugar

4 tbsp Worcestershire sauce

50g (1¾oz) plain flour

1.2 litres (2 pints) beef stock or 4 beef stock cubes dissolved in 1.2 litres (2 pints) water

salt and freshly ground black pepper

900g (2lb) Chantenay carrots

freshly chopped parsley, to garnish (optional)

1 Preheat the oven to 160°C (140°C fan/325°F/Gas 3). Meanwhile, heat the oil in a large non-stick frying pan or casserole, add the cubes of meat, and fry quickly until golden brown all over. Remove with a slotted spoon and drain on kitchen paper. You may need to do this in batches.

2 Add the onions and mushrooms to the pan and fry over a high heat, stirring occasionally, for 3 minutes or until starting to soften.

3 Put the mustard, curry powder, sugar, Worcestershire sauce, and flour into a bowl and add 75ml (2½fl oz) of the stock (150ml/5fl oz for 12). Whisk by hand until smooth.

4 Add the remaining stock to the pan and bring to the boil. Spoon about half the hot stock into the mustard mixture and whisk by hand to give a smooth paste. Pour the mixture back into the pan, whisking over a high heat until thickened.

5 Season with salt and freshly ground black pepper, then return the meat to the pan. Bring to the boil, cover with a lid, and transfer to the oven for 2–2½ hours (2½–3 hours for 12) or until the meat is tender.

6 While the meat is cooking, cook the carrots in boiling salted water for a few minutes or until just tender. Drain and refresh in cold water.

7 To serve, bring the casserole to the boil on the hob. Add the carrots, check the seasoning, and boil for a few minutes or until the carrots are hot. Sprinkle with parsley, if using, and serve.

Great for a crowd... Make in batches and freeze ahead of time.

CHANTENAY CARROTS

This variety of carrot is usually small, so you can use them whole. If yours are a little on the large size, slice them in half lengthways.

PREPARE AHEAD AND FREEZE

The dish can be made up to the end of step 5 up to 2 days ahead. Freeze without the carrots for up to 2 months.

IN THE AGA

Cook in the simmering oven for 2–2½ hours.

There's nothing nicer on a buffet table than slices of pink beef fillet. Serve with new potatoes and the salad on page 224.

Cold fillet of beef with mustard sauce

Serves 6

1.25kg (2¾lb) middle-cut fillet of beef

salt and freshly ground black pepper

1 tbsp olive oil

a small knob of butter

For the mustard sauce

200ml tub full-fat crème fraîche

2 tbsp Dijon mustard

1 tsp white wine vinegar

1 tsp black mustard seeds

1 tsp caster sugar

Serves 12

1.8kg (4lb) whole middle-cut fillet of beef

salt and freshly ground black pepper

2 tbsp olive oil

a knob of butter

For the mustard sauce

500ml tub full-fat crème fraîche

4 tbsp Dijon mustard

2 tsp white wine vinegar

2 tsp black mustard seeds

2 tsp caster sugar

1 Preheat the oven to 220°C (200°C fan/425°F/Gas 7). Meanwhile, season the beef with salt and freshly ground black pepper, then rub the oil over the meat.

2 Heat a wide-based frying pan over a high heat until very hot and brown the beef quickly on all sides.

3 Transfer to a small roasting tin, spread with the butter, and roast for 18–20 minutes (25 minutes for 12) or until medium rare. Set aside until cold.

4 To make the sauce, put all the ingredients into a bowl, season with salt and freshly ground black pepper, and stir to combine.

5 Thinly carve the beef and serve cold with the sauce.

Great for a crowd... Brown the fillets individually and roast two at a time.

CARVING THE BEEF

If carved too early and arranged on a platter, the meat will turn grey fairly quickly as it is exposed to the air. To prevent this, carve the cold beef up to 6 hours ahead, then reassemble into its original shape and wrap tightly in cling film. Chill until needed and arrange on the plate just before serving.

PREPARE AHEAD

The fillet can be roasted up to 2 days ahead. The sauce can be made up to 3 days ahead. Not suitable for freezing.

IN THE AGA

Roast on the second set of runners in the roasting oven for 18 minutes (25 minutes for 12).

Whether it's on a buffet table or at a supper party, vegetarians will love this. Serve with dressed salad leaves.

Mushrooms and spinach en croûte

Serves 6

1 tbsp olive oil
½ large onion, chopped
1 garlic clove, crushed
150g (5½oz) chestnut
  mushrooms, sliced
225g (8oz) baby spinach
125g (4½oz) ricotta
75g (2½oz) Gruyère cheese,
  grated

1 egg yolk
dash of Tabasco
salt and freshly ground
  black pepper
a little plain flour, to dust
½ x 500g packet ready-rolled
  all-butter puff pastry (freeze the
  other half for another occasion)
1 egg beaten with 1 tbsp milk

Serves 12

1 tbsp olive oil
1 large onion, chopped
2 garlic cloves, crushed
250g (9oz) chestnut
  mushrooms, sliced
450g (1lb) baby spinach
200g (7oz) ricotta
175g (6oz) Gruyère cheese,
  grated

1 egg
dash of Tabasco
salt and freshly ground
  black pepper
a little plain flour, to dust
375g packet ready-rolled
  all-butter puff pastry
1 egg beaten with 1 tbsp milk

1 Preheat the oven to 220°C (200°C fan/425°F/Gas 7) and put a baking sheet in the oven to get hot. Meanwhile, heat the oil in a non-stick frying pan, add the onion, and fry for 2 minutes. Lower the heat, cover with a lid, and cook for 15 minutes or until soft.

2 Add the garlic, mushrooms, and spinach and cook over a high heat for 3 minutes or until the spinach has wilted and the mushrooms have softened. Set aside to cool.

3 Meanwhile, put the ricotta, Gruyère, egg yolk (whole egg for 12), and Tabasco into a bowl, season with salt and freshly ground black pepper, and mix until combined. Stir into the cold spinach mixture.

4 Lay the sheet of pastry on a lightly floured work surface and roll it out into a 28 x 33cm (11 x 13in) rectangle (33 x 38cm/13 x 15in rectangle for 12).

5 Pile the spinach mixture into the middle, leaving a 4cm (1½in) gap around the edge. Brush the pastry with the egg mixture, then fold the ends over the filling and bring the sides up so they meet at the top. Crimp the ends together to seal, then brush the pastry with egg.

6 Transfer to the hot baking sheet and bake for 30 minutes (45 minutes for 12) or until golden all over. Leave to rest at room temperature for 5 minutes, then slice and serve hot.

Great for a crowd... Make more en croûtes and bake two to a baking sheet. Never make an en croûte larger than for 12, as the pastry may split.

PUFF PASTRY

Be sure to buy all-butter puff pastry, as it has a much better flavour than other kinds and is a little softer to handle.

PREPARE AHEAD

The en croûte can be made up to the end of step 5 up to 8 hours ahead. Not suitable for freezing.

IN THE AGA

Sit the en croûte on a cold baking sheet and bake on the floor of the roasting oven for 25–30 minutes.

This is great for vegetarians and meat-eaters alike – the mass of tasty mushrooms is delicious and the cornichons (baby gherkins) give a lovely texture and sweetness. Serve with rice.

Mushroom stroganoff

Serves 6

25g (scant 1oz) butter
1 large onion, thinly sliced
2 garlic cloves, crushed
1 tbsp paprika
1 tbsp plain flour
100ml (3½fl oz) Marsala
200g tub full-fat crème fraîche
650g (1lb 7oz) mixed
 mushrooms, such as oyster,
 chestnut, and portabella, sliced

salt and freshly ground
 black pepper
juice of ½ lemon
1 tsp tomato purée
1 tsp caster sugar
50g (1¾oz) cornichons,
 chopped

Serves 12

50g (1¾oz) butter
2 large onions, thinly sliced
4 garlic cloves, crushed
2 tbsp paprika
2 tbsp plain flour
200ml (7fl oz) Marsala
2 x 200g tubs full-fat
 crème fraîche
1.1kg (2½lb) mixed
 mushrooms, such as oyster,
 chestnut, and portabella, sliced

salt and freshly ground
 black pepper
juice of 1 lemon
2 tsp tomato purée
2 tsp caster sugar
100g (3½oz) cornichons,
 chopped

1 Melt the butter in a deep frying pan, add the onion, and fry for 1 minute. Lower the heat, cover with a lid, and simmer for 15 minutes or until soft.

2 Stir in the garlic, then sprinkle in the paprika and flour and mix well. Add the Marsala and crème fraîche and stir until thickened slightly.

3 Add the mushrooms, season with salt and freshly ground black pepper, and simmer over a low heat for 4 minutes (5–10 minutes for 12) or until the mushrooms are just cooked.

4 Stir in the lemon juice, tomato purée, and sugar and check the seasoning. Scatter over the cornichons and serve hot.

VARIATION
If you don't have any Marsala, you can use another fortified wine such as medium sherry or Port.

PREPARE AHEAD
This is best made and served immediately. Not suitable for freezing.

IN THE AGA
Soften the onion in the simmering oven for 15 minutes, then continue on the boiling plate.

We always try to keep the number of ingredients to a minimum, but by nature a curry has many – it's the blend of spices that give it flavour. Sorry! Serve with naan breads and Pilaf rice (pages 206–207).

GREAT FOR A CROWD

Vegetable korma

Serves 6

100g (3½oz) French beans, sliced into three

salt and freshly ground black pepper

2 tbsp olive oil

1 large onion, roughly chopped

2cm (¾in) piece fresh root ginger, peeled and grated

1 tsp cardamom seeds, crushed

1½ tbsp ground cumin

1½ tbsp ground coriander

1½ tbsp garam masala

450g (1lb) potatoes, chopped into 1½cm (⅝in) cubes

350g (12oz) carrots, chopped into 1½cm (⅝in) cubes

350g (12oz) cauliflower, cut into even-sized florets

400g can coconut milk

450ml (15fl oz) vegetable stock

100g (3½oz) ground almonds

juice of 1 lemon

2 tbsp mango chutney

Serves 12

175g (6oz) French beans, sliced into three

salt and freshly ground black pepper

3 tbsp olive oil

2 large onions, roughly chopped

5cm (2in) piece fresh root ginger, peeled and grated

2 tsp cardamom seeds, crushed

3 tbsp ground cumin

3 tbsp ground coriander

3 tbsp garam masala

900g (2lb) potatoes, chopped into 1½cm (⅝in) cubes

700g (1lb 9oz) carrots, chopped into 1½cm (⅝in) cubes

700g (1lb 9oz) cauliflower, cut into even-sized florets

2 x 400g cans coconut milk

900ml (1½ pints) vegetable stock

225g (8oz) ground almonds

juice of 2 lemons

4 tbsp mango chutney

1 Cook the beans in boiling salted water for 4 minutes or until just cooked. Drain, refresh in cold water, and set aside.

2 Heat the oil in a deep frying pan or casserole, add the onion, and fry over a high heat for 2 minutes.

3 Add the ginger and spices, stir to coat the onions, and fry for 1 minute. Add all the vegetables except the beans, then stir in the coconut milk and stock. Season well with salt and freshly ground black pepper and bring to the boil.

4 Cover with a lid and simmer over a low heat for 30–40 minutes (45 minutes for 12) or until the vegetables are tender.

5 Stir in the ground almonds (they will thicken the sauce), then add the reserved beans, the lemon juice, and chutney. Check the seasoning and serve.

Great for a crowd... This is perfect for making in one large batch if you have a saucepan big enough. Measure the spices accurately so you get the balance of flavours right. And remember to stir often.

PREPARE AHEAD

The korma can be made up to the end of step 4 up to 12 hours ahead. Not suitable for freezing.

IN THE AGA

At step 3, bring to the boil on the boiling plate, cover with a lid, and transfer to the simmering oven for 35 minutes.

Tiger prawns are expensive, but this is a great dish for a special occasion. Serve with Pilaf rice (page 207) or, as part of a buffet, with Vegetable korma (page 199) and Aromatic beef curry (page 203).

GREAT FOR A CROWD

Tiger prawn balti

Serves 6

3 tbsp sunflower oil

2 large onions, finely chopped

2 red peppers, halved, deseeded, and roughly chopped

6cm (2½in) piece fresh root ginger, peeled and finely grated

3 red chillies, halved, deseeded, and roughly chopped

1 tsp turmeric

2 tsp ground coriander

2 tsp garam masala

1 tsp black mustard seeds

2 x 400g cans chopped tomatoes

300ml (10fl oz) water

4 tbsp tomato purée

4 tsp lime pickle

juice of 1 lime

2 tbsp honey

salt and freshly ground black pepper

1kg (2¼lb) raw shelled tiger prawns

1 heaped tbsp freshly chopped coriander, to garnish

Serve 12

5 tbsp sunflower oil

4 large onions, finely chopped

4 red peppers, halved, deseeded, and roughly chopped

18cm (7in) piece fresh root ginger, peeled and finely grated

6 red chillies, halved, deseeded, and roughly chopped

2 tsp turmeric

4 tsp ground coriander

4 tsp garam masala

2 tsp black mustard seeds

4 x 400g cans chopped tomatoes

600ml (1 pint) water

8 tbsp tomato purée

2 heaped tbsp lime pickle

juice of 2 limes

4 tbsp honey

salt and freshly ground black pepper

2kg (4½lb) raw shelled tiger prawns

2 heaped tbsp freshly chopped coriander, to garnish

1 Heat the oil in a large frying pan or saucepan, add the onions, peppers, ginger, and chillies and fry over a high heat for 2 minutes or until starting to soften.

2 Cover with a lid, then reduce the heat and cook for 10 minutes or until the onions and peppers are nearly soft. Add the spices and stir over a high heat to coat the vegetables.

3 Add the tomatoes, water, tomato purée, lime pickle, lime juice, and honey. Bring to the boil and simmer for 10 minutes (15 minutes for 12). Season with salt and freshly ground black pepper, add the prawns, and cook for 5 minutes (5–10 minutes for 12) or until they turn pink and are cooked through. Garnish with the coriander and serve straightaway.

Great for a crowd... This is perfect for making in one large batch if you have a saucepan big enough. Measure the spices accurately so you get the balance of flavours right. And remember to stir often. Freezes well.

VARIATION

To cut costs, you could use a mixture of tiger prawns and other cooked seafood, such as mussels and squid.

PREPARE AHEAD AND FREEZE

The sauce can be made up to 1 day ahead. Reheat to serve, adding the prawns at the end. Freeze the sauce without the prawns for up to 1 month.

IN THE AGA

At step 2, cover with a lid and transfer to the simmering oven to soften for 30 minutes, then continue on the boiling plate.

Bright and full of flavour, this is one of the country's favourite curries. Serve with naan breads and Pilaf rice (pages 206–207).

Chicken tikka masala

Serves 6

12 skinless boneless chicken thighs, each cut into 6 pieces
1 tbsp medium curry powder
1 tsp paprika
1 tbsp olive oil
3 onions, roughly chopped
2 garlic cloves, crushed
6cm (2½in) piece fresh root ginger, peeled and finely grated
2 tbsp garam masala
½ tsp turmeric

200ml (7fl oz) water
500ml carton passata
2 tbsp tomato purée
1 tbsp sugar
salt and freshly ground black pepper
juice of ½ lime
200ml (7fl oz) double cream
1 heaped tbsp freshly chopped coriander, to garnish

Serves 12

24 skinless boneless chicken thighs, each cut into 6 pieces
2 tbsp medium curry powder
2 tsp paprika
2 tbsp olive oil
5 onions, roughly chopped
4 garlic cloves, crushed
7.5cm (3in) piece fresh root ginger, peeled and finely grated
4 tbsp garam masala
1 tsp turmeric

400ml (14fl oz) water
2 x 500ml cartons passata
4 tbsp tomato purée
2 tbsp sugar
salt and freshly ground black pepper
juice of 1 lime
300ml (10fl oz) double cream
2 tbsp freshly chopped coriander, to garnish

1 Put the chicken pieces into a bowl, sprinkle over the curry powder and paprika, cover, and chill for 15 minutes.

2 Heat the oil in a deep frying pan or casserole, add the chicken, and quickly brown all over. Remove with a slotted spoon and set aside. You may need to do this in batches.

3 Add the onions, garlic, and ginger and fry for 2 minutes or until starting to soften. Add the garam masala and turmeric and fry for 1 minute. Blend in the water, passata, tomato purée, and sugar, return the chicken to the pan, and season with salt and freshly ground black pepper.

4 Bring to the boil, cover with a lid, and simmer, stirring occasionally, for 30–40 minutes (1 hour for 12) or until the chicken is tender.

5 Add the lime juice, check the seasoning, bring to the boil again, then add the cream. Serve garnished with the coriander.

Great for a crowd... This is perfect for making in one large batch if you have a saucepan big enough. Measure the spices accurately so you get the balance of flavours right. And remember to stir often. Freezes well.

PREPARE AHEAD AND FREEZE
The curry can be made up to the end of step 4 up to 2 days ahead. Freeze without the lime juice and cream for up to 2 months.

IN THE AGA
At step 4, bring to the boil on the boiling plate, cover with a lid, and transfer to the simmering oven for 40–45 minutes or until the chicken is tender.

A warming curry with lots of spice. Serve with poppadoms, naan breads, and Pilaf rice (pages 206–207).

Aromatic beef curry with ginger and tomatoes

Serves 6

1 heaped tsp each ground cumin, ground coriander, and garam masala

½ tsp turmeric

10 cardamom pods, crushed, pods discarded, and seeds finely crushed

2 tbsp olive oil

900g (2lb) stewing beef, chopped into 2.5cm (1in) pieces

1 large onion, roughly chopped

1 red chilli, halved, deseeded, and chopped

4 garlic cloves, crushed

2cm (¾in) piece fresh root ginger, peeled and grated

400g can chopped tomatoes

300ml (10fl oz) beef stock

1 cinnamon stick

4 tbsp tomato purée

3 tbsp mango chutney

salt and freshly ground pepper

200g (7oz) okra or green beans, sliced into 2cm (¾in) pieces

Serves 12

2 heaped tsp each ground cumin, ground coriander, and garam masala

1 tsp turmeric

20 cardamom pods, crushed, pods discarded, and seeds finely crushed

4 tbsp olive oil

1.8kg (4lb) stewing beef, chopped into 2.5cm (1in) pieces

2 large onions, roughly chopped

2 red chillies, halved, deseeded, and chopped

8 garlic cloves, crushed

5cm (2in) piece fresh root ginger, peeled and grated

2 x 400g cans chopped tomatoes

600ml (1 pint) beef stock

2 cinnamon sticks

8 tbsp tomato purée

6 tbsp mango chutney

salt and freshly ground pepper

450g (1lb) okra or green beans, sliced into 2cm (¾in) pieces

1 Preheat the oven to 160°C (140°C fan/325°F/Gas 3). Heat a large frying pan or casserole over a high heat, add all the spices, and fry for 1 minute or until just toasted, then spoon into a small bowl.

2 Add the oil to the pan and quickly brown the beef until golden all over. Remove with a slotted spoon and set aside. You may need to do this in batches. Add the onion to the pan with the toasted spices, the chilli, garlic, and ginger and fry for 3–4 minutes.

3 Add the chopped tomatoes, stock, cinnamon, tomato purée, and chutney. Return the beef to the pan, season with salt and freshly ground pepper, cover with a lid, and transfer to the oven for 2–2¼ hours (2½ hours for 12) or until the beef is tender.

4 Cook the okra or green beans in boiling salted water for 3 minutes, drain, and stir into the pan. Fish out the cinnamon and discard and serve straightaway.

Great for a crowd... Make in batches. Don't try to brown too much beef in one go or it will go grey instead of golden brown. Freezes well.

TOASTING SPICES

Heat a frying pan until hot, add the spices, and fry, stirring constantly, until lightly coloured and toasted.

PREPARE AHEAD AND FREEZE

The curry can be made up to 2 days ahead. Freeze without the okra or green beans for up to 2 months.

IN THE AGA

Cook in the simmering oven for 2–2¼ hours or until tender.

Aromatic beef curry with ginger and tomatoes (see overleaf) ●●●

True naan breads are rather a palaver to make, so these are a bit of a cheat. But a really delicious one! Serve them with any of the curries on pages 199–203.

Garlic and coriander naan breads

Serves 6

3 large or 6 small plain
    naan breads
25g (scant 1oz) butter,
    at room temperature

2 garlic cloves, crushed
3 tbsp freshly chopped coriander
salt and freshly ground
    black pepper

Serves 12

6 large or 12 small plain
    naan breads
50g (1¾oz) butter,
    at room temperature

4 garlic cloves, crushed
6 tbsp freshly chopped coriander
salt and freshly ground
    black pepper

1 Preheat the oven to 200°C (180°C fan/400°F/Gas 6). Arrange the naan breads on a baking sheet without overlapping them.

2 Put the butter, garlic, and coriander into a bowl and mix until combined. Season with salt and freshly ground black pepper and mix again.

3 Spread evenly over the naan breads so the whole of each bread is covered.

4 Bake for 5–8 minutes (8 minutes for 12) or until the butter has melted and the bread is crisp.

PREPARE AHEAD AND FREEZE
The naan breads can be prepared up to the end of step 3 up to 12 hours ahead. Freeze for up to 3 months.

IN THE AGA
Bake on the top set of runners in the roasting oven for 6 minutes.

Pilaf (sometimes called pilaff or pilau) rice is a dish that originates from the near East. It's the perfect accompaniment to any of the curries on pages 199–203.

Pilaf rice

Serves 6

225g (8oz) basmati rice
salt and freshly ground
  black pepper
50g (1¾oz) butter
1 onion, roughly chopped
4 garlic cloves, crushed
1 red chilli, halved, deseeded,
  and finely chopped

225g (8oz) chestnut
  mushrooms, sliced
1 tsp paprika
juice of 1 lemon
50g (1¾oz) sultanas
25g (scant 1oz) flaked almonds
100g (3½oz) cooked petits pois

Serves 12

450g (1lb) basmati rice
salt and freshly ground
  black pepper
75g (2½oz) butter
2 onions, roughly chopped
6 garlic cloves, crushed
2 red chillies, halved, deseeded,
  and finely chopped

350g (12oz) chestnut
  mushrooms, sliced
2 tsp paprika
juice of 2 small lemons
100g (3½oz) sultanas
50g (1¾oz) flaked almonds
225g (8oz) cooked petits pois

1 Cook the rice in boiling salted water according to the packet instructions. Drain, refresh in cold water, and set aside.

2 Meanwhile, melt the butter in a large saucepan, add the onion, garlic, and chilli and fry for 2 minutes. Lower the heat, cover with a lid, and simmer for 20 minutes or until the onion is soft.

3 Add the mushrooms, turn up the heat, and fry for 3 minutes or until soft. Sprinkle in the paprika, lemon juice, sultanas, almonds, and petits pois and fry for a few minutes, stirring. Add the rice and stir until it is piping hot. Season with salt and freshly ground black pepper and serve.

PREPARE AHEAD
The pilaf can be cooked up to 12 hours ahead. To reheat, transfer to a buttered, wide-based ovenproof dish, cover with buttered foil, and place in an oven preheated to 200°C (180°C fan/ 400°F/Gas 6) for 15 minutes (25 minutes for 12) or until piping hot. Not suitable for freezing.

IN THE AGA
At step 2, cover with a lid and transfer to the simmering oven for 20 minutes. Return to the boiling plate at step 3.

Summer
in the garden

The warm-weather recipes in this chapter have all been chosen with sunny days and balmy evenings in mind. And if you're a city dweller, many of them are just as good at a picnic in the park.

Summer in the garden

Food needs to be gutsy to taste good outdoors. Kebabs and terrines, burgers and frittatas all fit the bill. When you're eating outside, it's often nice to dispense with cutlery, so the food should be easy to eat. No one's going to bother with a knife and fork in any case when they're tucking into finger food like chicken drumsticks.

Many of us prefer cold food or warm food when the weather hots up, so we've also included a selection of salads substantial enough to be served as a main course, along with a goat's cheese and onion marmalade galette that's as delicious warm as it is hot.

Food for every occasion

During the summer months we entertain in lots of different ways.

● Perhaps the most laid-back is laying food out buffet-style, either outside in the garden or in the kitchen if it backs on to the garden. See overleaf for our guide to laying a buffet table outside.

● Barbecues are always great fun, and you can't help but whet people's appetites with burgers and sausages sizzling on the grill. The cooking often becomes part of the entertainment, too, and can be shared – men, in particular, often like to show off their barbecuing skills.

● Placed in a shady spot, our garden tables and chairs are often the scene for a meal that lasts well into the afternoon or evening. If it's not quite warm enough to eat outside, we'll have lunch in the conservatory – but with the doors open, so we're reminded that summer's on its way.

● And a picnic in the country or in a town park never ceases to hold its appeal.

"You can't help but whet people's appetites with burgers and sausages sizzling on the grill. The cooking often becomes part of the entertainment at a barbecue, too."

Picnics

If you're venturing further afield than your own garden, there's no need to resort to sandwiches. Take the right food along and a picnic becomes an open-air feast.

● Keep the food simple and don't give too much choice – if it's been sitting outside in the sunshine for hours, it can't be used afterwards.

● Pick dishes that are easy to eat with your hands or just a plate and fork.

● Choose dishes you can transport in cool bags. If you've run out of ice blocks, freeze water in plastic bottles – they'll do the job just as well.

● If you're taking a dish such as a frittata, quiche, or galette, cut it into wedges or slices, then reassemble the pieces to transport it. Wrap it in foil then a tea towel to keep it warm. If the weather looks as if it might turn wet, however, wrap food in individual foil parcels.

● Keep food covered until you serve it or it will discolour, dry out, and attract flies.

● Dress salads when you get there. If you do it beforehand, the leaves will go soggy and limp. Coleslaw is a good choice because it can be taken along ready to serve.

● Take napkins and bin bags for rubbish.

Barbecuing

● Depending on the type of fuel you're using, light the barbecue at least an hour before you want to start cooking. If you're using a gas barbecue, follow the instructions carefully.

● Before you start, put a table next to the barbecue and gather together everything you'll need so you don't have to keep running into the house for utensils or whatever.

● If you're cooking lots of food, give chicken and sausages a headstart by part-cooking them in the oven until nearly done but not brown.

● Don't overbrown the outside of food before the middle is cooked.

● Have a clean plate or platter to put cooked meat on. And don't confuse it with the plate the raw meat was on or there could be a risk of food poisoning.

How to lay the table for a buffet in the garden

Arrange the food from right to left (as here) or left to right, whichever works best. To make it easier for guests to help themselves, place food in the order they'll put it on their plates, so main dishes first. If more than 30 people are coming and your garden is large, lay two tables with the same food on each.

Cutting board
Place whole pieces of meat on a cutting board with a carving knife and fork. Carve a few slices and lay them on the board, then leave guests to cut themselves more.

Bread basket
Cut the bread into evenly sized pieces and place it next to the butter.

Napkins and cutlery
To make them easier for people to carry, wrap the knives and forks in napkins.

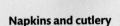

Salad bowls
Put bowls of salad at the end and supply serving implements for each one.

Salt and pepper
Place the salt and pepper after the food, so guests can season it as they wish.

Side dishes
Place the side dishes with serving spoons after the main dishes.

Finish ‹••••••••

‹••••••••

"With so much food on display, keep bugs at bay with a citronella candle. And never leave food unattended if your dog or cat is on the loose."

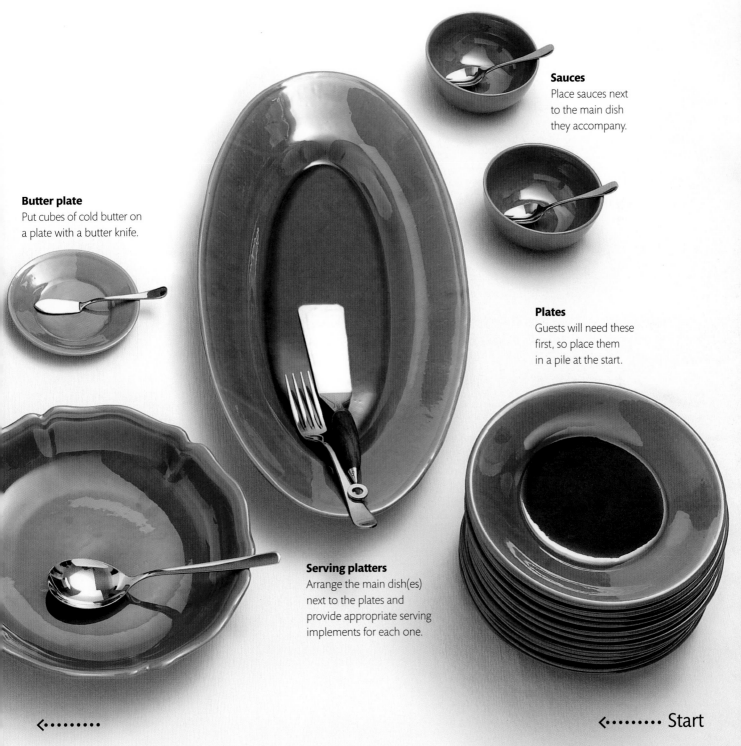

Sauces
Place sauces next to the main dish they accompany.

Butter plate
Put cubes of cold butter on a plate with a butter knife.

Plates
Guests will need these first, so place them in a pile at the start.

Serving platters
Arrange the main dish(es) next to the plates and provide appropriate serving implements for each one.

Small burgers are the perfect finger food and, with only half a bun, these are even easier to eat (and less stodgy). They are great for children's parties. Serve with a large bowl of chips and mayonnaise.

Manhattan mini burgers

Serves 6

Special equipment 6cm (2½in) *round cutter*

50g (1¾oz) fresh white breadcrumbs
500g (1lb 2oz) raw lean minced beef
½ onion, finely diced
4 small gherkins, finely chopped
2 tsp Dijon mustard
2 tbsp Worcestershire sauce
1 egg yolk

salt and freshly ground black pepper
sunflower oil, to fry

To serve

6 mini sesame burger buns
tomato ketchup
American-style mustard
6 small gherkins, sliced in half lengthways

Serves 12

Special equipment 6cm (2½in) *round cutter*

100g (3½oz) fresh white breadcrumbs
1kg (2¼lb) raw lean minced beef
1 onion, finely diced
8 small gherkins, finely chopped
1 heaped tbsp Dijon mustard
4 tbsp Worcestershire sauce
1 large egg

salt and freshly ground black pepper
sunflower oil, to fry

To serve

12 mini sesame burger buns
tomato ketchup
American-style mustard
12 small gherkins, sliced in half lengthways

1 Put the first seven ingredients into a large bowl and mix well with your hands. Season well with salt and freshly ground black pepper and shape into 12 round burgers (24 burgers for 12). Chill in the fridge for 30 minutes.

2 Heat a little sunflower oil in a frying pan, add the burgers, and fry for 3 minutes on each side or until golden brown on the outside and cooked through in the middle. You may need to do this in batches. Alternatively, cook them on a barbecue.

3 Slice the buns in half horizontally, then stamp out 12 rounds (24 rounds for 12) using a 6cm (2½in) round cutter. Use both the base and top of the buns.

4 Spread the cut side of the buns with ketchup, place a burger on top, then squirt with a little mustard and top with a slice of gherkin. Arrange on a large platter and serve.

PREPARE AHEAD AND FREEZE
The burgers can be made up to the end of step 1 up to 1 day ahead. Freeze the raw burgers for up to 2 months.

Drumsticks are always a favourite at a barbecue – with adults and children alike. Marinating aside, they are also quick to make. Serve hot or cold with salad and jacket potatoes.

Sticky chicken drumsticks

Serves 6

6 tbsp tomato ketchup
2 tbsp Worcestershire sauce
2 tbsp grainy mustard
2 tbsp runny honey

salt and freshly ground
  black pepper
6 chicken drumsticks (skin on)

Serves 12

175ml (6fl oz) tomato ketchup
4 tbsp Worcestershire sauce
4 tbsp grainy mustard
4 tbsp runny honey

salt and freshly ground
  black pepper
12 chicken drumsticks (skin on)

1 Put the first four ingredients into a bowl, mix together well, then season with salt and freshly ground black pepper.

2 Add the chicken and marinate for a minimum of 2 hours or overnight.

3 Preheat the oven to 220°C (200°C fan/425°F/Gas 7). Season the drumsticks with salt and freshly ground black pepper and cook for 30–40 minutes (45 minutes for 12) or until golden brown and sticky. Turn halfway through. Alternatively, cook on the barbecue.

PREPARE AHEAD AND FREEZE
The drumsticks can be marinated overnight. Freeze in the marinade for up to 2 months.

IN THE AGA
Cook on the second set of runners in the roasting oven for 20 minutes (30 minutes for 12), turning them over halfway through.

These lemony chicken burgers are so easy to make and are perfect for a barbecue. Make them larger if you prefer, but cook them for longer.

Mini chicken burgers

Serves 6

Special equipment 6cm (2½in) round cutter

2 slices white bread
500g (1lb 2oz) skinless boneless chicken breasts or thighs, roughly chopped
zest and juice of 1 small lemon
50g (1¾oz) freshly grated Parmesan cheese
small bunch of chives, snipped
1 egg yolk

salt and freshly ground black pepper
a little olive oil, to fry

To serve
6 sesame burger buns
grainy mustard
lettuce leaves
mayonnaise
2 tomatoes, sliced

Serves 12

Special equipment 6cm (2½in) round cutter

4 slices white bread
1kg (2¼lb) skinless boneless chicken breasts or thighs, roughly chopped
zest and juice of 2 small lemons
100g (3½oz) freshly grated Parmesan cheese
large bunch of chives, snipped
1 large egg

salt and freshly ground black pepper
a little olive oil, to fry

To serve
12 sesame burger buns
grainy mustard
lettuce leaves
mayonnaise
4 tomatoes, sliced

1 Put the bread into a food processor and whiz to fine breadcrumbs. Transfer to a large mixing bowl. Put the chicken into the processor and whiz till coarsely minced. You may need to do this in batches. Add to the bowl with the breadcrumbs.

2 Add the lemon zest, lemon juice, cheese, chives, and egg yolk (whole egg for 12) and mix together with your hands. Season with salt and freshly ground black pepper, then shape the mixture into 12 small burgers (24 for 12) and chill in the fridge for 30 minutes.

3 Heat a little oil in a frying pan and fry the burgers for 3–3½ minutes on each side or until lightly golden and cooked through. You may need to do this in batches. Alternatively, cook on a barbecue.

4 Slice the buns in half horizontally. Stamp out 12 rounds (24 for 12), using a 6cm (2½in) round cutter. Use the top and bottom of the buns. Spread each with a little mustard, then add a lettuce leaf. Place a burger on top, add a blob of mayonnaise, and garnish with a slice of tomato. Arrange the burgers on a platter and serve.

PREPARE AHEAD AND FREEZE
The burgers can be prepared up to the end of step 2 up to 1 day ahead. Freeze for up to 3 months.

In this chunky-textured terrine with a herby crust the chicken is kept in pieces. It is perfect for a picnic, lunch, or buffet.

French country terrine

Serves 6

Special equipment *450g (1lb) loaf tin*

1 tbsp olive oil
1 small onion, very finely chopped
1 garlic clove, crushed
175g (6oz) good pork sausagemeat
50g (1¾oz) lamb's liver
1½ tbsp brandy

225g (8oz) boneless skinless chicken breast, cut into thin even strips
1 heaped tbsp freshly chopped mixed herbs, such as parsley, thyme, and chives
salt and freshly ground black pepper
freshly chopped parsley and chives, to garnish

Serves 12

Special equipment *900g (2lb) loaf tin*

1 tbsp olive oil
1 medium onion, very finely chopped
2 garlic cloves, crushed
350g (12oz) good pork sausagemeat
100g (3½oz) lamb's liver
3 tbsp brandy

450g (1lb) boneless skinless chicken breast, cut into thin even strips
2 heaped tbsp freshly chopped mixed herbs, such as parsley, thyme, and chives
salt and freshly ground black pepper
freshly chopped parsley and chives, to garnish

1 Preheat the oven to 180°C (160°C fan/350°F/Gas 4). Meanwhile, heat the oil in a frying pan over a high heat, add the onion and garlic, and fry for 1 minute. Lower the heat, cover with a lid, and cook for 15 minutes or until the onion is soft. Set aside to cool slightly.

2 Put the sausagemeat, liver, and brandy into a processor and whiz until smooth. Spoon into a bowl. Add the cooled onion and garlic and stir well. Add the chicken and herbs and season with salt and freshly ground black pepper. Mix together with your hands.

3 Spoon into the loaf tin, making sure the chicken strips are lying horizontally. If you're making the small terrine, the mixture will only come two-thirds of the way up the side of the tin. Level the top with the back of a spoon, cover with foil, and seal tightly around the edges.

4 Sit the loaf tin in a small roasting tin and pour enough boiling water into the roasting tin to come halfway up the sides of the tin. Bake for 45 minutes–1 hour (1½ hours for 12) or until shrinking away from the sides of the tin and firm to the touch. Set aside to cool.

5 Sit weights or cans of soup on top of the foil to weigh the terrine down, then transfer to the fridge for a minimum of 4 hours.

6 To serve, turn the terrine out on to a plate and press the chopped parsley and chives on top. Cut into slices and serve.

SERVE WITH
The terrine goes really well with the Cumberland sauce on page 185, but it is equally delicious with good chutney. Serve some crusty bread alongside.

PREPARE AHEAD
The terrine can be made and garnished with herbs up to 2 days ahead. Wrap in foil. Not suitable for freezing.

IN THE AGA
Slide the roasting tin on to the lowest set of runners in the roasting oven, with the cold sheet on the second set of runners, and bake for 50 minutes (1–1¼ hours for 12).

A meal in itself. We serve it cold with crusty bread, but you can keep the bacon, croûtons, and chicken warm and add just before serving.

Chicken and bacon Caesar salad

Serves 6

200g packet smoked bacon lardons

4 thick slices white bread, crusts removed

3 tbsp olive oil

3 boneless skinless chicken breasts

2 romaine lettuces, cut into 5cm (2in) slices

50g (1¾oz) coarsely grated Parmesan cheese

salt and freshly ground black pepper

For the dressing

¼ garlic clove, crushed

2 tbsp white wine vinegar

½ tsp Dijon mustard

2 tbsp olive oil

6 tbsp mayonnaise

3 tbsp water

25g (scant 1oz) finely grated Parmesan cheese

1 tsp caster sugar

Serves 12

400g packet smoked bacon lardons

8 thick slices white bread, crusts removed

6 tbsp olive oil

6 boneless skinless chicken breasts

4 romaine lettuces, cut into 5cm (2in) slices

100g (3½oz) coarsely grated Parmesan cheese

salt and freshly ground black pepper

For the dressing

½ garlic clove, crushed

4 tbsp white wine vinegar

1 tsp Dijon mustard

4 tbsp olive oil

175ml (6fl oz) mayonnaise

4 tbsp water

50g (1¾oz) finely grated Parmesan cheese

2 tsp caster sugar

1 Preheat the oven to 220°C (200°C fan/425°F/Gas 7). Meanwhile, scatter the lardons over the base of a roasting tin. Cut each slice of bread into 20 even-sized cubes and scatter next to the lardons. Drizzle over two-thirds of the oil and cook in the oven for 15–20 minutes (20 minutes for 12) or until golden and crisp. Shake the tin occasionally.

2 Lay the chicken breasts between two sheets of cling film and bash with a rolling pin until half as thick. Heat the remaining oil in a frying pan, add the chicken, and fry for 3 minutes on each side or until golden all over and cooked through. You may need to do this in batches. Allow to cool slightly, then cut into thin slices.

3 Put the lettuce and Parmesan into a large salad bowl and season with salt and freshly ground black pepper. Add the lardons and croûtons and toss together.

4 To make the dressing, put the garlic, vinegar, mustard, and oil into a bowl and whisk by hand until smooth. Add all the other ingredients and whisk again. Season with salt and freshly ground black pepper. Pour the dressing over the salad and toss to combine. Arrange the chicken on top and serve at once.

PREPARE AHEAD

The lettuce and Parmesan can be placed in a bowl up to 6 hours ahead. The dressing can be made up to 3 days ahead. Not suitable for freezing.

IN THE AGA

Cook the lardons and croûtons on the floor of the roasting oven for 10–15 minutes or until golden and crisp.

Chicken and bacon Caesar salad (see overleaf) •••>

This is a wonderfully fresh light salad, perfect for a picnic or for eating al fresco. You can replace the chicken with turkey if you prefer. Serve with salad leaves and your favourite bread.

Mediterranean lemon and herb chicken salad

Serves 6

For the dressing

2 tbsp Dijon mustard
2 tbsp pesto
juice of 1 lemon
4 tbsp olive oil
1 tbsp caster sugar
salt and freshly ground
  black pepper

750g (1lb 10oz) cooked
  boneless skinless chicken,
  cut into thin strips

150g (5½oz) pitted green
  olives, halved
290g jar chargrilled red peppers,
  drained and thinly sliced
2 tbsp freshly chopped basil
2 tbsp freshly chopped
  flat-leaf parsley
200g (7oz) feta cheese, broken
  into small pieces

Serves 12

For the dressing

4 tbsp Dijon mustard
4 tbsp pesto
juice of 2 lemons
8 tbsp olive oil
2 tbsp caster sugar
salt and freshly ground
  black pepper

1.5kg (3lb 3oz) cooked
  boneless skinless chicken,
  cut into thin strips

300g (11oz) pitted green
  olives, halved
2 x 290g jars chargrilled
  red peppers, drained and
  thinly sliced
4 tbsp freshly chopped basil
4 tbsp freshly chopped
  flat-leaf parsley
400g (14oz) feta cheese,
  broken into small pieces

1 Put all the ingredients for the dressing into a large bowl and whisk by hand until well combined.

2 Add the chicken and toss well. Add the olives, half the peppers, the basil, parsley, and two-thirds of the feta. Season with salt and freshly ground black pepper and toss to combine.

3 Arrange on a platter and scatter the remaining peppers and feta attractively along the centre. Chill in the fridge before serving.

PREPARE AHEAD
The salad can be made up to 8 hours ahead.
Not suitable for freezing.

A frittata is a kind of Italian omelette and this one – cooked in the oven rather than in a frying pan – is ideal for picnics. Cut into wedges and serve warm or cold with dressed salad and bread.

Summer frittata

Serves 6

Special equipment *20cm (8in) round springform tin, greased and base-lined*

350g (12oz) potatoes, cut into 3cm (1¼in) cubes
1 small onion, roughly chopped
salt and freshly ground black pepper

8 large eggs
1 tsp freshly chopped thyme leaves
100g (3½oz) roll goat's cheese, cut into small cubes
75g (2½oz) Black Forest ham, cut into thin strips

Serves 12

Special equipment *2 x 20cm (8in) round springform tins, greased and base-lined*

700g (1lb 9oz) potatoes, cut into 3cm (1¼in) cubes
2 small onions, roughly chopped
salt and freshly ground black pepper

16 large eggs
2 tsp freshly chopped thyme leaves
2 x 100g (3½oz) rolls goat's cheese, cut into small cubes
150g (5½oz) Black Forest ham, cut into thin strips

1 Preheat the oven to 200°C (180°C fan/400°F/Gas 6). Cook the potatoes and onion in boiling salted water for 5–8 minutes or until tender. Drain and refresh in cold water.

2 Crack the eggs into a large mixing bowl, add the thyme, and season with salt and freshly ground black pepper. Whisk by hand until combined. Add the potatoes and onion and stir in the cheese.

3 Pour into the tin(s) and scatter over the strips of ham.

4 Bake for 12–15 minutes (15–20 minutes for 12) or until slightly risen and just firm. To make slicing easier, leave to cool slightly before serving.

VARIATION
Black Forest ham is one of the most reasonably priced cured hams. If you can't get hold of it, use Serrano ham or Parma ham.

PREPARE AHEAD
The frittata can be made up to 8 hours ahead. Not suitable for freezing.

IN THE AGA
Bake on the second set of runners in the roasting oven for 15 minutes (20 minutes for 12).

Buy the freshest peppers and aubergines you can find, with smooth skins, not wrinkly. Toast the pine nuts in a dry frying pan until golden. Watch them carefully, as they burn quickly. Serve with crusty bread.

Red pepper and aubergine salad with basil dressing

Serves 6

2 red peppers, cut in half and deseeded

2 large aubergines, sliced in half lengthways and cut into 5mm (¼in) slices

2 tbsp olive oil

salt and freshly ground black pepper

100g (3½oz) baby spinach

For the dressing

2 tbsp olive oil

2 tbsp balsamic vinegar

1½ tbsp fresh pesto

50g (1¾oz) pine nuts, toasted

Serves 12

4 red peppers, cut in half and deseeded

4 large aubergines, sliced in half lengthways and cut into 5mm (¼in) slices

4 tbsp olive oil

salt and freshly ground black pepper

200g (7oz) baby spinach

For the dressing

4 tbsp olive oil

4 tbsp balsamic vinegar

3 tbsp fresh pesto

75g (2½oz) pine nuts, toasted

1 Preheat the oven to 220°C (200°C fan/425°F/Gas 7). Arrange the pepper halves cut side down in a single layer on one end of a baking sheet, then lay the aubergine slices in a single layer at the other. (For 12, lay the peppers on one sheet and the aubergines on another sheet.) Drizzle over the oil and season with salt and freshly ground black pepper.

2 Roast for 25–30 minutes or until the peppers are chargrilled and the aubergines tender and golden. Put the hot peppers into a polythene bag, seal tightly, and set aside until cold. This allows them to sweat, which makes it easier to remove the skins.

3 Peel the skin from the peppers and discard. Cut the flesh into thin slices and transfer to a serving bowl. Add the aubergines and spinach and season with salt and freshly ground black pepper.

4 To make the dressing, put the oil, vinegar, and pesto into a jam jar, seal with a lid, and shake vigorously.

5 To serve, pour the dressing over the salad, toss well, then scatter with the pine nuts. For the flavours to infuse, it is best to do this about an hour before serving.

PREPARE AHEAD
The salad can be made up to the end of step 2 up to 12 hours ahead. The dressing can be made up to 4 days ahead. Not suitable for freezing.

IN THE AGA
Roast the peppers and aubergines on the top set of runners in the roasting oven for 30 minutes.

Packed with lentils, herbs, and vegetables, this side salad makes a fantastic accompaniment to barbecued meats and fish.

Globe artichoke and Puy lentil salad

Serves 6

200g (7oz) dried Puy lentils

2 large celery sticks, finely diced

½ small red onion, finely diced

100g tub chargrilled artichokes in oil, drained and sliced into large pieces

2 tbsp freshly chopped flat-leaf parsley

2 tbsp freshly chopped mint

225g (8oz) cherry tomatoes, quartered

For the dressing

2 tbsp white wine vinegar

4 tbsp olive oil

1 garlic clove, crushed

2 tbsp sun-dried tomato paste

1 tbsp balsamic vinegar

salt and freshly ground black pepper

Serves 12

400g (11oz) dried Puy lentils

4 large celery sticks, finely diced

1 small red onion, finely diced

195g tub chargrilled artichokes in oil, drained and sliced into large pieces

small bunch of flat-leaf parsley, chopped

small bunch of mint, chopped

500g (1lb 2oz) cherry tomatoes, quartered

For the dressing

4 tbsp white wine vinegar

8 tbsp olive oil

2 garlic cloves, crushed

4 tbsp sun-dried tomato paste

2 tbsp balsamic vinegar

salt and freshly ground black pepper

1 Cook the lentils in boiling water for 15–20 minutes or until tender. Don't add salt or they might not soften. Drain and refresh in cold water.

2 Put the celery, onion, artichokes, herbs, and tomatoes into a large mixing bowl and stir in the lentils.

3 Mix the ingredients for the dressing in a small bowl and pour over the salad.

4 Season well with salt and freshly ground black pepper and chill in the fridge for 1 hour before serving.

PREPARE AHEAD

The salad can be made up to the end of step 2 up to 12 hours ahead. Add the dressing up to 3 hours ahead. Not suitable for freezing.

This is a great main course for a picnic, but it's also good as a side dish – in which case it will feed more. Serve with French bread.

Tuna salade niçoise

Serves 6

100g (3½oz) French beans, trimmed

salt and freshly ground black pepper

6 eggs

3 small Baby Gem lettuces

6 tomatoes, quartered

225g (8oz) baby new potatoes, cooked and halved lengthways

2 x 200g cans tuna in oil, drained

12 canned anchovy fillets, drained

100g (3½oz) pitted black olives, halved lengthways

1 red onion, finely sliced

For the dressing

4 tbsp good olive oil

2 tbsp grainy mustard

2 tbsp white wine vinegar

2 tsp caster sugar

juice of 1 lemon

Serves 12

200g (7oz) French beans, trimmed

salt and freshly ground black pepper

12 eggs

6 small Baby Gem lettuces

12 tomatoes, quartered

450g (1lb) baby new potatoes, cooked and halved lengthways

2 x 400g cans tuna in oil, drained

24 canned anchovy fillets, drained

225g (8oz) pitted black olives, halved lengthways

2 red onions, finely sliced

For the dressing

8 tbsp good olive oil

4 tbsp grainy mustard

4 tbsp white wine vinegar

4 tsp caster sugar

juice of 2 lemons

1 Cook the beans in boiling salted water for 4 minutes or until just tender. Drain, refresh in cold water, and set aside.

2 Put the eggs into a saucepan, cover with water, and bring to the boil. Boil for 5 minutes, then drain and cover again with cold water. Peel, slice into quarters, and set aside.

3 Cut each lettuce into six wedges. Place in a serving bowl with the beans, tomatoes, potatoes, tuna, anchovies, olives, and onion and mix together. Season with salt and freshly ground black pepper.

4 Mix the ingredients for the dressing in a bowl, pour over the salad, and toss gently.

5 Scatter over the eggs and serve.

PREPARE AHEAD

The salad can be prepared up to the end of step 3 up to 6 hours ahead. Dress just before serving. Not suitable for freezing.

The sweet marinade for these kebabs helps the vegetables and cheese turn golden. Serve with salad and jacket potatoes.

Chargrilled vegetable and halloumi skewers

Serves 6

Special equipment *6 metal or wooden skewers (soak wooden skewers in water for 12 hours beforehand to prevent them burning)*

2 medium red onions

salt

1 yellow pepper, halved, deseeded, and cut into 12 large pieces

1 red pepper, halved, deseeded, and cut into 12 large pieces

250g (9oz) halloumi cheese, cut into 18 cubes

12 small cherry tomatoes

2 tbsp olive oil, for frying

For the marinade

2 tbsp soy sauce

1 tbsp runny honey

1 red chilli, halved, deseeded, and finely chopped

1 large garlic clove, crushed

Serves 12

Special equipment *12 metal or wooden skewers (soak wooden skewers in water for 12 hours beforehand to prevent them burning)*

4 medium red onions

salt

2 yellow peppers, halved, deseeded, and cut into 12 large pieces each

2 red peppers, halved, deseeded, and cut into 24 large pieces

450g (1lb) halloumi cheese, cut into 36 cubes

24 small cherry tomatoes

4 tbsp olive oil, for frying

For the marinade

4 tbsp soy sauce

2 tbsp runny honey

2 red chillies, halved, deseeded, and finely chopped

2 large garlic cloves, crushed

1 Slice each onion into six wedges, leaving the root end intact on each wedge so that the layers stay together during cooking. Bring a pan of salted water to the boil, add the onion wedges, the pieces of yellow pepper and the pieces of red pepper, and bring back to the boil. Boil for 5 minutes, then drain, refresh in cold water, and drain again.

2 In the order of your choice, thread two onion wedges, two pieces of yellow pepper, two pieces of red pepper, and three cubes of cheese on to each skewer. Place in a shallow dish.

3 Put all the ingredients for the marinade into a small bowl and mix well. Pour over the kebabs and leave to marinate for at least 1 hour and up to 8 hours.

4 Heat the oil in a large frying pan or griddle pan, add the kebabs, and fry for 2–3 minutes on each side or until chargrilled and brown and the cheese is just soft. You may need to do this in batches. Alternatively, cook under the grill or on a barbecue. Serve hot on the skewers.

PREPARE AHEAD
The kebabs can be made up to the end of step 2 up to 1 day ahead. They can be marinated for up to 8 hours. Not suitable for freezing.

This unusual salad goes well with barbecued meat or fish.
To allow the flavours to infuse, make it up to six hours ahead.

Spicy roast squash and feta salad

Serves 6

1 large butternut squash
1 red onion, thinly sliced
2 tbsp olive oil
salt and freshly ground
   black pepper
1 tsp ground cumin
100g (3½oz) feta cheese,
   crumbled
2 tbsp freshly chopped parsley

For the dressing

1 tbsp white wine vinegar
2 tbsp olive oil
1 tsp honey
½ garlic clove, crushed

Serves 12

2 large butternut squash
2 red onions, thinly sliced
4 tbsp olive oil
salt and freshly ground
   black pepper
1 tbsp ground cumin
200g (7oz) feta cheese,
   crumbled
4 tbsp freshly chopped parsley

For the dressing

2 tbsp white wine vinegar
4 tbsp olive oil
2 tsp honey
1 garlic clove, crushed

1 Preheat the oven to 220°C (200°C fan/425°F/Gas 7). Cut the squash in half lengthways, scoop out the seeds and discard, then peel and cut the flesh into thin half-moon slices.

2 Scatter the squash and onion over the base of a roasting tin. Drizzle with the oil, season with salt and freshly ground black pepper, and toss to combine.

3 Roast for 25–30 minutes (30–35 minutes for 12) or until pale golden and just tender. Transfer to a mixing bowl with a slotted spoon, scatter over the cumin, and toss together. Set aside to cool.

4 When completely cool, stir in the feta and parsley. Put the ingredients for the dressing into a clean jam jar, tighten the lid, and shake well.

5 Pour the dressing over the salad and mix together. Transfer to a salad bowl and chill for up to six hours before serving.

PREPARE AHEAD
The salad can be made up to 6 hours ahead.
Not suitable for freezing.

IN THE AGA
Roast the squash on the floor of the roasting
oven for 20–25 minutes (25–30 minutes for 12).

PREPARING SQUASH

STEP 1 Cut the squash in half
lengthways, then scoop out the
seeds and fibres with a spoon.

STEP 2 Cut into sections and use a
peeler to remove the skin. You may
need a knife for larger squash.

A fantastic vegetarian lunch. Make two separate galettes for 12. Allow to cool slightly before slicing and serving warm with salad.

Goat's cheese, thyme, and onion marmalade galette

Serves 6

2 red peppers, halved and deseeded

1 tbsp olive oil

salt and freshly ground black pepper

375g packet ready-rolled puff pastry

a little plain flour, to dust

2 x 150g tubs soft goat's cheese

1 tbsp fresh thyme leaves, plus a few sprigs to garnish

1 egg, beaten

For the onion marmalade

2 tbsp olive oil

3 large onions, sliced

1 tbsp caster sugar

1 tbsp balsamic vinegar

Serves 12

4 red peppers, halved and deseeded

2 tbsp olive oil

salt and freshly ground black pepper

2 x 375g packets ready-rolled puff pastry

a little plain flour, to dust

4 x 150g tubs soft goat's cheese

2 tbsp fresh thyme leaves, plus a few sprigs to garnish

1 egg, beaten

For the onion marmalade

3 tbsp olive oil

6 large onions, sliced

2 tbsp caster sugar

2 tbsp balsamic vinegar

1 Preheat the oven to 200°C (180°C fan/400°F/Gas 6). Arrange the peppers cut side down on a baking sheet, drizzle over the oil, and season with salt and freshly ground black pepper. Roast for 25–30 minutes or until blackened. Transfer to a polythene bag, seal, and set aside.

2 Meanwhile, make the onion marmalade. Heat the oil in a non-stick frying pan over a high heat, add the onions, and fry for 3 minutes or until starting to soften. Sprinkle in the sugar and vinegar and season with salt and freshly ground black pepper. Cover with a lid, lower the heat, and cook for 20 minutes or until the onions are soft. Set aside to cool.

3 Pop a baking sheet in the oven to get hot (two sheets for 12). Lightly flour a piece of baking parchment (two pieces for 12) and roll the pastry out into a 23 x 33cm (9 x 13in) rectangle (two rectangles for 12). Prick the base with a fork, leaving a border of 5cm (2in). Spread the cheese inside the border, scatter over the thyme, and spoon the onion marmalade on top. Peel the peppers, cut into strips, and scatter over the top. Brush the border with beaten egg.

4 Transfer the baking parchment and galette(s) to the baking sheet and bake for 20–25 minutes (30–35 minutes for 12) or until the pastry is golden. Garnish with thyme sprigs.

CHEAT

If you don't have the time to roast the peppers and make the onion marmalade, use shop-bought, but buy the best you can.

PREPARE AHEAD

The galette can be made up to the end of step 3 up to 8 hours ahead. Not suitable for freezing.

IN THE AGA

Roast the peppers on the second set of runners in the roasting oven for 15–20 minutes. At step 2, transfer to the simmering oven for 20 minutes. Bake the galette on the floor of the roasting oven for 25–30 minutes. Bake two galettes individually.

Coleslaw should be light and fresh rather than rich and sloppy. This recipe comes from our lovely friend Joanna.

Sweet chilli coleslaw

Serves 6

300g (11oz) white cabbage
1 small white onion
2 celery sticks
2 carrots, coarsely grated
salt and freshly ground
    black pepper

3 tbsp cider vinegar
2 tsp Dijon mustard
8 tbsp light or full-fat
    mayonnaise
5 tbsp sweet chilli dipping sauce

Serves 12

600g (1lb 5oz) white cabbage
1 large white onion
4 celery sticks
4 carrots, coarsely grated
salt and freshly ground
    black pepper

6 tbsp cider vinegar
1 heaped tbsp Dijon mustard
250ml (8fl oz) light or full-fat
    mayonnaise
150ml (5fl oz) sweet chilli
    dipping sauce

1 Slice the cabbage, onion, and celery in a food processor, using the slicing blade. If you have a mandolin, use the thin blade. Alternatively, slice them very finely by hand.

2 Transfer to a bowl, add the carrots, and season with salt and freshly ground black pepper.

3 Put the vinegar, mustard, mayonnaise, and dipping sauce into a jam jar. Seal with a lid and shake vigorously to combine.

4 Pour over the dressing and toss well. Transfer to the fridge for a minimum of 3 hours. Serve chilled or at room temperature.

SWEET CHILLI DIPPING SAUCE
Look for this in the oriental section of the supermarket. It gives coleslaw a sweet kick and stops the sauce being too thick.

PREPARE AHEAD
The dressing can be made and kept in the jar for up to 4 days. The coleslaw can be made up to 1 day ahead. The flavours improve, in fact. Not suitable for freezing.

Some classic recipes are unbeatable, but our quiche lorraine – with added parsley – has the edge, we think. Serve warm with salad.

Quiche lorraine

Serves 6

Special equipment 20cm (8in) round 5cm (2in) deep loose-bottomed tart tin or quiche dish

175g (6oz) plain flour, plus a little extra to dust
85g (3oz) cold butter, cubed
1 egg

For the filling
a knob of butter
1 large onion, roughly chopped
225g (8oz) unsmoked bacon, snipped into small pieces
1 heaped tbsp freshly chopped flat-leaf parsley
75g (2½oz) mature Cheddar cheese, grated
3 eggs
200ml tub full-fat crème fraîche
150ml (5fl oz) double cream
salt and freshly ground black pepper

Serves 12

Special equipment 28cm (11in) round 5cm (2in) deep loose-bottomed tart tin or quiche dish

225g (8oz) plain flour, plus a little extra to dust
115g (4oz) cold butter, cubed
1 egg
1–2 tbsp water

For the filling
a knob of butter
2 large onions, roughly chopped
350g (12oz) unsmoked bacon, snipped into small pieces
2 heaped tbsp freshly chopped flat-leaf parsley
175g (6oz) mature Cheddar cheese, grated
6 eggs
300ml (10fl oz) full-fat crème fraîche
300ml (10fl oz) double cream
salt and freshly ground black pepper

1 Put the flour and butter into a processor and whiz until the mixture resembles breadcrumbs. Add the egg (and the water if you're making the larger one) and whiz again until you have a smooth dough. Dust a work surface with flour and knead the dough lightly. Roll the dough out and use to line the flan tin (see page 243). Prick the base all over with a fork and chill for 15 minutes.

2 Preheat the oven to 200°C (180°C fan/400°F/Gas 6). Pop a baking sheet in to get hot. Line the pastry case with baking parchment, fill with dried beans, and bake for 15–20 minutes (see page 275). Remove the beans and paper, lower the temperature to 160°C (140°C fan/325°F/Gas 3), and return the pastry case to the oven to dry out for 5–10 minutes. Set aside to cool. Turn the oven up to 190°C (170°C fan/375°F/Gas 5).

3 To make the filling, melt the butter in a frying pan, add the onion and bacon, and fry over a high heat for 2 minutes or until starting to crisp. Cover with a lid, lower the heat, and cook slowly for 15–20 minutes or until the onion is tender and the bacon cooked. Spoon into the pastry case and spread out evenly. Scatter with half the parsley and half the cheese.

4 Put the eggs, crème fraîche, and double cream into a mixing bowl and whisk by hand until combined. Add the remaining parsley and season with salt and freshly ground black pepper. Pour into the flan case and sprinkle over the remaining cheese.

5 Bake in the oven for 25 minutes (30–35 minutes for 12) or until golden brown and the egg mixture is just set.

PREPARE AHEAD AND FREEZE
The quiche lorraine can be made up to 2 days ahead. Freeze for up to 2 months.

IN THE AGA
Skip step 2. Make the filling and pour into the unbaked pastry case. Bake on the floor of the roasting oven for 25 minutes (35 minutes for 12).

From left Hazelnut meringue
roulade with raspberries (page 272),
Individual tiramisus (page 256),
Exotic fruit salad (page 265).

Our favourite puddings

The grand finale to any feast is the pudding. In this chapter, you'll find desserts of all kinds – wicked and indulgent, delicate and fruity, warm and comforting.

Our favourite puddings

We're huge fans of puddings. We love the classics like soufflés and crème brûlées, possets and pavlovas, tarts and tiramisus, as well as our own variations on family favourites such as apple crumble and lemon meringue pie. In fact, the only thing we dislike about puddings is having to choose which ones to cook!

In general, for 8–12 people we'll serve one pudding that's rich and indulgent and another that's light and fruity – a fresh fruit salad or a fruit compote perhaps. These are always popular and if there's any left over it's delicious for breakfast the following day. Go to town with the decoration – fresh mint leaves, lime wedges, or a sprinkling of pomegranate seeds all look fantastic.

Serving puddings

● Plates must be hot if you're serving a warm dessert.

● So you know there'll be enough to go around, cut large puddings such as cheesecakes, pies, tarts, and roulades into wedges or slices. Place them on a flat platter or cakestand – the pieces can be fiddly to remove from a bowl – and reassemble them so they look whole.

● If you're offering a selection of puddings on one plate, keep the portions small and arrange them in an attractive way.

● Take containers of ice cream out of the freezer and leave at room temperature for an hour or until beginning to thaw at the edges. Scoop balls of the ice cream on to a cold tray, cover with cling film, and return to the freezer until required. Serve piled into a mound.

Cutlery
Provide both dessert forks and dessert spoons so that guests can help themselves to the ones they need.

Finish

Jug of cream or custard
If you're worried about drips, sit the jug on a plate. Put crème fraîche, ice cream, or whipped cream, into a small bowl.

How to lay a buffet table of puddings

Puddings should be presented in the same way as main courses – from right to left (as here) or from left to right, depending on the layout of your room – and in the order guests will put them on their plates, so the puddings themselves should come before any cream or custard.

Doing it like this makes it quicker and easier for people to serve themselves. For a buffet of a dozen guests or more, we offer two puddings, plus a fruit salad. If you've invited over 30 people and have enough room, lay two buffet tables with the same puddings on each.

Large puddings
Cut cheesecakes and tarts into slices or wedges and place on a flat platter or cakestand with a spatula to serve them with. Present other puddings in the dish you've made them in.

Table decoration
Place the table decoration in a prominent position, but well out of guests' way.

Start

Fruit salad
A glass bowl will show off the jewel-bright colours of a fruit salad to their best advantage. Provide a serving spoon.

Individual puddings
Serve individual puddings in tumblers, wine glasses, Martini glasses, shot glasses, or ramekins. Place them on a tray to make them easier to take to the table.

Bowls and plates
Provide pudding bowls and dessert plates. Which people take will depend on the pudding they choose – although most guests will likely eat more than one!

This is also very good made with thinly sliced unpeeled eating apples instead of apricots. Use about three per galette. Serve the pudding warm with cream.

Apricot and almond galette

Makes 1 (serves 6)

a little plain flour, to dust
½ x 375g packet all-butter
    puff pastry
a little milk
400g can apricots in natural
    juices, drained

150g (5½oz) golden marzipan,
    coarsely grated
1 tbsp apricot jam
1 tsp water

Makes 2 (serves 12)

a little plain flour, to dust
375g packet all-butter puff pastry
a little milk
2 x 400g cans apricots in natural
    juices, drained

250g (9oz) golden marzipan,
    coarsely grated
2 tbsp apricot jam
2 tsp water

1 Preheat the oven to 220°C (200°C fan/425°F/Gas 7). Pop a baking sheet in to get hot. Lightly flour a piece of baking parchment and roll the pastry out into a 12.5 x 30cm (5 x 12in) rectangle. For 12, roll it out into a 25 x 30cm (10 x 12in) rectangle, cut it in half lengthways to make two strips, then arrange them neatly side by side.

2 With a knife, score a 1cm (½in) border around the rectangle(s), taking care not to cut all the way through – this allows the strip to rise up around the apricots and stops any liquid or fruit leaking out. Brush the border(s) with a little milk.

3 Slice each apricot into four slices and arrange them in rows inside the border(s). Sprinkle over the marzipan.

4 Slide the paper on to the hot baking sheet and bake for 20 minutes (20–25 minutes for two galettes) or until golden brown. Check halfway through cooking and, if they are getting too brown, cover loosely with foil.

5 Heat the apricot jam in a pan with the water, whisking until smooth. Brush the apricots with a thin layer to glaze them. Serve warm.

COLD IS BEST
Take the pastry and marzipan straight from the fridge – they are easier to handle when cold. If you're not using all the pastry immediately, freeze any left over until needed.

PREPARE AHEAD AND FREEZE
The galette(s) can be made up to 2 days ahead. Freeze for up to 1 month.

IN THE AGA
Bake the galette on the grid shelf on the floor of the roasting oven for 15–20 minutes (20–25 minutes for two galettes).

These individual crumbles are scrumptious and so easy to make.
Serve with cream, crème fraîche, or warm custard.

Mini apple, apricot, and hazelnut crumbles

Serves 6

Special equipment 6 x size 1
(150ml/5fl oz) ramekins

900g (2lb) Bramley apples, peeled
and cut into 1cm (½in) cubes

175g (6oz) ready-to-eat
dried apricots, snipped
into small pieces

100ml (3½fl oz) apple juice
100g (3½oz) demerara sugar
100g (3½oz) plain flour
50g (1¾oz) cold butter, cubed
30g (1oz) hazelnuts, chopped

Serves 12

Special equipment 12 x size 1
(150ml/5fl oz) ramekins

1.8kg (4lb) Bramley apples, peeled
and cut into 1cm (½in) cubes

350g (12oz) ready-to-eat
dried apricots, snipped
into small pieces

200ml (7fl oz) apple juice
200g (7oz) demerara sugar
200g (7oz) plain flour
100g (3½oz) cold butter, cubed
50g (1¾oz) hazelnuts, chopped

1 Preheat the oven to 200°C (180°C fan/400°F/Gas 6). Put the apples, apricots, apple juice, and all but 1 heaped tablespoon (3 level tablespoons for 12) of the demerara sugar into a saucepan. Bring to the boil, cover with a lid, and simmer for 5–7 minutes or until the apples are just soft. Remove from the heat and divide among the ramekins.

2 Put the flour and butter into a mixing bowl and rub together. Add the remaining sugar and the hazelnuts and mix together.

3 Sprinkle the crumble topping over the apples in the ramekins, then place on a baking sheet and bake for 15 minutes or until the crumble is light golden brown and the fruit is bubbling around the edges.

MAKING CRUMBLE TOPPING

Using the tips of your fingers, rub the cold butter into the flour until the mixture resembles breadcrumbs.

PREPARE AHEAD AND FREEZE
The crumbles can be made up to 2 days ahead. Freeze for up to 1 month.

IN THE AGA
Bake the crumbles in the middle of the roasting oven for 15 minutes or until golden.

VARIATION
You could equally make one large crumble. Use a 1.2 litre (2 pint) ovenproof dish for six or a 2.4 litre (4 pint) dish for 12. Bake for 30 minutes (45 minutes for 12).

What makes this crumble so unusual is the layer of creamy custard in the middle. Serve it as it is or with a little more cream.

Apricot custard crumble pie

Makes a 28cm (11in) pie (serves 8–10)

Special equipment *28cm (11in) round tart tin*

175g (6oz) plain flour, plus a little extra to dust
75g (2½oz) butter
2 tbsp caster sugar
1 egg

For the filling

150ml (5fl oz) soured cream
3 egg yolks
200g (7oz) caster sugar
25g (scant 1oz) plain flour
2 x 400g cans apricot halves in natural juices, drained and each apricot cut into three

For the crumble topping

50g (1¾oz) butter
60g (2oz) plain flour
50g (1¾oz) caster sugar

1 Preheat the oven to 220°C (200°C fan/425°F/Gas 7). Put a baking sheet in to get hot. Meanwhile, make the pastry. Put the flour and butter into a processor and whiz until the mixture resembles breadcrumbs. Add the sugar and egg and whiz again to form a ball.

2 Place the base of the tart tin on a work surface. Lightly dust the base of the tart tin and the work surface with flour, then roll the pastry out and line the tart tin.

3 To make the filling, put the soured cream, egg yolks, sugar, and flour into a mixing bowl and whisk by hand until smooth.

4 Arrange the apricots over the base of the pastry case and pour the custard filling over the top. Sit the pie on the hot baking sheet and bake for 20 minutes or until the filling is just beginning to set.

5 Meanwhile, make the crumble topping. Put the butter, flour, and sugar into a mixing bowl and rub with your fingertips until the mixture resembles coarse breadcrumbs.

6 Sprinkle the crumble topping over the just-set custard. Return to the oven and bake for a further 15 minutes or until golden and the custard is completely set. If the crumble topping starts to get too brown, cover with foil. Serve warm or cold.

PREPARE AHEAD
The pie can be made the day before and gently reheated. Not suitable for freezing.

IN THE AGA
At step 4, bake on the floor of the roasting oven for 20 minutes. Add the topping and return to the floor of the oven for 15 minutes. If the pastry is getting too brown, slide on to the grid shelf on the floor. If the topping is getting too brown, slide the cold sheet on to the second set or runners.

LINING A TART TIN

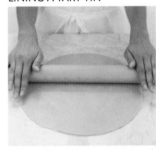

STEP 1 Place the ball of pastry in the middle of the base of the tin and roll into a circle 5cm (2in) bigger. Carefully fold in the edge all around.

STEP 2 Return the base of the tin to the surround, then unfold the edge and neaten. Prick the disc of pastry all over with a fork.

Crisp, short pastry packed with fruit – this apple pie is perfect for a special Sunday lunch. Serve warm with custard, cream, or ice cream.

Melt-in-the-mouth apple pie

Makes a 24cm (9½in) pie (serves 8)

Special equipment 5cm (2in) deep round pie dish with a 19cm (7½in) base and a 24cm (9½in) top

225g (8oz) plain flour, plus
  a little extra to dust
150g (5½oz) cold butter, cubed
25g (scant 1oz) caster sugar,
  plus a little extra to decorate
1 egg, beaten
1–2 tbsp water

For the filling

1.35kg (3lb) Bramley apples,
  peeled, cored, and thinly sliced
175g (6oz) caster sugar
½ tsp ground cinnamon

1 egg, beaten, to glaze

1 Preheat the oven to 200°C (180°C fan/400°F/Gas 6). Meanwhile, put the flour, butter, and sugar into a processor and whiz until the mixture resembles breadcrumbs. Add the egg and water and whiz again until it forms a ball. The dough will weigh about 450g (1lb). Divide it into a 250g (9oz) piece and a 200g (7oz) piece.

2 Lightly flour a work surface and roll the larger piece out very thinly, then use to line the inside of the dish, leaving a little hanging over at the sides.

3 To make the filling, put the apples, sugar, and cinnamon into a bowl, mix well, then spoon into the base of the dish. The apples will be higher than the pastry, but they will sink down as they cook.

4 Lightly flour the work surface and roll the remaining pastry out slightly larger than the surface of the dish. Brush the top of the pastry rim in the dish with water, then sit the pastry circle on top and gently push down to seal the edges. Using a small sharp knife, trim off any excess pastry and crimp the edges together with your fingertips. Use any leftover pastry for decoration (see right). Brush the pie with the beaten egg.

5 Bake for 45–50 minutes or until golden brown and crisp. Allow to cool slightly, then sprinkle with a little extra caster sugar and serve.

PASTRY DECORATIONS

Roll any leftover pastry out thinly, then place on a piece of baking parchment and pop in the freezer for 15 minutes or until frozen. When crisp, use a knife to cut into the shapes or letters you want.

PREPARE AHEAD AND FREEZE

The pie can be made up to the end of step 4 up to 1 day ahead. Freeze for up to 2 months.

IN THE AGA

Bake on the floor of the roasting oven for 15 minutes, then slide the grid shelf on the floor underneath the pie and bake for 30 minutes. If the pie is getting too brown, slide the cold sheet on to the second set of runners.

These individual soufflés look impressive and, despite their rather complicated-sounding name, are extremely simple to make.

Twice-baked lemon soufflés

Serves 6

Special equipment 6 x size 1 (150ml/5fl oz) ramekins, greased and base-lined with a disc of baking parchment

3 eggs, separated
175g (6oz) caster sugar
25g (scant 1oz) cornflour
finely grated zest of
  2 large lemons

juice of 1 large lemon
250g (9oz) half-fat cream cheese
1 large tbsp luxury lemon curd

For the lemon sauce
300ml (10fl oz) double cream
1 tbsp luxury lemon curd
finely grated zest and juice
  of 1 lemon

Serves 12

Special equipment 12 x size 1 (150ml/5fl oz) ramekins, greased and base-lined with a disc of baking parchment

6 eggs, separated
350g (12oz) caster sugar
50g (1¾oz) cornflour
finely grated zest of
  4 large lemons

juice of 2 large lemons
500g (1lb 2oz) half-fat
  cream cheese
2 large tbsp luxury lemon curd

For the lemon sauce
600ml (1 pint) double cream
2 tbsp luxury lemon curd
finely grated zest and juice
  of 2 lemons

1 Preheat the oven to 190°C (170°C fan/375°F/Gas 5). Put the egg yolks and half the sugar into a mixing bowl and whisk with an electric whisk until pale, thick, and frothy.

2 Mix the cornflour, lemon zest, and lemon juice in a bowl until smooth. Fold in the egg-yolk mixture, then beat in the cream cheese and lemon curd with a spatula.

3 Whisk the egg whites with an electric whisk until they resemble clouds. Whisking constantly, add the remaining sugar a teaspoon at a time until the whites are stiff and shiny.

4 Carefully fold the egg-white mixture into the mixing bowl, then spoon into the ramekins. Run a knife around the edge of each one to ensure they rise evenly. Sit the ramekins snugly in a roasting tin, then pour in enough boiling water to come halfway up the sides of the tin.

5 Bake for 15–20 minutes or until the soufflés have risen well and are just cooked. Set aside to cool completely.

6 Turn the soufflés out of the ramekins, remove the paper bases, and arrange snugly in one layer in an ovenproof dish.

7 To make the sauce, put all the ingredients into a mixing bowl and whisk until smooth. Pour the sauce around the soufflés in the dish, then bake in an oven preheated to 200°C (180°C fan/400°F/Gas 6) for 10 minutes (20–25 minutes for 12). Serve at once.

PREPARE AHEAD
The soufflés can be made up to the end of step 6 and the sauce poured around them up to 8 hours ahead. Not suitable for freezing.

IN THE AGA
At step 5, bake on the second set of runners in the roasting oven for 15 minutes. At step 7, bake on the second set of runners in the roasting oven for 8–10 minutes.

This is a truly wonderful LMP. It takes a bit of time to make but, for a really special occasion, it's worth it. Serve warm or cold, but not hot, as the pie will be too soft to cut.

Lemon meringue pie

Makes a 28cm (11in) pie (serves 8–10)

Special equipment 28cm (11in) fluted loose-bottomed tart tin

225g (8oz) plain flour, plus a little extra to dust
175g (6oz) cold butter, cubed
45g (1½oz) icing sugar
1 large egg, beaten
1 tbsp water

For the lemon filling
finely grated zest and juice of 6 lemons
65g (2¼oz) cornflour
450ml (15fl oz) water
250g (9oz) caster sugar
6 egg yolks

For the topping
4 egg whites
225g (8oz) caster sugar
2 level tsp cornflour

JUICING LEMONS
To get the most juice from lemons, cut them in half and pop them in the microwave. Heat until hot (3 minutes should be about right for six lemons), then squeeze. Not only will you get more juice from them, they'll be easier to squeeze, too.

1 Put the flour and butter into a processor and whiz until the mixture resembles breadcrumbs. Add the icing sugar, egg, and water and whiz until it forms a ball. Transfer to a lightly floured work surface and roll the dough out thinly until slightly larger than the tin, then use to line the tin. Cover with cling film and chill for about an hour.

2 Preheat the oven to 200°C (180°C fan/400°F/Gas 6). Line the pastry case with baking parchment, fill with dried beans, and bake for 15 minutes (see page 275). Remove the beans and parchment and return to the oven for 5 minutes to dry out, then remove from the oven and set aside. Reduce the oven temperature to 180°C (160°C fan/350°F/Gas 4).

3 To make the filling, mix the lemon zest, lemon juice, and cornflour to a smooth paste in a small bowl. Bring the water to the boil in a pan, add the lemon mixture, and stir over the heat until thickened, then boil for 1 minute. Mix the sugar and yolks in a bowl and carefully add to the pan. Stir over a medium heat until you have a thick custard. Set aside to cool slightly, then pour into the pastry case.

4 To make the topping, whisk the egg whites with an electric whisk until they look like clouds. Gradually add the caster sugar, whisking on maximum speed until the whites are stiff and glossy. Add the cornflour and whisk to combine.

5 Spoon the meringue on top of the lemon filling, spreading to cover it completely and swirling the top. Bake for 30 minutes or until the filling is completely set and the meringue is lightly golden and crisp.

PREPARE AHEAD
The pastry case can be made up to 2 days ahead. The pie can be made completely up to 1 day ahead. Not suitable for freezing.

IN THE AGA
Skip step 2. At the end of step 3, slide on to the floor of the roasting oven, with the cold sheet on the second set of runners, and bake for 20 minutes or until the filling is just set. At step 5, bake on the grid shelf on the floor of the roasting oven, with the cold sheet on the second set of runners, for 5–10 minutes.

This is similar to sticky toffee pudding and it's truly scrumptious. If you're serving 12, bake the pudding in two tins.

Toffee pudding with warm toffee sauce

Serves 6

Special equipment 23 x 33cm (9 x 13in) traybake tin, greased, lined with baking parchment, and greased

100g (3½oz) butter, at
  room temperature
175g (6oz) light muscovado sugar
2 eggs
225g (8oz) self-raising flour
2 tbsp black treacle
150ml (5fl oz) milk
50g (1¾oz) walnuts, chopped

For the toffee sauce

150g (5½oz) light muscovado
  sugar
150g (5½oz) golden syrup
50g (1¾oz) butter
170g can evaporated milk

Serves 12

Special equipment Two 23 x 33cm (9 x 13in) traybake tins, greased, lined with baking parchment, and greased

225g (8oz) butter, at
  room temperature
350g (12oz) light muscovado
  sugar
4 eggs
450g (1lb) self-raising flour
4 tbsp black treacle
300ml (10fl oz) milk
100g (3½oz) walnuts, chopped

For the toffee sauce

300g (11oz) light muscovado
  sugar
300g (11oz) golden syrup
100g (3½oz) butter
2 x 170g cans evaporated milk

1 Preheat the oven to 180°C (160°C fan/350°F/Gas 4). Put the butter, sugar, eggs, flour, and treacle into a bowl and whisk with an electric whisk until combined. Slowly add the milk, whisking until smooth. Pour into the lined tin and sprinkle with the walnuts.

2 Bake for 30–35 minutes (40 minutes for two puddings) or until well risen, just firm in the middle, and lightly golden brown. Keep warm.

3 To make the sauce, put the sugar, syrup, and butter into a saucepan and stir over a low heat until the sugar has dissolved, the butter has melted, and all the ingredients are combined. Simmer for 5 minutes, then remove from the heat and stir in the evaporated milk.

4 Cut the pudding into squares and serve warm with the warm toffee sauce.

PREPARE AHEAD AND FREEZE

The pudding can be made up to 1 day ahead. Freeze for up to 2 months. The sauce can be made up to 5 days ahead. Not suitable for freezing.

IN THE AGA

Bake on the grid shelf on the floor of the roasting oven, with the cold sheet on the second set of runners, for 25–30 minutes (30–35 minutes for two puddings).

Becca is a great friend of ours. She has her own catering company and has given us great advice on cooking for numbers.

Becca's white chocolate and orange mousses

Serves 6

Special equipment *6 x 7cm (2¾in) round metal cooking rings*

75g (2½oz) HobNobs, crushed
45g (1½oz) butter, melted
1 tbsp demerara sugar

150g (5½oz) Belgium or Continental 100 per cent white chocolate
1 tbsp Cointreau
1 large orange

For the mousse
100g (3½oz) full-fat cream cheese
150ml (5fl oz) double cream

Serves 12

Special equipment *12 x 7cm (2¾in) round metal cooking rings*

175g (6oz) HobNobs, crushed
75g (2½oz) butter, melted
1½ tbsp demerara sugar

300g (11oz) Belgium or Continental 100 per cent white chocolate
3 tbsp Cointreau
2 large oranges

For the mousse
250g (9oz) full-fat cream cheese
300ml (10fl oz) double cream

1 Put the HobNobs into a mixing bowl, add the butter and sugar, and mix to combine.

2 Line a baking sheet with cling film and sit the rings on top. Spoon the biscuit mixture evenly into the rings and level the tops with the back of a teaspoon. Transfer to the fridge to chill while you make the mousse.

3 Put the cream cheese and cream into a mixing bowl and whisk with an electric whisk until thick and holding its shape.

4 Gently melt the chocolate in a bowl set over a pan of just-simmering water until smooth.

5 Add the chocolate to the cream mixture and stir in the Cointreau. Finely grate the zest of the orange(s) and add to the mousse.

6 Spoon the mousse into the rings and level the tops. Chill for a minimum of 4 hours to firm up. Meanwhile, peel the orange(s) with a small knife. Cut the segments free and place in a bowl. Squeeze over the juice from the peel.

7 Remove the rings and serve the mousses with the orange segments arranged on top.

VARIATION
If you don't have cooking rings, you can make one large mousse. Follow the recipe for 12 and spoon the mousse into a 20cm (8in) round springform tin. Cut into 12 wedges and decorate with the orange segments.

PREPARE AHEAD
You can make the mousses up to 12 hours ahead. Not suitable for freezing.

ON THE AGA
To melt the chocolate, break it up into a bowl and place on the back of the Aga until melted.

This is so impressive – two small puddings, a little of each on one plate, served with some glazed summer berries. Your friends will think they are in a three-star restaurant.

A rather special dessert collection

Serves 12

Glazed summer berries

250g (9oz) small strawberries, hulled and halved
250g (9oz) raspberries
100g (3½oz) blueberries
3 tsp icing sugar

1 Place the berries in a large mixing bowl and toss together gently.

2 Sift the icing sugar over the top and gently combine. Cover and chill in the fridge for up to 4 hours. The sugar will dissolve in the strawberry juices to form a shimmering glaze.

Crème brûlée

Special equipment 18cm (7in) square cake tin, greased

600ml (1 pint) double cream
4 egg yolks
25g (scant 1oz) caster sugar
½ tsp vanilla extract
100g (3½oz) demerara sugar

1 Preheat the oven to 140°C (120°C fan/275°F/Gas 1). Heat the double cream gently in a saucepan until hand hot. Put the egg yolks, sugar, and vanilla extract into a bowl and whisk until combined. Pour the mixture into the hot cream and whisk until smooth. Transfer to a jug, then strain into the cake tin.

2 Sit the cake tin in a roasting tin, pour enough boiling water into the roasting tin to come halfway up the sides of the cake tin, then transfer to the oven and bake for 30–35 minutes or until the cream mixture has just set. Set aside to cool.

3 Once cold, sprinkle the demerara sugar on top and slide under a hot grill until the sugar dissolves and becomes caramel-coloured. Set aside to firm up in the fridge for at least 1 hour and up to 5 hours.

4 When ready to serve, cut into even-sized squares with a fish slice.

If you're serving fewer than 12 people, make just one of these special puddings – it will serve six. Cut the crème brûlée into six servings rather than 12. And make the chocolate pots in six 150ml (5fl oz) ramekins or wine glasses. Serve with or without the glazed summer berries.

Chocolate pots

Special equipment 12 shot glasses, about 75ml (2½fl oz) in capacity

300g (11oz) Bournville chocolate
300ml (10fl oz) double cream
200ml (7fl oz) full-fat crème fraîche

TO SERVE
The desserts look particularly attractive on long white plates. Arrange a chocolate pot at one end, place a pile of the berries in the centre, and a square of crème brûlée at the other end.

1 Reserve two squares of chocolate for decoration, then put the rest in a bowl set over a pan of simmering water. Add 200ml (7fl oz) of the double cream and stir until the chocolate has melted. Set aside to cool slightly.

2 Stir in the crème fraîche, then pour into the shot glasses. Leave to set in the fridge for at least 2 hours.

3 Once set, pour the remaining double cream over the top. Coarsely grate the reserved chocolate and sprinkle on top.

PREPARE AHEAD
The custard for the crème brûlée can be made up to 2 days ahead. Add the topping up to 5 hours before serving. The chocolate pots can be made up to 2 days ahead. The berries can be prepared up to 4 hours ahead. Not suitable for freezing.

IN THE AGA
Bake the custard for the crème brûlée on the grid shelf on the lowest set of runners in the roasting oven for 8 minutes. Transfer to the simmering oven and cook for 40 minutes or until just set.

A rather special dessert collection (see overleaf) ●●●▶

The combination of rhubarb and lemon is delicious. This pudding looks particularly pretty made with young pink rhubarb, which is available in the shops towards the end of the winter.

Rhubarb and lemon pots

Serves 6

750g (1lb 10oz) rhubarb, sliced into 4cm (1¾in) pieces

finely grated zest of ½ orange, plus 2 tbsp orange juice

25g (scant 1oz) caster sugar

For the lemon topping

300ml (10fl oz) double cream

50g (1¾oz) caster sugar

finely grated zest and juice of 1½ lemons

six mint leaves, to decorate

Serves 12

1.5kg (3lb 3oz) rhubarb, sliced into 4cm (1¾in) pieces

finely grated zest of 1 orange, plus 4 tbsp orange juice

50g (1¾oz) caster sugar

For the lemon topping

600ml (1 pint) double cream

100g (3½oz) caster sugar

finely grated zest and juice of 3 lemons

12 mint leaves, to decorate

1 Put the rhubarb, orange zest, orange juice, and sugar into a saucepan. Stir over a high heat for 2 minutes, cover with a lid, lower the heat, and simmer for 10 minutes (15 minutes for 12) or until the rhubarb is just tender. Set aside to cool.

2 To make the topping, put the cream, sugar, and lemon zest into a pan. Heat gently over a low heat until the sugar dissolves and the mixture reaches simmering point. Remove from the heat, stir in the lemon juice, and set aside to cool slightly.

3 Spoon the rhubarb and a little of the liquid into the base of some pretty glasses or tumblers. Pour the lemon topping on top, then transfer to the fridge for a minimum of 4 hours to set.

4 Serve chilled, decorated with mint leaves.

PREPARE AHEAD

The pots can be made up to 12 hours ahead.

Not suitable for freezing.

We all love tiramisu. This version is served individually, with the added decadence of a splash of Baileys Irish Cream. Serve the tiramisus in tumblers or wine, martini, or champagne glasses.

Individual tiramisus

Serves 6

1½ tsp instant coffee granules
120ml (4fl oz) boiling water
3 tbsp Baileys Irish Cream
2 eggs
75g (2½oz) caster sugar
300ml (10fl oz) double cream
250g tub full-fat mascarpone

3 squares from a packet
   of trifle sponges
75g (2½oz) plain chocolate,
   coarsely grated

Serves 12

1 tbsp instant coffee granules
300ml (10fl oz) boiling water
6 tbsp Baileys Irish Cream
4 eggs
150g (5½oz) caster sugar
600ml (1 pint) double cream
2 x 250g tubs full-fat mascarpone

6 squares from a packet
   of trifle sponges
150g (5½oz) plain chocolate,
   coarsely grated

1 Put the coffee granules and boiling water into a jug and stir to dissolve. Allow to cool slightly, then stir in the Baileys.

2 Break the eggs into a mixing bowl, add the sugar, and whisk with an electric whisk until pale, thick, and frothy and the whisk leaves a trail on the surface when lifted.

3 Whip the cream till just lightly whipped and holding its shape.

4 Put the mascarpone into a bowl, stir in 2 tablespoons of the whipped cream, and mix with a spatula. Gently fold in the rest of the whipped cream, followed by the egg mixture, taking care not to knock out any of the air.

5 Cut the trifle sponges in half horizontally and then in half crossways. Push a piece into the base of each tumbler or glass, drizzle over half the coffee mixture, then spoon over half the cream mixture. Repeat to give another layer of sponge, coffee, and cream. Finish with a sprinkling of the grated chocolate.

6 Cover and chill in the fridge for a minimum of 4 hours.

VARIATION

If you don't have any Baileys Irish Cream, you can replace it with the same quantity of brandy.

PREPARE AHEAD AND FREEZE
The tiramisus can be made up to 12 hours ahead.
Freeze for up to 1 month.

A rich, indulgent cheesecake that requires no gelatine – ideal for vegetarians. Serve on its own or with fresh summer fruits such as raspberries and strawberries.

Chocolate truffle cheesecake

Serves 12

Special equipment *19cm (7½in) square tin or an 18cm (7in) round springform tin, lined with cling film*

200g (7oz) Bournville chocolate
2 eggs, separated
50g (1¾oz) caster sugar
175g (6oz) full-fat cream cheese

½ tsp vanilla extract
150ml (5fl oz) double cream, lightly whipped
175g (6oz) chocolate digestive biscuits, crushed
75g (2½oz) butter, melted

1 Break the chocolate into small pieces into a bowl. Sit the bowl over a pan of hot water on a low heat and stir until melted. Take care not to allow the chocolate to get too hot or it will lose its shine and become too thick.

2 Put the egg yolks and sugar into a large bowl and whisk with an electric whisk until light and thick and a trail is left when the whisks are lifted from the bowl.

3 Mix the cream cheese and vanilla extract in a bowl, then stir in the melted chocolate. Fold in the whisked egg yolks and sugar, taking care not to knock out any air. Fold in the whipped cream.

4 Whisk the egg whites with an electric hand whisk until like clouds. Stir a spoonful of egg whites into the chocolate mixture with a spatula, then cut and fold the rest in until smooth.

5 Spoon into the prepared tin and level the top. Transfer to the fridge for 1 hour or until just set.

6 Mix the biscuits and butter together until combined. Carefully press on top of the cheesecake in an even layer. Return to the fridge for a minimum of 6 hours.

7 To serve, turn the cheesecake upside-down on to a board or plate and cut into 12 fingers or wedges.

FOLDING IN EGG WHITES

STEP 1 Cut down through the spoonful of egg white and bring some chocolate mixture up over it.

STEP 2 Continue the cut, lift, and sweep and, when no whites are visible, add the rest and repeat.

PREPARE AHEAD AND FREEZE
The cheesecake can be made up to the end of step 6 up to 2 days ahead. Freeze for up to 3 months.

ON THE AGA
To melt the chocolate, break it up into a bowl and place on the back of the Aga until melted.

This was the favourite pudding at a charity buffet for 40 that Mary was a guest at – it went like lightning. The other good news is that once you've collected the ingredients together, it takes 10 minutes.

Heavenly lemon cheesecake on a ginger crust

Makes a 20cm (8in) cheesecake (serves 8)

Special equipment 20cm (8in) round loose-bottomed cake tin, greased and base-lined with baking parchment

100g (3½oz) ginger biscuits, crushed
50g (1¾oz) butter, melted
2 x 250g tubs mascarpone
325g jar luxury lemon curd
juice of 1 small lemon
fresh raspberries and blueberries, to decorate
icing sugar, to dust

1 Mix the biscuits with the butter in a bowl, then press into the base of the tin (but not up the sides).

2 Put the mascarpone, lemon curd, and lemon juice in a bowl and beat with a spatula until smooth.

3 Spoon on to the biscuit base and level the top. Chill in the fridge for at least 4 hours and up to 24 hours to firm up.

4 To serve, remove the cheesecake from the tin, peel off the baking parchment, and arrange on a platter. Decorate with the fruit and dust with icing sugar.

Great for a crowd... You can make up to three cheesecakes in one go (but take care not to overbeat the mixture at step 2). If you're making more cheesecakes than that, prepare them in separate batches.

PREPARE AHEAD
The cheesecake can be made up to the end of step 3 up to 1 day ahead. Not suitable for freezing.

This unusual chilled cheesecake has a delicious raspberry-ripple filling. If we don't have any Framboise raspberry liqueur to hand, we make a cherry-ripple cheesecake, using kirsch instead.

Chilled marbled raspberry cheesecake

Makes a 23cm (9in) cheesecake (serves 8)

Special equipment 23cm (9in) round springform tin, greased and base-lined with baking parchment

100g (3½oz) digestive biscuits, crushed
50g (1¾oz) butter, melted
25g (scant 1oz) demerara sugar

For the raspberry filling
500g (1lb 2oz) fresh raspberries
2 tsp powdered gelatine
2 tbsp water
2 tbsp Framboise liqueur

For the creamy filling
3 tsp powdered gelatine
3 tbsp water
250g (9oz) full-fat cream cheese, at room temperature
2 eggs, separated
200g (7oz) half-fat crème fraîche
100g (3½oz) caster sugar

1 Mix the biscuits, butter, and sugar together in a bowl and press into the base of the tin. Transfer to the fridge to chill.

2 Meanwhile, make the raspberry filling. Whiz the raspberries in a processor until smooth, then push through a sieve into a bowl. Put the gelatine into another bowl and add the water. Allow to soak until the gelatine becomes spongy, then stand the bowl in a saucepan of hot water until it dissolves. Once dissolved, add the Framboise, then pour into the raspberry purée. Stir and set aside.

3 To make the creamy filling, prepare the gelatine and water as above. Put the cream cheese, egg yolks, and crème fraîche into a bowl and stir to combine.

4 Spoon 2 tablespoons of the creamy mixture into the liquid gelatine and mix, then pour the whole lot into the creamy mixture and stir until smooth.

5 Whisk the egg whites with an electric hand whisk until stiff, then add the caster sugar a teaspoon at a time, whisking constantly until shiny and stiff. Fold the egg whites into the creamy mixture until smooth.

6 Carefully fold the raspberry filling into the creamy mixture to give a ripple effect.

7 Spoon into the tin and chill in the fridge for a minimum of 6 hours or until firm.

8 To serve, remove from the tin, discard the disc of paper, and cut into slices.

PREPARE AHEAD AND FREEZE
The cheesecake can be made up to the end of step 7 up to 2 days ahead. Freeze for up to 3 months.

One of the great things about this ice cream (apart from its flavour) is that you don't need an ice-cream maker. It's made with raw meringue, which means it doesn't need whisking as it freezes.

Rum and raisin ice cream

Serves 10–12

Special equipment 1.5 litre (2¾ pint) freezerproof container

175g (6oz) lexia raisins
5 tbsp dark rum
4 eggs, separated
100g (3½oz) caster sugar
300ml (10fl oz) double cream

LEXIA RAISINS

These large plump raisins are lovely in ice cream. If you can't find them, you can use any other kind of raisin.

SERVING TIP

To make serving speedier, once the ice cream is frozen, scoop out the number of balls of ice cream you need and arrange on a tray (make sure it fits in the freezer first). Cover with cling film and slide the tray into the freezer. Then all you need to do is arrange the balls in the bowls when you are ready to serve.

1 Put the raisins into a bowl and add the rum. Leave to soak – ideally overnight.

2 Put the egg yolks into a small bowl and whisk with a fork until blended.

3 Whisk the egg whites with an electric whisk until stiff. Whisking on maximum speed, add the sugar a teaspoon at a time until the whites are stiff and glossy.

4 Whip the cream until soft peaks form, then fold into the egg-white mixture until smooth. Stir in the egg yolks and soaked raisins. If there is any rum left in the bowl, add this too.

5 Transfer to the freezerproof container and freeze for a minimum of 24 hours.

6 Remove from the freezer 10 minutes before serving to make scooping easier.

PREPARE AHEAD AND FREEZE

Freeze for up to 2 months.

A fruit-based pudding is so welcome after a rich main course and these poached pears make a great change from fruit salad. The sauce for them is vivid and vibrant in colour.

Poached pears with blackberry sauce

Serves 6

350g (12oz) granulated sugar
1.2 litres (2 pints) water
a few strips of lemon zest
6 pears, peeled, but stalk left on

For the blackberry sauce

450g (1lb) blackberries
100g (3½oz) granulated sugar

Serves 12

700g (1lb 9oz) granulated sugar
2.5 litres (4¼ pints) water
a few strips of lemon zest
12 pears, peeled, but stalk left on

For the blackberry sauce

900g (2lb) blackberries
200g (7oz) granulated sugar

1 Put the sugar, water, and lemon peel into a saucepan just large enough to take the pears upright in a single layer.

2 Heat gently, stirring until the sugar has dissolved, then boil rapidly for 2 minutes.

3 Place the pears in the hot syrup, cover with a wet sheet of greaseproof paper (this ensures the top of the pears do not dry out), and bring to the boil. Cover with a lid and simmer gently for 30–45 minutes (50 minutes for 12) or until the pears are just tender. Set aside to cool.

4 Put the blackberries and sugar into a pan and cook for 5 minutes or until the juices start to run. Push through a sieve into a bowl to get a thickish purée.

5 When the pears are cold, remove from the syrup and pat dry with kitchen paper.

6 Serve one pear per person or cut each one in half lengthways through the stem, remove the core, and serve two halves. Drizzle over the sauce.

VARIATION

Blackcurrants work just as well as blackberries. Whichever fruit you use, make the pudding extra special by adding 1 tablespoon of crème de cassis to the purée.

PREPARE AHEAD AND FREEZE

The pears can be poached up to 12 hours ahead and kept in the syrup until ready to serve. The sauce can be made up to 3 days ahead. Freeze the sauce for up to 2 months.

IN THE AGA

At step 3, bring to the boil, cover with a lid, and transfer to the simmering oven for 40 minutes (50 minutes for 12).

One of the quickest, most delicious puddings you'll ever make! Serve with shortbread biscuits to make it extra special.

Magenta fruit compote with white chocolate sauce

Serves 6

30g (1oz) caster sugar

2 tbsp crème de cassis or blackcurrant liqueur

4 tbsp water

225g (8oz) blueberries

225g (8oz) raspberries

225g (8oz) strawberries, quartered

150g (5oz) Belgian or Continental 100 per cent white chocolate

300ml (10fl oz) double cream

Serves 12

50g (1¾oz) caster sugar

4 tbsp crème de cassis or blackcurrant liqueur

8 tbsp water

500g (1lb 2oz) blueberries

500g (1lb 2oz) raspberries

500g (1lb 2oz) strawberries, quartered

300g (11oz) Belgian or Continental 100 per cent white chocolate

600ml (1 pint) double cream

1 Put the sugar, crème de cassis, and water into a shallow saucepan. Gently heat, then add the blueberries and simmer for a few minutes or until just starting to soften. Remove from the heat and add the raspberries and strawberries. Mix together and leave in the pan to cool completely.

2 Put the chocolate and cream into a bowl set over a pan of just-simmering water and stir until runny. Take care not to overheat the chocolate or it will lose its shine and split. Leave to cool and thicken slightly.

3 Divide the fruit among wine or cocktail glasses. Pour the white chocolate sauce over the top, then place in the fridge for 2 hours to set slightly.

PREPARE AHEAD

The fruit can be prepared up to 2 days ahead and the puddings assembled up to 12 hours ahead. Not suitable for freezing.

This is a lovely refreshing fruit salad and any left over is a real treat for breakfast the next day. Serve on its own or with cream.

Exotic fruit salad

Serves 6

½ large cantaloupe melon

1 large mango, stone removed
  and flesh cut into cubes
  (see page 273)

3 passion fruit

3 oranges

1 grapefruit

225g (8oz) black
  seedless grapes

4 tbsp Cointreau or Grand
  Marnier (optional)

Serves 12

1 large cantaloupe melon,
  cut in half

2 large mangoes, stones removed
  and flesh cut into cubes
  (see page 273)

6 passion fruit

6 oranges

2 grapefruits

500g (1lb 2oz) black
  seedless grapes

8 tbsp Cointreau or Grand
  Marnier (optional)

1 Scoop the seeds from the melon and discard. Using a sharp knife, cut into wedges and remove the skin. Slice the flesh into 2.5cm (1in) chunks and put into a serving bowl with the mango cubes.

2 Slice the passion fruit in half and scoop the seeds into the bowl.

3 Remove the skin from the oranges and grapefruit(s) and cut the flesh into segments, making sure you catch the juices. Add to the bowl.

4 Slice the grapes in half and add to the bowl.

5 Add the Cointreau or Grand Marnier, if using, and mix lightly together, then chill in the fridge until you are ready to serve.

PREPARE AHEAD
The salad can be made up to 12 hours ahead.
Not suitable for freezing.

OTHER FRUITS TO USE
Raspberries and strawberries are good in a fruit salad, but add them at the last minute or they will bleed into the other fruits and turn mushy. Bananas go soft after a while, too. Avoid apples, pears, and peaches, as they discolour.

SEGMENTING ORANGES

STEP 1 Cut a piece from the top and base, then slice down around the flesh, removing skin and pith.

STEP 2 Slide the knife down one side of a segment, then cut down the other side and pull it free.

A classic dessert that's brilliant for serving numbers. For a recipe for six, turn to page 250. This is delicious served with soft summer fruits such as raspberries or a fruit coulis.

Party crème brûlée

Serves 12–16

Special equipment *2.4 litre (4 pint) shallow wide-based ovenproof dish, greased*

85g (3oz) caster sugar
12 egg yolks
3 tsp vanilla extract
1.2 litres (2 pints) double cream
300ml (10fl oz) single cream
225g (8oz) demerara sugar
100g (3½oz) raspberries, to decorate
mint leaves, to decorate

1 Preheat the oven to 160°C (140°C fan/325°F/Gas 3). Meanwhile, put the sugar, egg yolks, and vanilla extract into a large mixing bowl and whisk together by hand.

2 Put the double cream and single cream into a saucepan and heat until just below boiling point (just hot enough to put your finger in).

3 Pour the hot cream into the egg yolk mixture, whisking quickly until combined.

4 Pour the custard through a sieve into the prepared ovenproof dish.

5 Put the dish into a large roasting tin and pour enough boiling water into the tin so that it comes halfway up the sides of the dish.

6 Carefully slide into the oven and cook for 35–45 minutes or until set but with a slight wobble in the middle. Check after 30 minutes to see how it's doing.

7 Remove from the oven and leave to cool in the roasting tin, then place in the fridge and chill until stone cold.

8 Sprinkle over the demerara sugar, then pop under a hot grill, watching it very carefully, for 20–25 minutes or until melted and golden brown. You could also use a blowtorch to do this. To give the topping time to soften slightly, chill in the fridge for at least 5 hours and up to 10 hours, but no more or it will turn to liquid.

9 To serve, cut into portions with a fish slice and decorate with raspberries and mint leaves.

Great for a crowd... Make in batches and store in the fridge for 5–10 hours.

VARIATION

You could also serve the crème brûlée in individual portions – there will be enough for 12 size 1 (150ml/5fl oz) ramekins. The baking time will be shorter, though – around 20 minutes – but keep an eye on them when they're in the oven.

PREPARE AHEAD

The custard can be made up to the end of step 7 up to 2 days ahead. Not suitable for freezing.

IN THE AGA

Slide the tin on to the lowest set of runners in the roasting oven, with the cold sheet on the second set of runners, and bake for 15 minutes or until just set around the edges, then transfer to the simmering oven for 45 minutes. At step 8, add the demerara sugar and brown with a blowtorch.

Pear and ginger is one of our all-time favourite combinations. This pavlova is sprinkled with pomegranate seeds just before serving – they look so pretty and glisten like little gems.

Pear and ginger pavlova

Serves 6

3 egg whites
175g (6oz) caster sugar
1 level tsp cornflour
1 tsp white wine vinegar

For the topping

5 fairly ripe pears, peeled, cored, and chopped into chunky slices
juice of ½ lemon

50g (1¾oz) caster sugar
300ml (10fl oz) double cream, whipped
6 bulbs stem ginger (from a jar), drained and coarsely chopped
1 small pomegranate

Serves 12

6 egg whites
350g (12oz) caster sugar
2 level tsp cornflour
2 tsp white wine vinegar

For the topping

10 fairly ripe pears, peeled, cored, and chopped into chunky slices

juice of 1 lemon
100g (3½oz) caster sugar
600ml (1 pint) double cream, whipped
12 bulbs stem ginger (from a jar), drained and coarsely chopped
2 small pomegranates

1 Preheat the oven to 160°C (140°C fan/325°F/Gas 3). Whisk the egg whites with an electric whisk until they look like clouds. Gradually add the sugar a little at a time, whisking on maximum speed until the whites are stiff and glossy. Mix the cornflour and vinegar in a cup until smooth, then stir into the pavlova mixture.

2 Line a baking sheet with baking parchment and draw a 20 x 30cm (8 x 12in) rectangle on it (two rectangles side by side for 12). Spread the pavlova mixture out into the rectangle(s) with a knife, then create a well in the middle by building up the sides.

3 Slide the baking sheet into the oven, immediately reduce the temperature to 150°C (130°C fan/300°F/Gas 2), and bake for 1 hour. Turn the oven off and leave the pavlova in the oven for a further hour to dry out.

4 To make the topping, put the pears, lemon juice, and sugar into a small pan and barely cover with water from the tap. Simmer gently over a low heat for 10 minutes or until the pears are just tender. Leave in the liquid until needed, then drain, reserve a few for decoration, and stir the rest into the whipped cream with the ginger.

5 Arrange the pavlova on a serving plate, spoon the cream into the well, and decorate with the reserved pears. Cut the pomegranate(s) in half, pick out the seeds, and sprinkle over the top. Serve at room temperature.

PREPARE AHEAD AND FREEZE
The pavlova can be made up to the end of step 3 up to 1 month ahead. Wrap in cling film and then foil and keep in a cool place. The pears can be poached up to 8 hours ahead. The pavlova can be assembled up to 4 hours ahead. Freeze the pavlova without the topping for up to 6 months.

IN THE AGA
Bake the pavlova in the simmering oven for 2–2½ hours, then sit it by the side of the Aga until cold.

You don't get successful pavlovas if you use more than six egg whites at one time, which is why we make them in two batches for this party pyramid. It is the most spectacular dessert you'll ever make.

Party pavlova pyramid

Serves 35–40

2 x 6 egg whites
2 x 350g (12oz) caster sugar
2 x 1 tsp white wine vinegar
2 x 1 tsp cornflour

For the filling
1.7 litres (3 pints) double cream
500g tub Greek yogurt
900g (2lb) strawberries, hulled

750g (1lb 10oz) raspberries
450g (1lb) blueberries
a few mint leaves, to decorate, optional

1 Preheat the oven to 160°C (140°C fan/325°F/Gas 3). Make a first batch of pavlova by putting six egg whites into a mixing bowl and whisking with an electric whisk until they look like clouds. Gradually add the sugar a little at a time, whisking on maximum speed until they are stiff and glossy. Mix the vinegar and cornflour in a cup until smooth, then stir into the bowl.

2 Line a baking sheet with baking parchment and spread the pavlova mixture out – it should be about 30cm (12in) in diameter and about 5cm (2in) thick. This will be the base for the pyramid.

3 Slide into the oven, then immediately reduce the temperature to 150°C (130°C fan/300°F/Gas 2) and bake for 1 hour. Turn the oven off and leave the pavlova inside for an hour or overnight to dry.

4 Prepare a second batch of pavlova mixture in the same way. Use to make one pavlova measuring 25cm (10in) in diameter, another measuring 20cm (8in) in diameter, and a third that is 12cm (5in) in diameter. The smallest one can be fairly thin and should fit on a baking sheet with the 20cm (8in) pavlova.

5 Cook in the same way: put the 25cm (10in) pavlova in the oven and bake for 15 minutes, then pop the two smaller pavlovas in as well and bake for a further 45 minutes. Switch off the oven and leave to dry out for an hour or overnight.

6 To assemble, whip the cream until just stiff and mix with the yogurt. Place the largest pavlova on a foil-covered board or tray (it needs to be sturdy), then cover with whipped cream and half the fruit. Make sure the fruit can be seen around the edge, so the pyramid will look attractive.

7 Place the next-largest pavlova on top and cover with cream and fruit. Continue in the same way with the other pavlovas. Finish with the last of the cream and a pretty arrangement of fruit and mint leaves on top, if using. To serve, cut in wedges, starting from the top.

Great for a crowd... To make a larger pyramid, add another meringue layer as opposed to making larger meringues.

PREPARE AHEAD AND FREEZE
The pavlovas can be made up to 1 month ahead and stored (see page 268). Freeze for up to 6 months. The pyramid can be assembled up to 4 hours ahead. This is best done in situ, so you don't need to move it.

IN THE AGA
Bake the largest pavlova in the simmering oven for 2½ hours, then sit it by the side of the Aga until cold. Bake the 25cm (10in) pavlova for 1 hour, add the two smaller pavlovas, and bake for a further hour. Sit them by the Aga until cold.

Party pavlova pyramid (see overleaf) ●●●>

Meringue roulade is such a classic pudding. As a twist, we've added chopped roasted hazelnuts to give a lovely nutty flavour that goes sublimely well with raspberries and cream.

Hazelnut meringue roulade with raspberries

Makes a 33cm (13in) roulade (serves 8–10)

Special equipment 23 x 33cm (9 x 13in) Swiss roll tin, greased and lined with baking parchment

4 egg whites
225g (8oz) caster sugar

50g (1¾oz) roasted hazelnuts, chopped
300ml (10fl oz) double cream, whipped
200g (7oz) fresh raspberries

1 Preheat the oven to 200°C (180°C fan/400°F/Gas 6). Meanwhile, put the egg whites into a large clean bowl and whisk with an electric whisk on full speed until very stiff. With the whisk still on full speed, gradually add the sugar a teaspoon at a time, whisking well between each addition. The meringue is ready when it is glossy and very, very stiff.

2 Spread the mixture into the prepared tin and sprinkle with the hazelnuts. Bake for 8 minutes or until very golden.

3 Remove the meringue from the oven and turn hazelnut side down on to a sheet of non-stick baking parchment. Remove the paper from the base of the meringue and allow to cool for 10 minutes.

4 Spread the whipped cream over the meringue and scatter over the raspberries. Using the parchment to help you, roll the meringue up fairly tightly from one of the long ends to form a roulade. Wrap in non-stick baking parchment and chill well before serving.

5 To serve, unwrap and cut into slices.

Great for a crowd... Prepare individual roulades rather than multiplying the quantities and making one big one. Bake one at a time. The roulades freeze well, remember.

PREPARE AHEAD AND FREEZE
The roulade can be made up to 12 hours ahead. Freeze without the raspberries for up to 2 months. Serve with the raspberries on the side.

IN THE AGA
Bake on the grid shelf on the floor of the roasting oven, with the cold sheet on the second set of runners, for 12–15 minutes.

Eton mess is a favourite pudding of meringues, cream, and fruit. We love the combination of lime and mango in our version. Don't crush the meringues too much – the pieces should be the size of grapes.

Mango Eton mess

Serves 6

1 large ripe mango
300ml (10fl oz) double cream
25g (scant 1oz) icing sugar

finely grated zest and juice
  of 1 lime
100g (3½oz) meringues, crushed

Serves 12

2 large ripe mangoes
600ml (1 pint) double cream
50g (1¾oz) icing sugar

finely grated zest and juice
  of 2 limes
200g (7oz) meringues, crushed

1 Cut the mango(es) in half, then remove the flesh (see right). Put half the cubes into a processor and whiz to a smooth purée. Put the other half to one side.

2 Whip the cream until it just holds its shape. Carefully fold in the mango purée, the reserved mango cubes, icing sugar, lime zest, lime juice, and meringues.

3 Spoon into pretty wine glasses or tumblers or into one large glass bowl and serve chilled.

PREPARE AHEAD
The cream can be whipped and folded with all the ingredients except the meringues up to 12 hours ahead. Fold in the meringues a maximum of 6 hours ahead. Not suitable for freezing.

PREPARING A MANGO

STEP 1 Sit the mango on its side, then slice it in half at either side of the large flat stone in the centre.

STEP 2 Cut the flesh into cubes, but don't cut through the skin. Press the skin so the cubes burst upwards.

These creamy desserts are one of those foolproof puds you'll go back to time and again and all your friends will ask for the recipe.

Lemon and lime possets

Serves 6

600ml (1 pint) double cream
150g (5½oz) caster sugar
finely grated zest and juice
  of 2 lemons

finely grated zest and juice
  of 2 limes
lime zest, sprigs of mint, or
  borage flowers, to decorate

Serves 12

1.2 litres (2 pints) double cream
300g (11oz) caster sugar
finely grated zest and juice
  of 4 lemons

finely grated zest and juice
  of 4 limes
lime zest, sprigs of mint, or
  borage flowers, to decorate

1 Put the cream, sugar, lemon zest, and lime zest into a wide-based saucepan.

2 Heat gently over a low heat, stirring until the sugar has dissolved and the cream is just under scalding point (just hot enough to touch).

3 Remove from the heat and stir in the lemon juice and lime juice.

4 Pour into small coffee cups or shot glasses and leave to set in the fridge for at least 6 hours.

5 Serve chilled, decorated with lime zest, sprigs of mint, or borage flowers.

PREPARE AHEAD
The possets can be made up to the end of step 4 up to 2 days ahead. Not suitable for freezing.

This looks stunning and makes the most of all the lovely summer fruits. It's a top favourite of Lucy's.

Summer berry tart

Makes a 28cm (11in) tart (serves 8–10)

Special equipment 28cm (11in) loose-bottomed fluted tart tin

225g (8oz) plain flour, plus a little extra to dust
100g (3½oz) cold butter, cubed
25g (scant 1oz) icing sugar
1 egg
2 tbsp water

For the crème pâtissière

3 eggs
75g (2½oz) caster sugar
1 tsp vanilla extract
50g (1¾oz) plain flour
400ml (14fl oz) milk

For the topping

400g (14oz) strawberries, hulled and quartered
225g (8oz) raspberries
225g (8oz) blueberries
6–8 tbsp redcurrant jelly
1 tbsp water

1 Preheat the oven to 200°C (180°C fan/400°F/Gas 6). Put the flour, butter, and icing sugar into a processer and whiz until the mixture resembles breadcrumbs. Add the egg and water and whiz again until it forms a smooth dough. Lightly dust a work surface with flour and knead the dough for a few minutes or until it forms a smooth ball. Roll it out and use to line the tart tin (see page 243). Chill while you make the crème pâtissière.

2 Put the eggs, sugar, vanilla extract, and flour into a mixing bowl and mix with a wooden spoon until smooth. Add 2 tablespoons of the milk and stir again. Heat the remaining milk until just below boiling, then pour into the mixing bowl and whisk until smooth. Return to the pan and gently heat, whisking until thick and nearly simmering, but don't let it boil. Set aside to cool.

3 Bake the pastry case blind for 20 minutes, then remove the beans and paper (see right). Lower the oven temperature to 160°C (140°C fan/325°F/Gas 3) and return the tart case to the oven for 10 minutes to dry out. Set aside to cool.

4 Pour the crème pâtissière into the tart case and arrange the fruit in circles on top – strawberries on the outside, then a circle of raspberries, and the blueberries in the centre.

5 Heat the redcurrant jelly and water together in a pan over a gentle heat, whisking until smooth. Brush this glaze over the fruit, then place the tart in the fridge and serve chilled.

PREPARE AHEAD

The pastry case can be baked up to 2 days ahead. The crème pâtissière can be made up to 1 day ahead. The tart can be assembled up to 8 hours ahead. Not suitable for freezing.

IN THE AGA

Skip step 3. Fill the uncooked pastry case and bake on the grid shelf on the floor of the roasting oven, with the cold sheet on the second set of runners, for 25 minutes, then transfer to the simmering oven for 15 minutes.

BAKING BLIND

STEP 1 Cut a baking parchment circle just larger than the tin. Fold into a triangle and snip the edge.

STEP 2 Line the pastry case with the baking parchment, pushing it into the rim. Fill with dried beans.

STEP 3 After 20 minutes' baking, the case is partially cooked and won't go soggy when the filling is added.

Tea for a crowd

Plates of neatly cut sandwiches, tiers of home-made biscuits and cakes – it's everyone's idea of a traditional English tea. In this chapter you'll find all the recipes you need to make it.

Tea for a crowd

Birthdays, christenings, and funerals, friends dropping by at the weekend, a visit from granny – it's at times like these that a reviving cup of tea and a selection of sweet and savoury treats go down well. As it is likely to be a special occasion, it seems only fitting to pull out all the stops and go with tradition. And if you don't have a reason for inviting people round for tea, invent one! We often do – as a way of catching up with family, friends, and neighbours.

Small is best

At teatime, forget those huge slices of cake and oversized biscuits you so often see in tea shops and fast-food outlets. Keep the food small, so it's easier for guests to eat, particularly if they'll be standing up.

● When making sandwiches, remove the crusts, then cut across into neat squares, triangles, or fingers.

● Cut large cakes into manageable wedges and traybakes into smallish squares or slices.

● Offer a selection of individual items such as cupcakes and muffins, biscuits and scones – these are simple to eat as you stand and chat.

"If you don't have a reason for inviting people round for tea, invent one! We often do – as a way of catching up with family, friends, and neighbours."

For freshness

● Bake scones on the day. If you do have to prepare them in advance, freeze them and then gently reheat in a low oven once defrosted. At a buffet, serve them with bowls of jam and cream (there's no need for butter) for guests to help themselves. Otherwise top them before you serve them.

● Although you can ice cakes ahead, the icing will be at its shiniest if you do it on the day itself. Serve forks with iced cakes as they can be messy to eat with your hands.

● Depending on the filling you're using, most sandwiches can be prepared up to a day ahead. Kept correctly, they will taste as fresh as the moment you made them. Other sandwiches, such as cucumber and tomato, are best made no more than 10 hours ahead. For more on this, turn to page 283.

Make it an occasion

● Use cups and saucers, never mugs (unless you're outside – at a sporting event, say – or having something from the back of the car).

● Provide napkins – tea is as much of a meal as any other.

● Arrange cakes, scones, and biscuits on tiered cakestands. They look so pretty presented like that. You'll find lots of designs in the shops and they won't cost the earth if you buy them from charity shops.

● To give cakes a final flourish, decorate them with a sprinkling of icing sugar. You can do it before or after you've arranged them on the plates or stands – it doesn't much matter. Fresh flowers and crystallized fresh flowers look great as decorations, too.

Quantities

● For a tea with cakes, serve one round of sandwiches (two slices of bread) per person.

● Most people will drink a couple of cups of tea. For 20 cups, you'll need about 15 teabags (although it depends of course on how strong you make it) and 600ml (1 pint) milk.

WHICH TEAS TO SERVE *We always make a pot of builders' tea and one of Earl Grey. We also provide a pot of boiling water, a selection of fancy herbal teas, and a jar of instant coffee. Sprigs of fresh mint or lemon balm make a refreshing cuppa in summer.*

How to lay a table for a buffet tea

Place the table against a wall, with just enough room behind it for someone to stand and pour guests a cup of tea. Alternatively, you can let people serve themselves. Depending on the layout of your room, display the food from right to left (as here) or from left to right, and in the order guests will eat it, so sandwiches should come before cakes, traybakes, and scones. This will make it quicker. If you've invited over 30 people and have enough room, lay two buffet tables with the same food on each.

Individual cakes
Arrange individual cakes such as muffins and cupcakes on a tiered cakestand.

Large traybakes or cakes
Cut large cakes or traybakes into small wedges or slices and arrange on a flat platter.

Scones or biscuits
Arrange scones or biscuits on a serving platter.

Jam
Serve the jam for scones in a bowl with a spoon.

Napkins
Place a pile of napkins at the end of the table.

Cream
Serve the cream for scones in a bowl with a teaspoon.

Plates
Stand a pile of tea plates next to the sandwiches.

Finish <·········

<·········

Pots of tea
Stand the teapots on a tray to catch any drips. If you're serving more than one kind of tea, label them so guests know what's what.

Table decoration
Place the table decoration in a prominent position, but well out of guests' way.

Sugar
Put the sugar in a bowl with a teaspoon.

Cups
The first thing your guests will want is a cup of tea, so place cups and saucers at the start.

Sandwiches
Arrange the sandwiches on serving platters or plates and present them before the biscuits and cakes.

Lemon
Put lemon slices in a bowl with a small fork.

Milk
Use a large jug so you don't have to keep refilling it.

Teaspoons
Place teaspoons handle up in a jug or mug. Provide cake forks as well for iced cakes.

At teatime, sandwiches should be small rather than filling. Some fillings can be added up to 10 hours ahead. Others can be added up to one day ahead with no compromise on freshness or taste.

Sandwiches

Makes 24 (serves 6)

soft butter
12 slices bread from a thin-cut or
    medium-cut white or brown loaf
the filling(s) of your choice (see below)
salt and freshly ground black pepper

Fillings you can add 1 day ahead

Rare roast beef with horseradish sauce
    and rocket
Egg mayonnaise with lots of mustard cress
Smoked salmon and cream cheese
Hummus, olive, and grated carrot
Ham and English mustard
Cream cheese, mango chutney,
    and watercress
Gravadlax and mustard mayonnaise
    (see page 81)
Mature Cheddar, pickle, and watercress
Goat's cheese, rocket, and sun-dried
    tomato paste
Thin strips of pan-fried steak and mustard
Crispy bacon with egg mayonnaise

Fillings to add on the day

Prawns with lemon mayonnaise
Feta cheese, sun-dried tomato paste,
    and cucumber
Cucumber and black pepper
Sardine, mayonnaise, and lemon
Fresh salmon and cucumber
Avocado and bacon
Crab and avocado with lime mayonnaise
Pastrami and sweet dill pickle with cream
    cheese and horseradish sauce
Tomato, basil, and mozzarella
Smoked mackerel, tomato, and aïoli

1 Butter the bread on one side, top half the slices with the filling(s) of your choice, and sandwich together. Leave the crusts on.

2 Arrange the sandwiches in piles of four on a large tray (check first that it will fit in your fridge). Cover with a layer of damp kitchen paper, then cover tightly with cling film, and place the tray in the fridge.

3 Two hours before serving, slice off the crusts and cut the sandwiches into fingers or quarters – either triangles or squares. Cover with cling film and keep at room temperature until ready to serve. They will taste as fresh as the moment you made them.

CUCUMBER AND TOMATOES
Fillings containing cucumber or tomato should only ever be added on the day. To stop the bread going soggy, you also need to remove the seeds. Slice the cucumber in half lengthways and scoop out the seeds with a teaspoon. To deseed tomatoes, see page 166.

Cut into squares, traybakes are great at large gatherings.
This unusual recipe has a wonderful zesty taste.

Lime marmalade traybake

Cuts into 12 squares

Special equipment 23 x 30cm (9 x 12in) traybake tin, lined with foil and greased

225g (8oz) butter, at room temperature
225g (8oz) caster sugar
300g (11oz) self-raising flour
4 eggs
2 tsp baking powder
finely grated zest of 1 lime, plus
    2 tbsp lime juice
2 tbsp lime marmalade

For the icing

350g (12oz) icing sugar
100g (3½oz) full-fat cream cheese
50g (1¾oz) butter, at room temperature
2 tbsp lime marmalade
juice and finely grated zest of 1 small lime

1 Preheat the oven to 180°C (160°C fan/350°F/Gas 4). Put all the ingredients for the cake into a mixing bowl and beat by hand or with an electric whisk until combined and smooth.

2 Spoon into the traybake tin and level the top.

3 Bake for 30–35 minutes or until risen and golden. Set aside to cool completely.

4 To make the icing, sift the icing sugar into a mixing bowl, add all the other ingredients, and beat with a wooden spoon or an electric whisk until well combined and smooth.

5 Spread the icing over the cake, making a pretty pattern on it with a palette knife. Cut into 12 squares and serve.

PREPARE AHEAD AND FREEZE
The cake can be made up to 1 day ahead and iced on the day. Freeze without the icing for up to 3 months.

IN THE AGA
Bake on the grid shelf on the floor of the roasting oven, with the cold sheet on the second set of runners, for 30 minutes.

A lemon traybake is always a big hit and we think this variation with orange is particularly delicious. It's also very easy to make.

Iced orange and lemon traybake

Cuts into 12 squares

Special equipment 23 x 30cm (9 x 12in) traybake tin, lined with foil and greased

225g (8oz) butter, at room temperature
225g (8oz) caster sugar
300g (11oz) self-raising flour
2 tsp baking powder
4 eggs
4 tbsp milk
grated zest of ½ lemon
grated zest of ½ small orange

For the icing

225g (8oz) icing sugar
1 tbsp lemon juice
2 tbsp orange juice
grated zest of ½ lemon
grated zest of ½ small orange

1 Preheat the oven to 180°C (160°C fan/350°F/Gas 4). Put the butter, sugar, flour, baking powder, eggs, and milk into a bowl and mix with a wooden spoon or electric hand whisk until smooth. Stir in the lemon zest and orange zest and pour into the traybake tin. Level the top.

2 Bake for 30 minutes or until shrinking away from the sides of the tin and springy to the touch. Leave to cool in the tin.

3 To make the icing, sift the icing sugar into a bowl, mix in the lemon juice and orange juice, and beat until smooth. Spread evenly over the cold cake, then sprinkle with the lemon zest and orange zest and leave to set. To serve, cut into 12 squares.

PREPARE AHEAD AND FREEZE
The traybake can be made and iced up to 1 day ahead. Freeze without the icing for up to 3 months.

IN THE AGA
Bake on the grid shelf on the floor of the roasting oven, with the cold sheet on the second set of runners, for 30 minutes or until golden brown.

These are as delicious with a cup of coffee as they are at teatime. If you're preparing them ahead, stop them going soggy by storing them in a tin with pieces of kitchen paper between the layers.

Almond biscuits

Makes 30–35

Special equipment 5cm (2in) fluted scone cutter

100g (3½oz) butter, at room temperature
75g (2½oz) caster sugar
150g (5½oz) plain flour, plus
  a little extra to dust
75g (2½oz) ground almonds
½ tsp almond extract
50g (1¾oz) flaked almonds

1 Put the butter and sugar into a mixing bowl and whisk with an electric whisk until light and fluffy. Add the flour, ground almonds, and almond extract and whisk again until smooth.

2 Lightly dust a work surface with flour and knead the dough for a few minutes until smooth. Wrap in cling film and chill for 30 minutes.

3 Preheat the oven to 180°C (160°C fan/325°F/Gas 4). Grease two baking sheets or line with baking parchment. Lightly flour the work surface again and roll the dough out until it is 5mm (¼in) thick. Using a 5cm (2in) fluted scone cutter, cut out 30–35 rounds.

4 Transfer to the baking sheets with a palette knife. Sprinkle a few flaked almonds on top of each biscuit and press them down gently so they stick to the dough.

5 Bake for 10–12 minutes (checking after 8 minutes) or until lightly golden. Leave to cool slightly, then transfer to a wire rack to cool completely.

PREPARE AHEAD AND FREEZE
The biscuits can be made up to 4 days ahead. Keep, layered with kitchen paper, in a biscuit tin. Freeze for up to 3 months.

IN THE AGA
Bake on the grid shelf on the floor of the roasting oven, with the cold sheet on the second set of runners, for 10 minutes.

Everyone loves cookies. And no one will be able to resist this deliciously gooey combination of pecan nuts and chocolate. The cookies keep well in a tin for a couple of days.

Pecan and chocolate chip cookies

Makes 24

100g (3½oz) butter, at room temperature
50g (1¾oz) caster sugar
150g (5½oz) self-raising flour, plus a little extra to dust
½ tsp vanilla extract
50g (1¾oz) milk chocolate chips
50g (1¾oz) pecan nuts, chopped

1 Preheat the oven to 180°C (160°C fan/350°F/Gas 4). Put the butter and sugar into a bowl and mix together with a wooden spoon until light and fluffy. Stir in the flour, then add the vanilla extract, chocolate chips, and pecans and mix to a soft dough.

2 Knead the dough lightly on a floured work surface, then divide into 24 balls. Flatten the balls with the palm of your hand and arrange on two baking sheets lined with baking parchment. Space them out so they have room to spread.

3 Bake for 20–25 minutes or until lightly golden. Transfer to a wire rack to cool.

PREPARE AHEAD AND FREEZE
The cookies can be made up to 2 days ahead and kept in a sealed container. Freeze the raw mixture or the cooked cookies for up to 2 months.

IN THE AGA
Bake on the grid shelf on the floor of the roasting oven, with the cold sheet on the second set of runners, for 15 minutes.

Cupcakes are the cake of the moment, with some shops specializing in just them. These are made in muffin tins, which are fairly large, but make them in bun tins if you wish – you should get 18 fairy cakes.

Coffee and walnut cupcakes

Makes 12

Special equipment 12-hole muffin tin lined with 12 paper muffin cases

1 tbsp instant coffee granules
1 tbsp boiling water
115g (4oz) butter, softened
140g (5oz) self-raising flour
140g (5oz) caster sugar
2 tbsp milk
2 large eggs
25g (scant 1oz) walnuts, chopped

For the coffee icing

2 tsp instant coffee granules
2 tsp boiling water
100g (3½oz) butter, at room temperature
225g (8oz) icing sugar
12 walnut halves, to decorate

SOFTENING BUTTER

To make sure the butter is soft enough to work with, cut it into small cubes and pop into a bowl of lukewarm water. After 10 minutes or so, squeeze one of the cubes – it should be lovely and soft. You can then drain them and use them.

1 Preheat the oven to 180°C (160°C fan/350°F/Gas 4). Put the coffee granules and water into a mixing bowl and stir until smooth. Add the butter, flour, sugar, milk, and eggs and mix with an electric whisk until smooth. Stir in the walnuts, then spoon into the muffin cases.

2 Bake in the centre of the oven for 20–25 minutes or until risen and golden brown. Transfer to a wire rack until stone cold.

3 To make the icing, put the coffee granules and boiling water into a bowl and stir until smooth. Add the butter, sift in the icing sugar, and stir until smooth and free of streaks.

4 Spoon on to the cupcakes, then decorate each one with a walnut half.

PREPARE AHEAD AND FREEZE

The cupcakes can be made and iced up to 1 day ahead. Freeze without the icing for up to 1 month.

IN THE AGA

Bake on the grid shelf on the floor of the roasting oven, with the cold sheet on the second set of runners, for 15–20 minutes.

Arranged on a tiered cakestand, a dozen cupcakes (see page 288) make a spectacular centrepiece for any tea party. We like to bake them in silver or floral muffin cases. Serve one per person.

Cupcake tier

Serves 12

For the glacé icing

juice of 1 lemon
225g (8oz) icing sugar

For the chocolate curls

bar of white chocolate, at room
    temperature
bar of plain chocolate, at room
    temperature

DECORATING CUPCAKES

When it comes to decorating cupcakes, let your imagination run riot. But keep the tier looking elegant and classy – not chaotic. Crystallized flowers look pretty, as do silver balls or silver hearts. Or decorate the edges of the cakestand with fresh flowers. The beauty of the cupcake tier is that you can match the decorations to suit the occasion. For a child's birthday party, for instance, you could decorate one of the cupcakes with a candle. Hundreds & Thousands or tiny coloured sweets such as Jelly Beans and Smarties also work well.

1 Make a dozen cupcakes, following the recipe on page 288. You won't need the coffee icing and walnuts.

2 To make the glacé icing, warm the lemon juice in a pan. Put the icing sugar into a mixing bowl and gradually add enough lemon juice to make a smooth glossy icing. Spoon the icing on to the cupcakes and leave to set.

3 Meanwhile, shave curls from the chocolate bars with a vegetable peeler.

4 Once the icing has set, decorate the cupcakes with a mixture of white chocolate curls and plain chocolate curls.

PREPARE AHEAD AND FREEZE

The cupcakes can be iced up to 1 day ahead.
Freeze without the icing for up to 1 month.

Fairy cakes are always so popular. These are a basic vanilla sponge mix with lemon icing. Decorate them with creative flair. We like to use Jelly Babies, Jelly Tots, and Maltesers.

Fairy cakes

Makes 24

Special equipment 2 x 12-hole bun tins, greased or lined with paper cases

150g (5½oz) butter, softened
  (see page 288)
150g (5½oz) caster sugar
150g (5½oz) self-raising flour
1½ tsp baking powder
1½ tsp vanilla extract
3 eggs

For the icing

150g (5½oz) icing sugar
about 3 bsp lemon juice

To decorate

sweets of your choice

1 Preheat the oven to 180°C (160°C fan/350°F/Gas 4). Put all the ingredients for the cakes into a large mixing bowl and beat with an electric whisk until smooth. Spoon evenly into the tins.

2 Bake for 12–15 minutes or until risen and pale golden brown. Set aside to cool, then remove the cakes from the tins.

3 To make the icing, sift the icing sugar into a bowl and add enough lemon juice to make a fairly stiff paste. Spoon a circle of the icing on the top of each cake. While the icing is still soft, decorate with the sweets of your choice.

PREPARE AHEAD AND FREEZE
The cakes can be made and iced up to 1 day ahead. Freeze for up to 2 months.

IN THE AGA
Bake on the grid shelf on the floor of the roasting oven for 10–12 minutes or until well risen and golden. If the cakes are getting too brown, slide the cold sheet on to the second set of runners.

VARIATIONS

Chocolate chip fairy cakes
Add 25g (scant 1oz) dark chocolate chips to the basic sponge mix.

Lemon party cakes
Add the grated zest of 1 lemon to the basic sponge mix.

Orange fairy cakes
Add the grated zest of 1 orange to the basic sponge mix. For the icing, use orange juice or orange blossom water instead of lemon juice.

Rosewater fairy cakes
For the icing, use 2 tbsp rosewater and 1 tbsp water instead of the lemon juice.

This lovely cake has no flour – just cocoa powder – so it is as light as a feather. For children, replace the Cointreau with orange juice. Bake it at Easter and decorate with mini eggs.

Chocolate and orange mousse cake

Serves 8

Special equipment *23cm (9in) springform tin, greased and base-lined*

200g (7oz) bar orange milk chocolate
50g (1¾oz) butter
6 eggs, separated
75g (2½oz) caster sugar
2–3 tbsp Cointreau
2 level tbsp cocoa powder

For the topping

100g (3½oz) orange milk chocolate, coarsely grated
1–2 tbsp Cointreau
200ml (7fl oz) double cream, lightly whipped
cocoa powder, to dust

1 Preheat the oven to 180°C (160°C fan/350°F/Gas 4). Meanwhile, break the chocolate into pieces and place in a small heatproof bowl with the butter. Sit the bowl over a pan of hot water and stir until the chocolate and butter have melted. Set aside to cool slightly.

2 Whisk the egg whites with an electric whisk until stiff. Put the egg yolks and sugar into a separate bowl and whisk until light and creamy.

3 Pour the melted chocolate into the egg-yolk mixture, add the Cointreau, and gently fold together, taking care not to knock out any of the air. Add the egg whites and gently fold to combine. Sift in the cocoa powder and fold until combined. Spoon evenly into the tin.

4 Bake for 40 minutes or until risen, shrinking away from the sides of the tin, and just firm to the touch in the centre. Leave to cool, then remove from the tin.

5 For the topping, stir half the chocolate and the Cointreau into the cream. Spread over the top of the cake and sprinkle with the remaining chocolate. Sift the cocoa powder on top.

BASE-LINING THE TIN

Put baking parchment over the base of the tin, clip the ring in place, and trim the parchment with scissors.

PREPARE AHEAD
The cake can be made up to the end of step 4 up to 1 day ahead. Add the topping on the day of serving. Freeze without the topping for up to 2 months.

IN THE AGA
Bake the cake in two 23cm (9in) sandwich tins on the grid shelf on the floor of the roasting oven, with the cold sheet on the second set of runners, for 25 minutes. Use just under half the topping to sandwich the cakes together.

Seeded bars are extremely popular in the shops. They are also healthier than a slice of cake, so why not make your own. When we were testing these, the whole lot went in one go!

Figgy seeded bites

Makes 12 bars or 24 bites

Special equipment 18cm (7in) square shallow tin, lined with baking parchment and greased

75g (2½oz) butter
50g (1¾oz) golden syrup
100g (3½oz) caster sugar
175g (6oz) porridge oats
25g (scant 1oz) sunflower seeds
25g (scant 1oz) pumpkin seeds
25g (scant 1oz) desiccated coconut
100g (3½oz) dried figs, snipped
  into tiny pieces
50g (1¾oz) dried apricots, snipped
  into tiny pieces

1 Preheat the oven to 180°C (160°C fan/350°F/Gas 4). Heat the butter, syrup, and sugar in a pan over a gentle heat, stirring until melted and dissolved.

2 Put the remaining ingredients into a large mixing bowl, add the melted butter mixture, and stir well. Pour into the tin and level the top.

3 Bake for 30–35 minutes or until lightly golden and firm in the middle. Leave to cool slightly, then cut into 12 rectangles or 24 squares. Leave in the tin to harden, then transfer to a wire rack to cool completely.

PREPARE AHEAD
The bites can be made up to 3 days ahead and kept in a cool place. Not suitable for freezing.

IN THE AGA
Bake on the grid shelf on the floor of the roasting oven, with the cold sheet on the second set of runners, for 15–20 minutes.

These are perfect for a children's tea party. For a slightly more sophisticated touch, replace the white chocolate chips with dark chocolate chips.

White chocolate and strawberry muffins

Makes 12

Special equipment *Deep 12-hole muffin tin lined with paper muffin cases*

300g (11oz) self-raising flour
1 tsp baking powder
175g (6oz) caster sugar
2 eggs
225ml (7½fl oz) milk
100g (3½oz) butter, melted
2 tsp vanilla extract
100g (3½oz) white chocolate chips
12 tsp strawberry jam
icing sugar, to dust

1 Preheat the oven to 200°C (180°C fan/400°F/Gas 6). Put all the ingredients except the chocolate chips and jam into a large bowl and whisk with an electric whisk until smooth. Stir in the chocolate chips.

2 Divide half the mixture evenly between the cases, spoon 1 teaspoon of jam on top of each one, then spoon the remaining mixture on top.

3 Bake for 25–30 minutes or until well risen and lightly golden brown.

4 Dust with a little icing sugar and serve warm or cold.

PREPARE AHEAD AND FREEZE
The muffins can be made up to 2 days ahead. Freeze for up to 1 month.

IN THE AGA
Bake on the grid shelf on the floor of the roasting oven, with the cold sheet on the second set of runners, for 20–25 minutes.

White chocolate and strawberry muffins (see overleaf) ●●>

Mincemeat buns are traditional at Christmas, but there's no reason why you shouldn't make them at any time of year. Use vegetarian mincemeat if you don't eat meat.

Mincemeat buns

Makes 24

Special equipment 2 x 12-hole bun tins, lined with paper cases

150g (5½oz) butter, softened (see page 288)
150g (5½oz) caster sugar
225g (8oz) self-raising flour
2 eggs
2 tbsp milk
100g (3½oz) currants
100g (3½oz) mincemeat
50g (1¾oz) flaked almonds

1 Preheat the oven to 180°C (160°C fan/350°F/Gas 4). Put all the ingredients except the almonds into a bowl and beat well with a wooden spoon to combine.

2 Spoon the mixture into the paper cases, level the tops, and make sure there are no drips over the sides of the cases. Sprinkle with the almonds.

3 Bake for 15 minutes or until well risen and lightly golden.

4 Leave the buns in the tins for a few minutes, then transfer them to a cooling rack and leave to cool completely.

PREPARE AHEAD AND FREEZE
The buns can be made up to 1 day ahead and kept in the fridge. Freeze for up to 2 months.

IN THE AGA
Bake on the grid shelf on the floor of the roasting oven, with the cold sheet on the second set of runners, for 15 minutes or until golden.

Small loaf cakes are always lovely to make and are quicker to bake than large ones. This recipes makes two. If you don't need both straightaway, you can eat one and freeze the other.

Apricot and cherry loaf cakes

Makes 2

Special equipment 2 x 450g (1lb) loaf tins, greased and the bases and sides lined with a long strip of baking parchment

175g (6oz) self-raising flour

115g (4oz) butter, softened (see page 288)

115g (4oz) caster sugar

3 large eggs, beaten

150g (5½oz) ready-to-eat apricots, snipped into small pieces

50g (1½oz) raisins

50g (1½oz) glacé cherries, snipped into small pieces

1 Preheat the oven to 180°C (160°C fan/350°F/Gas 4). Put the flour, butter, sugar, and eggs into a mixing bowl and whisk with an electric whisk until combined. Stir in the dried fruit and cherries, then spoon into the tins and level the tops.

2 Bake for 45–50 minutes or until golden brown and well risen. Transfer to a wire rack to cool completely.

PREPARE AHEAD AND FREEZE

The cakes can be baked up to 2 days ahead, although they are best made and eaten on the same day. Freeze for up to 3 months.

IN THE AGA

Sit the loaf tins in a roasting tin (the sides of it will prevent the cake burning) and bake on the lowest set of runners, with the cold sheet on the second set of runners, for 45 minutes.

Passing through the village of Ashburton, in Devon, Mary stopped at a tea shop and had a piece of wonderful carrot cake. The owner kindly gave Mary the recipe and it's loved by one and all.

Ashburton carrot cake

Makes a 23cm (9in) cake (serves 8)

Special equipment 2 x 23cm (9in) sandwich tins, greased and lined with a disc of baking parchment

200g (7oz) self-raising flour
300g (11oz) granulated sugar
1 tsp baking powder
1½ tsp ground cinnamon
175ml (6fl oz) sunflower oil
2 eggs, lightly beaten

1 tsp vanilla extract
100g (3½oz) raw carrots, grated
100g (3½oz) chopped walnuts
60g (2oz) desiccated coconut
220g can pineapple slices, drained, chopped, and dried thoroughly

For the icing
200g (7oz) full-fat cream cheese
100g (3½oz) butter, softened (see page 288)
200g (7oz) icing sugar
1 tsp vanilla extract

1 Preheat the oven to 180°C (160°C fan/350°F/Gas 4). Put the flour into a large mixing bowl, add the sugar, baking powder, and cinnamon and stir together.

2 Add the oil, eggs, and vanilla extract and beat well with a wooden spoon or spatula. Fold in the carrots, walnuts, coconut, and pineapple and beat until smooth.

3 Spoon evenly into the sandwich tins and bake for 45–50 minutes or until well risen and golden brown. To check that the cakes are cooked in the middle, insert a skewer into the centre – if it comes out clean, they are done. Transfer to a wire rack and leave to cool.

4 To make the icing, put the cream cheese and butter into a bowl, sift in the icing sugar, add the vanilla extract, and whisk with an electric whisk until smooth.

5 Remove the cakes from the tins and peel off the baking parchment. Turn one cake upside down on to a serving plate and spread with half the icing. Sit the other cake on top and spread the remaining icing over the top.

PREPARE AHEAD AND FREEZE
The cake can be made up to 1 day ahead, although it is best made on the day. Freeze without the icing for up to 2 months.

IN THE AGA
Bake on the grid shelf on the floor of the roasting oven, with the cold sheet on the second set of runners, for 30 minutes. Keep an eye on it – you may need to replace the cold sheet halfway through cooking to stop it getting too brown.

BASE-LINING THE TINS

STEP 1 Stand the tin on baking parchment, draw round the base with a pencil, then cut the disc out.

STEP 2 Place the disc of baking parchment in the bottom of the greased sandwich tin.

Scones are so quintessentially English and a traditional part of tea. For success every time, make sure the dough is good and sticky rather than dry. Serve warm with clotted cream and strawberry jam.

Buttery scones

Makes 12

Special equipment 7.5cm (3in) scone cutter

225g (8oz) self-raising flour, plus a little extra to dust
2 tsp baking powder
45g (1½oz) butter, at room temperature
25g (scant 1oz) caster sugar
1 egg
about 150ml (5fl oz) milk

1 Preheat the oven to 200°C (180°C fan/400°F/Gas 6). Put the flour, baking powder, and butter into a processor and whiz until the mixture resembles breadcrumbs. Add the sugar.

2 Break the egg into a measuring jug and beat with a fork, then pour in enough of the milk to make just over 150ml (5fl oz). Beat again to mix.

3 Switch the processor on and gradually pour in the milk and egg mixture, leaving about 1 tablespoon in the jug for glazing. Whiz until combined – the mixture should be slightly sticky. Add a little more milk if it isn't.

4 Transfer the dough to a lightly floured work surface and knead until smooth, then roll it out until it is 1cm (½in) thick. Using a 7.5cm (3in) scone cutter, cut out 12 scones, re-rolling the dough until it is all used up.

5 Arrange on a greased baking sheet and brush the tops with the remaining milk and egg mixture to glaze.

6 Bake for 15–20 minutes or until well risen and golden.

CUTTING THE SCONES OUT
Be careful not to twist the cutter when cutting the scones out or the scones won't rise evenly during baking.

PREPARE AHEAD AND FREEZE
The scones can be made up to 1 day ahead. Freeze for up to 3 months.

IN THE AGA
Bake on the floor of the roasting oven for 15 minutes or until well risen and golden.

Most brownies are dense and dark, but we use milk chocolate so ours are very light in colour and texture, with gooey pieces of melted chocolate. Simply delicious.

Best-ever brownies

Makes 12

Special equipment 23 x 33cm (9 x 13in) traybake tin, lined with baking parchment and well greased

225g (8oz) butter, softened
350g (12oz) milk chocolate
4 eggs
450g (1lb) light muscovado sugar
150ml (5fl oz) milk
225g (8oz) self-raising flour

1 Preheat the oven to 180°C (160°C fan/350°F/Gas 4). Melt the butter and 225g (8oz) of the milk chocolate in a bowl set over a pan of hot water until the mixture is smooth and glossy.

2 Break the eggs into a mixing bowl, add the sugar, milk, and the melted chocolate mixture, and beat with a wooden spoon to combine. Sift in the flour and mix until smooth.

3 Stir in the remaining chocolate, then pour into the tin and bake for 45–50 minutes or until well risen and cooked in the middle. Leave to cool, then cut into 12 squares.

PREPARE AHEAD AND FREEZE

The brownies can be made up to 2 days ahead. Freeze for up to 3 months.

IN THE AGA

Bake on the grid shelf on the floor of the roasting oven, with the cold sheet on the second set of runners, for 45 minutes or until well risen and cooked in the middle.

Menu planners

Winter drinks parties

On a cold winter's day there's nothing lovelier than presenting your guests with a glass of hot mulled wine the moment they arrive. To balance your work load, serve a selection of hot eats with some cold party bites that you can prepare completely in advance. At Christmas or New Year, decorate the platters with holly and sprigs of heather tied together with swatches of tartan ribbon. As a sign that it's time for your guests to go, serve them brownies or cupcakes in pretty, individual truffle cases.

"We love the idea of giving the food for our drinks parties a theme, as with these four party bites that all have a hint of the orient."

A hint of the orient

Allow a total of 8–10 bites per person. Serve the chicken satays first – these are the most impressive. Remember to use platters that aren't heavy to hold.

PARTY BITES

Mini chicken satays (page 36)

Pork meatballs with oriental dipping sauce (page 38)

Duck and hoisin spring rolls (page 41)

Scorching chilli dip with a choice of dippers (page 49)

FOR WHEN IT'S TIME TO GO

Coffee and walnut cupcakes (page 288)

Prepare ahead

Scorching chilli dip 4 days ahead.

Mini chicken satays 2 days ahead.

Pork meatballs 2 days ahead.

Coffee and walnut cupcakes 1 day ahead.

Duck and hoisin spring rolls 8 hours ahead.

New Year's Day

Allow a total of 8–10 bites per person. Bring out the sausage rolls first – these are the showstoppers. Serve mixed platters as the canapés start to disappear.

PARTY BITES

Sausage and apple filo rolls (page 34)

Golden dough balls with cheese and chutney (page 35)

Bacon and water chestnut bites with mango chutney (page 42)

Crostini with slow-roasted tomatoes and herbs (page 51)

FOR WHEN IT'S TIME TO GO

Best-ever brownies (page 303)

Prepare ahead

Best-ever brownies 2 days ahead.
Bacon and water chestnut bites 1 day ahead.
Sausage and apple filo rolls 12 hours ahead.
Golden dough balls 12 hours ahead.
Crostini with slow-roasted tomatoes 6 hours ahead.

Summer drinks parties

Drinks parties are always a big hit in summer when the weather is good and your guests can spill out into the garden or on to a patio, roof terrace, or balcony. Set the scene with pot plants or flowers in season and decorate serving platters with bunches of fresh herbs and edible blooms such as violets, pansies, and nasturtiums. When it's time for your guests to go, bring out some brownies or cupcakes in individual truffle cases.

"Buy in plenty of bags of ice to keep wine, beer, and a variety of non-alcoholic drinks cool. You could even chill them in the bath tub if you have a really huge crowd coming."

Mediterranean

Cold eats are ideal in summer and are great for preparing ahead. Allow a total of 8–10 per person.

PARTY BITES
Beef remoulade rolls (page 45)

Garlicky herb dip with a choice of dippers (page 49)

Crostini with slow-roasted tomatoes and herbs (page 51)

Crostini with Parma ham and peppered cream cheese (page 52)

FOR WHEN IT'S TIME TO GO
Coffee and walnut cupcakes (page 288)

Prepare ahead
Garlicky herb dip 3 days ahead.
Coffee and walnut cupcakes 1 day ahead.
Beef remoulade rolls 8 hours ahead.
Crostini with slow-roasted tomatoes 6 hours ahead.
Crostini with Parma ham 6 hours ahead.

Smart

A sophisticated selection of meat, fish, and vegetarian canapés. Allow 8–10 per person.

PARTY BITES

FOR WHEN IT'S TIME TO GO

Prepare ahead

Best-ever brownies 2 days ahead.
Asparagus filo rolls 12 hours ahead.
Duck and hoisin spring rolls 8 hours ahead.
Smoked salmon on rye 6 hours ahead.
Hummus and feta tartlets 4 hours ahead.

Winter lunch parties

For lunch, two courses – a main dish and pudding – are often enough. But for a special occasion, or if it's cold out there, we like to kick off with a hot starter or some piping hot soup. When serving three courses, we choose a main dish that can look after itself in the oven. A roast is ideal on Sundays and this is one of our favourite times to entertain family and friends.

Warming

A hearty meal of two upmarket pies, plus a rich and flavoursome soup to start with.

STARTER
Honey-glazed parsnip soup (page 66)

MAIN COURSE AND SIDE DISH
Loch Fyne haddock bake (page 136)
Green salad or green vegetable

PUDDING
Lemon meringue pie (page 247)

Prepare ahead
Honey-glazed parsnip soup 2 days ahead.
Lemon meringue pie 1 day ahead.
Haddock bake 8 hours ahead.

*"If you're going to Mary's for lunch on Sunday,
you can expect roast leg of lamb."*

Italian

You can't go wrong with Italian food. It's the food of love and everyone adores it.

STARTER

*Bruschette with Reblochon
and roasted vegetables* (page 73)

MAIN COURSE AND SIDE DISHES

Italian farmhouse chicken (page 161)

*Rice or mashed potatoes
Green vegetable*

PUDDING

Individual tiramisus (page 256)
and/or
Exotic fruit salad (page 265)

Prepare ahead

Italian farmhouse chicken 12 hours ahead.

Individual tiramisus 12 hours ahead.

Fruit salad 12 hours ahead.

Bruschette with Reblochon 3 hours ahead.

Sunday roast

If you're going to Mary's for lunch after church on Sunday, this is what you can expect.

STARTER

*French onion soup with mustard
Gruyère croûtons* (page 64)

MAIN COURSE AND SIDE DISHES

Slow-roast leg of lamb (page 119)

*Roast potatoes with chilli
and thyme* (page 126)

Green vegetable

PUDDING

*Mini apple, apricot, and hazelnut
crumbles* (page 242)
or
Melt-in-the mouth apple pie (page 244)

Prepare ahead

French onion soup 3 days ahead.

Mini crumbles 2 days ahead.

Leg of lamb 1 day ahead.

Roast potatoes 1 day ahead.

Apple pie 1 day ahead.

Summer lunch parties

One of the most popular times of year for having a lunch party is in the summer, and it's not hard to figure out why. From May to September a fabulous range of fresh ingredients comes into season – asparagus, Jersey Royal potatoes, soft fruits, lamb. We can't get enough of them! If three courses seem too much, serve two – a main dish plus pudding.

Cold but smart

No emerging hot and bothered from the kitchen with this menu – you'll be as cool as a cucumber.

STARTER
Crab, avocado, and smoked salmon tians (page 77)

MAIN COURSE AND SIDE DISHES
Cold fillet of beef with mustard sauce (page 196)

Spicy roast squash and feta salad (page 229)

Baby new potatoes

PUDDING
A rather special dessert collection (page 250)
or
Chilled marbled raspberry cheesecake (page 260)

Prepare ahead
Cold fillet of beef 2 days ahead.
Dessert collection 2 days ahead.
Chilled marbled raspberry cheesecake 2 days ahead.
Crab tians 6 hours ahead.
Spicy roast squash salad 6 hours ahead.

"Charity events are a huge part of our summer. It's where we got the idea for our 'Ladies that lunch' menu."

Vegetarian

We both love meat and fish, but, with recipes as special as these, how could we miss them.

STARTER

Asparagus with Parmesan and mustard sauce (page 70)

MAIN COURSE AND SIDE DISHES

Goat's cheese, thyme, and onion marmalade galette (page 230)

Globe artichoke and Puy lentil salad (page 226)

Green salad

PUDDING

Magenta fruit compote with white chocolate sauce (page 264)
or
Mango Eton mess (page 273)

Ladies that lunch

Just two courses to this menu – and fairly light ones at that – for obvious reasons.

MAIN COURSE AND SIDE DISHES

Mediterranean lemon and herb chicken salad (page 222)
or
Hot baked trout with tomato and basil salsa (page 101)

Baby new potatoes and green salad

PUDDING

Pear and ginger pavlova (page 268)
or
Rhubarb and lemon pots (page 254)

Prepare ahead
Asparagus with Parmesan 1 day ahead.
Globe artichoke and lentil salad 12 hours ahead.
Fruit compote 12 hours ahead.
Goat's cheese galette 8 hours ahead.
Mango Eton mess 6 hours ahead.

Prepare ahead
Rhubarb and lemon pots 12 hours ahead.
Mediterranean salad 8 hours ahead.
Hot baked trout 8 hours ahead.
Pear and ginger pavlova 4 hours ahead.

Tea for a crowd

Tea's back in fashion. Hurrah! Could there be a more perfect afternoon treat? In the summer, tea parties in the garden are such fun. While in winter, it's so cosy gathering in front of the fire as daylight turns to dusk. We adore a full English tea – neatly cut sandwiches followed by small cakes, large cakes, scones, jam, and cream. All washed down – of course – with pots of Rosy Lee.

"Tea can be as special as any lunch or dinner. Use it as an excuse to get out granny's china. 'Tea tastes better from a fine china cup,' as they say."

Buffet tea

An afternoon feast. Lay the table along the lines we suggest on pages 280–281.

Sandwiches (page 283)

Ashburton carrot cake (page 300)

Buttery scones (page 302)

Best-ever brownies (page 303)

Prepare ahead
Best-ever brownies 2 days ahead.
Ashburton carrot cake 1 day ahead.
Buttery scones 1 day ahead.
Sandwiches 1 day–10 hours ahead, depending on the filling.

Family tea

Serve just one kind of sandwich at an informal tea with cakes. Allow one round (two slices) per person.

Sandwiches (page 283)

Iced orange and lemon traybake
(page 285)

White chocolate and strawberry muffins (page 295)

Prepare ahead
White chocolate and strawberry muffins 2 days ahead.
Iced orange and lemon traybake 1 day ahead.
Sandwiches 1 day–10 hours ahead, depending on the filling.

Winter dinner parties

We love finding a reason to go all out in the kitchen, and dinner parties provide the perfect excuse. For us, winter is a time for casseroles and warming bakes, rich gravies and roasted meats. Set the scene with fresh flowers, candles, and music, and these meals will be special wherever you entertain your guests – in the kitchen, dining room, or conservatory.

Posh

Allow 1–2 blinis per person if you're serving four courses; three if you're not offering a starter.

PARTY BITES
Home-made blinis with salmon and crème fraîche (page 50)

STARTER
Roquefort and parsley mousseline creams (page 71)

MAIN COURSE AND SIDE DISHES
Mini pork en croûtes (page 120)

Heavenly potato gratin (page 123)

Green salad or green vegetable

PUDDING
Lemon and lime possets (page 274)

Magenta fruit compote with white chocolate sauce (page 264)

Prepare ahead
Lemon and lime possets 2 days ahead.
Heavenly potato gratin 1 day ahead.
Mini pork en croûtes 12 hours ahead.
Fruit compote 12 hours ahead.
Smoked salmon and dill blinis 6 hours ahead.
Roquefort mousseline creams 6 hours ahead.

*"With the starter on the table and the candles
lit, it's time to seat your guests."*

Supper in the kitchen

There's no need to be lavish to turn out a special
meal. Guests feel so comfortable at the kitchen table.

STARTER
Rustic mushroom liver pâté (page 82)

MAIN COURSE AND SIDE DISHES
Hot mustard spiced beef (page 195)

*Cheese-topped dauphinois potatoes
(page 125)*

Green vegetable

PUDDING
*Toffee pudding with warm toffee
sauce (page 248)*
or
Exotic fruit salad (page 265)

Festive

Serve both of these scrumptious puddings if
you're expecting a dozen people or more.

STARTER
Celebratory fish platter (page 81)

MAIN COURSE AND SIDE DISHES
*Pheasant breasts with mushrooms
and Madeira (page 109)*

*Roast potatoes with chilli
and thyme (page 126)*

Green salad or green vegetable

PUDDING
Chocolate truffle cheesecake (page 257)
and/or
*Poached pears with blackberry sauce
(page 263)*

Prepare ahead
Rustic mushroom liver pâté 3 days ahead.
Hot mustard spiced beef 2 days ahead.
Toffee pudding 1 day ahead.
Fruit salad 12 hours ahead.
Cheese-topped dauphinois potatoes 8 hours ahead.

Prepare ahead
Chocolate truffle cheesecake 2 days ahead.
Pheasant breasts with mushrooms 1 day ahead.
Roast potatoes 1 day ahead.
Poached pears 12 hours ahead.
Fish platter 4 hours ahead.

Summer dinner parties

Make the most of the warm summer evenings by serving supper or dinner in the garden. If the weather starts to get chilly, have your canapés and starter outside, then come in for the main course. Or you could do what we do – brave it and give everyone a pashmina or rug! Here's a choice of summer menus – smart or casual – to serve inside or out.

Posh

Allow three crostini per person if you're not offering a first course; one or two if you are.

PARTY BITES
Crostini with slow-roasted tomatoes and herbs (page 51)

STARTER
Roasted figs with Parma ham and goat's cheese (page 68)

MAIN COURSE AND SIDE DISHES
Duck breasts with a piquant lime and ginger sauce (page 111)

Cheese-topped dauphinois potatoes (page 125)

Green vegetable

PUDDING
Becca's white chocolate and orange mousses (page 249)
and/or
Exotic fruit salad (page 265)

Prepare ahead
Duck breasts 1 day ahead.
Roasted figs 12 hours ahead.
White chocolate and orange mousses 12 hours ahead.
Fruit salad 12 hours ahead.
Cheese-topped dauphinois potatoes 8 hours ahead.
Crostini with slow-roasted tomatoes 6 hours ahead.

"Or you could do what we do – brave the evening chill and give everyone a pashmina or rug!"

Fresh and light

A showcase for the new potatoes, carrots, and soft fruits that are at their best in the summer months.

STARTER
Smoked mackerel and watercress pâté (page 79)

MAIN COURSE AND SIDE DISHES
Sardinian chicken (page 160)

Baby new potatoes and carrots

PUDDING
Magenta fruit compote with white chocolate sauce (page 264)
and/or
Heavenly lemon cheesecake on a ginger crust (page 259)

Vegetarian

Our meat-free take on two classics from Italy with a choice of fruity puds.

STARTER
Bruschette with Reblochon and roasted vegetables (page 73)

MAIN COURSE AND SIDE DISH
Butternut squash lasagne (page 147)

Green salad

PUDDING
Hazelnut meringue roulade with raspberries (page 272)
and/or
Exotic fruit salad (page 265)

Prepare ahead
Smoked mackerel pâté 2 days ahead.
Sardinian chicken 2 days ahead.
Lemon cheesecake 1 day ahead.
Fruit compote 12 hours ahead.

Prepare ahead
Butternut squash lasagne 2 days ahead.
Hazelnut meringue roulade 12 hours ahead.
Fruit salad 12 hours ahead.
Bruschette with Reblochon 3 hours ahead.

Buffets

The goal when planning a buffet is to provide a variety of dishes that will delight your guests, but that won't require much last-minute assembly from you. These two menus are just right! To speed up serving at larger gatherings, ask some friends to help. Position them out of the way at the back of the table and tell them how much food to serve per person so you don't run out. They'll find it easier to serve the correct amount from two dishes for 12 rather than one dish for 24. For our guide to laying a buffet table, turn to pages 178–179.

"Help-yourself and hassle-free, buffets are the ultimate way of feeding a crowd – all through the year, indoors or out."

Christmas time

Unapologetically lavish. Tis the season to be jolly!

PARTY BITES
Bacon and water chestnut bites with mango chutney (page 42)
and/or
Smoked salmon on rye with cucumber pickle (page 46)

MAIN COURSES AND SIDE DISHES
Classic poached salmon (page 182)
and/or
Watercroft glazed ham with Cumberland sauce (page 184–185)
Baby new potatoes and/or Green salad

PUDDING
Party pavlova pyramid (page 269)
or
Pear and ginger pavlova (page 268)
Exotic fruit salad (page 265)

Prepare ahead
Party pavlova pyramid 1 month ahead.
Pear and ginger pavlova 1 month ahead.
Cumberland sauce 1 week ahead.
Glazed ham 5 days ahead.
Bacon bites 1 day ahead.
Classic poached salmon 1 day ahead.
Fruit salad 12 hours ahead.
Smoked salmon bites 6 hours ahead.

Mary's summer feast

There's a special something for everyone here.

PARTY BITES

Golden dough balls with cheese and chutney (page 35)
and/or
Smoked salmon on rye with cucumber pickle (page 46)

MAIN COURSES AND SIDE DISHES

Thai beef with lime and chilli (page 114)

Thai green rice (page 116)
and/or
21st-century coronation chicken (page 187)

Roasted Mediteranean vegetables (page 127)

Baby new potatoes and/or Green salad

PUDDING

Heavenly lemon cheesecake on a ginger crust (page 259)

Exotic fruit salad (page 265)

Prepare ahead

Coronation chicken 1 day ahead.
Mediterranean vegetables 1 day ahead.
Cheesecake 1 day ahead.
Dough balls 12 hours ahead.
Thai beef and **Thai rice** 12 hours ahead.
Fruit salad 12 hours ahead.
Smoked salmon bites 6 hours ahead.

Bowl parties

With little choice and no fuss, bowl parties make entertaining easy. So don't worry if your bowls don't all match – these are such relaxed occasions. Use whatever bowls you have to hand – pasta bowls, cereal bowls, soup bowls, the kind you find in fancy restaurants, the kind folk drink their coffee from in the morning in France. If you don't have enough, ask your friends to bring some along.

"Just about any dish your guests can eat with a fork from a bowl while they stand and chat is perfect bowl food."

Winter curry party

Serve two of the curries for the main course. Make both for the number of people coming – it's better to have too much food than too little.

STARTER
Garlicky herb dip with dippers (page 49)

MAIN COURSES AND SIDE DISHES
Chicken tikka masala (page 202)
and/or
Aromatic beef curry with ginger and tomatoes (page 203)
and/or
Vegetable korma (page 199)

Garlic and coriander naan breads (page 206)

Pilaf rice (page 207)

PUDDING
Rum and raisin ice cream (page 261)
and/or
Exotic fruit salad (page 265)

Prepare ahead
Rum and raisin ice cream 2 months.
Garlicky dip 3 days ahead.
Chicken tikka masala 2 days ahead.
Aromatic beef curry 2 days ahead.
Vegetable korma 12 hours ahead.
Naan breads and **Pilaf rice** 12 hours ahead.
Fruit salad 12 hours ahead.

Lucy's budget bowl party

We think the starter and main course are pretty hot, but if your guests eat jalapeño peppers for breakfast, put out the Tabasco for them to help themselves.

STARTER

Scorching chilli dip with dippers (page 49)

MAIN COURSE AND SIDE DISHES

Chilli con carne (page 192)

Rice or jacket potatoes
Green salad

PUDDING

Party crème brûlée (page 266)
and/or
Exotic fruit salad (page 265)

Prepare ahead
Scorching chilli dip 4 days ahead.
Chilli con carne 2 days ahead.
Party crème brûlée 2 days ahead.
Fruit salad 12 hours ahead.

Pot luck parties

If you're preparing a dish to take to a pot luck gathering, be careful not to let it slop all over the car seats as you transport it. For a shepherd's pie or lasagne, wrap the ovenproof dish in foil and place it in a cardboard box or basket in the boot of the car or inside on the floor. Insulated bags are great for keeping coronation chicken cool, but they'll also keep goulash hot (without the ice blocks, naturally). Alternatively, you could put the food in plastic containers or polythene bags and transfer it to the cooking pot or serving platter when you get there.

"Pot luck parties are all about keeping it simple – you and your friends sharing the load with dishes that are easy to prepare, transport, and serve."

Winter gathering

Choose either one main and a pudding and ask everyone to prepare them or ask people to make a different dish from the menu so you have a choice.

MAIN COURSES AND SIDE DISHES
Shepherd's pie dauphinois (page 141)
and/or
Paprika pork goulash (page 183)
with
Rice or mashed potatoes
Green vegetable

PUDDING
Apricot and almond galette (page 240)
and/or
Chocolate truffle cheesecake (page 257)

Prepare ahead
Apricot and almond galette 2 days ahead.
Chocolate truffle cheesecake 2 days ahead.
Shepherd's pie 1 day ahead.
Pork goulash 1 day ahead.

Summer get-together

Serve this menu as you can the winter one – with one main course and a pudding or all the dishes, prepared by various people.

MAIN COURSES AND SIDE DISHES

Butternut squash lasagne (page 147)
and/or
21st-century coronation chicken (page 187)
with
New potatoes
Green salad

PUDDING

*Hazelnut meringue roulade
with raspberries* (page 272)
and/or
Summer berry tart (page 275)

Prepare ahead

Butternut squash lasagne 2 days ahead.

Coronation chicken 1 day ahead.

Hazelnut meringue roulade 12 hours ahead.

Summer berry tart 8 hours ahead.

Useful information

Eggs

We use large eggs for the recipes in this book unless we state otherwise.

Spoon measurements

All spoon measurements have been measured with standard measuring spoons and are level unless otherwise stated.

Volume equivalents

METRIC	IMPERIAL	METRIC	IMPERIAL
30ml	1fl oz	450ml	15fl oz
60ml	2fl oz	500m	16fl oz
75ml	2½fl oz	600ml	1 pint
100ml	3½fl oz	750ml	1¼ pints
120ml	4fl oz	900ml	1½ pints
150ml	5fl oz (¼ pint)	1 litre	1¾ pints
175ml	6fl oz	1.2 litres	2 pints
200ml	7fl oz (⅓ pint)	1.4 litres	2½ pints
240ml	8fl oz	1.5 litres	2¾ pints
300ml	10fl oz (½ pint)	1.7 litres	3 pints
350ml	12fl oz	2 litres	3½ pints
400ml	14fl oz	3 litres	5¼ pints

Weight equivalents

METRIC	IMPERIAL	METRIC	IMPERIAL
15g	½oz	150g	5½oz
20g	¾oz	175g	6oz
25g	scant 1oz	200g	7oz
30g	1oz	225g	8oz
45g	1½oz	250g	9oz
50g	1¾oz	300g	11oz
60g	2oz	450g	1lb
75g	2½oz	500g	1lb 2oz
85g	3oz	675g	1½lb
100g	3½oz	900g	2lb
115g	4oz	1kg	2¼lb
125g	4½oz	1.5kg	3lb 3oz
140g	5oz	1.8kg	4lb

Oven temperature equivalents

CELSIUS	FAN	FAHRENHEIT	GAS	DESCRIPTION
110°C	90°C	225°F	¼	Cool
130°C	110°C	250°F	½	Cool
140°C	120°C	275°F	1	Very low
150°C	130°C	300°F	2	Very low
160°C	140°C	325°F	3	Low
180°C	160°C	350°F	4	Moderate
190°C	170°C	375°F	5	Moderately hot
200°C	180°C	400°F	6	Hot
220°C	200°C	425°F	7	Hot
230°C	210°C	450°F	8	Very hot
240°C	220°C	475°F	9	Very hot

Index

Index entries in *italics* refer
to techniques and tips.

Acknowledgments

Authors' acknowledgments

Firstly, a huge thank you to the lovely Lucinda McCord, who was an essential part of the team that created the recipes with us for this book. She was also the home economist for the photography. Lucinda, thank you for your dedication, passion for your work, and friendship.

Thank you to Izzie Forrest and Rebecca Reed for their help with recipe ideas and catering tips.

Thank you, too, to Mary-Clare Jerram at Dorling Kindersley, who commissioned us to write this book and could see our vision for it. She has worked closely with us at every stage and always with a smile.

And a huge thank you to Michael Fullalove, who edited the book with such dedication and commitment, and always with humour and great understanding. It has been a joy to work with you.

Thank you to Bill Reavell for the stunning photography and the wonderful shoot.

We would also like to thank our agents, Felicity Bryan and Michele Topham, who never seem to worry about our problems, but just sort them out fast!

Finally, thank you to you our readers. You continue to support us with your emails, letters, and photos. It is always lovely to hear from you – it makes each book more and more enjoyable.

Publisher's acknowledgments

Dorling Kindersley would like to thank Barbara Shepherd at Lakeland (products available at time of going to print, www.lakeland.co.uk), Divertimenti (www.divertimenti.co.uk), Sue Rowlands and Liz Hippisley the prop stylists, Lucinda McCord and Jane Lawrie the food stylists, Liz Cook for the index, Nicky Collings for art directing the photoshoot, and Romaine Werblow for picture research.

All images © Dorling Kindersley
For further information see: www.dkimages.com